CAPTAIN HARRY WHEELER
ARIZONA LAWMAN

BILL O'NEAL

EAKIN PRESS  Austin, Texas

For my daughter and fellow college teacher,
Dr. Shellie O'Neal.

Contents

Introduction to a Lawman / 1

ONE / Early Life on the Frontier / 5

TWO / Family Man and Cavalryman / 16

THREE / Arizona Ranger / 25

FOUR / Ranger Captain / 45

FIVE / The Last Ranger / 76

SIX / Sheriff of Cochise County / 87

SEVEN / The Bisbee Deportation / 111

EIGHT / Captain in the Great War / 131

NINE / A New Family / 142

Endnotes / 161

Bibliography / 175

Index / 183

Harry Wheeler, while serving as sheriff of Cochise County. (Courtesy Arizona Historical Society)

Introduction to a Lawman

"Hold on there. I arrest you. Give me that gun."

—Lt. Harry Wheeler to armed troublemaker J.A. Tracy

Joe Bostwick pulled a mask over his face, cocked his long-barreled Colt .45, and stealthily entered the door of Tucson's Palace Saloon. It was late on Sunday night, October 23, 1904, and only eight men were in the barroom. Bostwick menacingly ordered all of them to raise their hands, but M. D. Beede slipped outside and sprinted down the street. When he encountered Sgt. Harry Wheeler of the Arizona Rangers, Beede blurted out that a robbery was in progress. Seeing Wheeler turn toward the saloon, he added: "Don't go in there—there's a holdup going on!"

"All right," Wheeler calmly replied, "that's what I'm here for."

Wheeler pulled his single-action Colt and stalked to the front door of the saloon. Bostwick spotted the lawman and whirled to fire his revolver, but Wheeler triggered the first shot. The heavy .45-caliber slug grazed Bostwick's forehead above the right eye. Bostwick fired wildly as Wheeler drilled him in the right side of the chest. The stricken bandit groaned and collapsed to the floor.

When interviewed by a reporter for the Tucson *Citizen,* Wheeler commented: "I am sorry that this happened, but it was either his life or mine, and if I hadn't been just a little quicker on the draw than he was, I might be in his position now. Under the circumstances, if I had to do it all over again I think I would do exactly the same thing."[1]

These words and actions were typical of one of the most dedicated, controversial, and lethal peace officers ever to serve Arizona. Harry Wheeler was the only member of the Arizona Rangers to hold every rank in that notable company. He won election three times as sheriff of Cochise County; he also served on the Douglas police force and as a mounted customs officer. Wheeler was driven by a powerful sense of duty and an inner need for public service. An extraordinary marksman with pistol or rifle, he employed his skills with firearms on the side of law and order, wearing one badge after another throughout his career. Emulating his father, Wheeler also served his country, joining the U. S. Cavalry during the 1890s, then obtaining a commission when the United States entered the Great War. The constant fulfillment of duty was the framework of Harry Wheeler's life.

My personal introduction to Harry Wheeler came when I researched *The Arizona Rangers,* a history published by Eakin Press in 1987. At the Arizona State Archives in Phoenix, with the expert assistance of Wilma Smallwood, Carol Downy and Shirley Macias, I photocopied hundreds of pages of Ranger records and correspondence. A majority of the letters were from Capt. Harry Wheeler to the governor's office. The State Archives permitted me to borrow microfilm of Arizona newspapers, four reels at a time, through interlibrary loan. I scoured newspapers from 1901 through 1909 for stories about the Arizona Rangers. But I was most intrigued by Wheeler, and I continued to borrow reels of Arizona newspapers through 1925, the year of his death. Guided by Lori Davisson, research specialist of the Arizona Heritage Center in Tucson (Lori has since retired), I gathered a great deal of information about the Rangers and Wheeler.

By the time I completed research for my Ranger book, I also had accumulated files for a biography of Harry Wheeler. At the old courthouse in Tombstone, where Sheriff Wheeler was headquartered, I learned that an unidentified daughter of Wheeler (I assumed it was Jessie Jacqueline Wheeler) and her children had visited in 1980. She left no forwarding information, but I realized that no suitable biography could be written without establishing contact with surviving family members. Unable to locate Wheeler's descendants, I proceeded on to other book projects, always hoping to make the connection that would allow me to complete my biographical files.

On a visit to Arizona in 2001, I met Sgt. Dave Bruce of the modern Arizona Rangers. Sergeant Bruce told me about Mrs. Pam Hamlett of Tucson, granddaughter of Harry Wheeler. Her mother was Jessie Jacqueline Wheeler Morrison, who passed away shortly before the publication of this book. Pam responded to my queries, then graciously consented to a personal visit and granted me access to Wheeler family artifacts, documents, and correspondence. Pam's interest in presenting her grandfather's story was the key to my completion of Harry Wheeler's biography, and I am deeply grateful for her invaluable assistance.

Art Austin, assistant park manager at the Tombstone Courthouse National Historic Site, twice allowed me to prevail upon his exceptional fund of knowledge, in the 1980s and again in 2002. Tom and Virginia Messer of Eakin Press encouraged me to produce this book, and I offer them heartfelt appreciation for their friendship and professional support. My wife Karon—as always—was instrumental in this project, accompanying me on research trips, chasing down leads on the Internet, and preparing the manuscript, with the able assistance of Panola College students Rachel Reed and Stacy Blanton.

Each of these people assisted in various ways to introduce me to one of the most remarkable lawmen in western history, and I am profoundly grateful for the help they gave me in following Harry Wheeler's trail.

CHAPTER ONE

Early Life on the Frontier

"I always got a licking."

—Harry Wheeler

Harry Cornwall Wheeler was born in Jacksonville, Florida, on July 23, 1875.[1] His father was 2nd Lt. William Baker Wheeler, a West Point graduate, Class of 1871, and his mother was Annie Cornwall Wheeler, daughter of Judge Harry Cornwall of Virginia. William and Annie both were born in 1847, on August 12 and November 28, respectively. A family coat of arms proclaims the English heritage of the Wheelers and the Cornwalls, and baby Harry was given his mother's maiden name. The oldest of three children, Harry later had a sister, Sallie, and a brother, William D.

Lieutenant Wheeler was a native of New York, who may have served as a seventeen-year-old enlisted man late in the Civil War. At the age of nineteen, on July 1, 1867, he was sworn in as a cadet at the United States Military Academy. During the next four years, among the gray stone buildings overlooking the Hudson River, the classic virtues of "Duty, Honor, Country" were drilled into Wheeler, and later he would instill these and other military concepts into his sons. Graduating thirty-first in his class, Lieutenant Wheeler was posted to the Eighteenth Infantry.[2]

The post-Civil War army which Lieutenant Wheeler entered had been reduced to an authorized strength of 25,000 enlisted men, but a one-third desertion rate kept the actual roster totals around 19,000 men. Since the ten cavalry regiments bore the brunt of combat against the horseback warriors of the West, a troop of 100 was authorized (in practice, active troop rosters usually numbered about sixty men). Infantry companies, on the other hand, were allotted merely thirty-seven enlisted men, along with a captain, first lieutenant, and second lieutenant. The year before 2nd Lt. Wheeler entered active service, a pay reduction went into effect, with privates receiving $13 per month, sergeants $22 per month, and second lieutenants about $116 per month ($1,400 per year).[3]

Once assigned to a regiment and company, soldiers remained with those units permanently. When officers finally reached high rank, promotion often sent them to a rare vacancy in another regiment. But a strict seniority system and a retirement age of sixty-four kept promotions at a glacial pace, with officers stuck in the same rank for a decade or more.

William B. Wheeler spent over three decades in the Eighteenth Infantry, including nearly eleven years as a second lieutenant. He married and had three children while still a second lieutenant. Finally promoted in 1882, he remained a first lieutenant for nine years. Not until 1891, when he was forty-three, was he elevated to captain. But like many other officers, loyalty and devotion to duty kept Wheeler in the service, and his children observed and absorbed these and other admirable qualities.

From 1871 until 1878, Lieutenant Wheeler was stationed in the troubled South, at Yorkville and Columbia, South Carolina (a state still enduring military Reconstruction) and at Atlanta, Georgia. He was on duty in Columbia in 1875 when Harry was born in Jacksonville, Florida, apparently at a family home of

Left: Cadet William Wheeler, West Point, Class of 1871. Right: Harry's mother, Annie Cornwall Wheeler. This image was taken in Hays City, Kansas, and the Wheeler family was transferred to Fort Hays in 1885, when Annie was thirty-eight. (Courtesy Pam Hamlett)

Annie Wheeler. In 1878, when Harry was three, his father was transferred with the Eighteenth to the West. Lieutenant Wheeler was assigned to Fort Assiniboine in northern Montana, a new post still under construction.

The previous year the Nez Perce War had climaxed at the Battle of Bear Paw Mountain, about thirty miles east of the fort site. Also, in the wake of the Battle of Little Bighorn, Sitting Bull had led a large body of Sioux nearby into Canada, and Montana settlers feared they might return at any time. In response to appeals from citizens of northern Montana, Congress appropriated $100,000 in 1878 to build a fort about thirty-five miles south of the Canadian border. Brick kilns were built near the fort site, and other construction materials were shipped up the Missouri River. Fort Assiniboine took shape rapidly. Six sets of two-story brick barracks were erected on the north side of a vast parade ground, while stables and storehouses were placed behind the barracks to the north. A big hospital dominated the east end of the parade, while an impressive officers' row formed a long line across the south side. Set after set of brick duplexes were flanked on each end by a two-story multiplex, each of which

From ages three to ten, 1878-85, Harry lived at Fort Assiniboine, Montana. Perhaps the Wheelers lived in the turreted brick building at right, which had apartments for six officers. (Courtesy National Archives)

housed six apartments and boasted a three-story, crenelated tower. Fort Assiniboine became the largest post in Montana.[4]

This sprawling military town was young Harry Wheeler's home from the ages of three through ten. The day was framed by military routine, from reveille each morning to retreat in the evening, when the colors slid down a ninety-foot flagpole to the sounds of the regimental band and the sunset gun. Little Harry watched troops drill on the parade ground, observed the garrison's salute of the flag, heard the stirring strains of martial music. He experienced his first few years of education at the school for officers' children, who were his playmates around the post. Winters were frigid and snowy, while the short summers were plagued by mosquitoes. Twice Lieutenant Wheeler was granted long furloughs, from March through August 1880, and from May through August 1883, when there were trips, probably to visit family. In February 1882 William Wheeler finally received his first promotion, to first lieutenant.

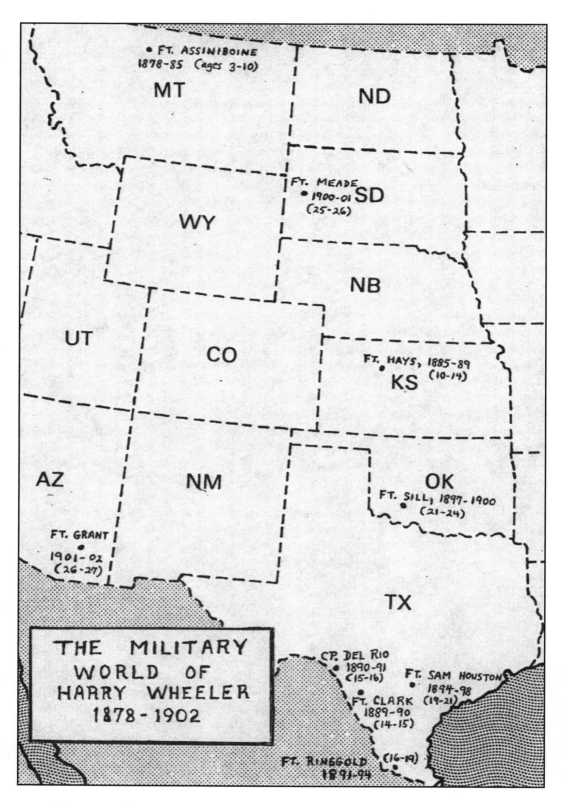

THE MILITARY
WORLD OF
HARRY WHEELER
1878-1902

• FT. ASSINIBOINE
1878-85 (ages 3-10)

MT

ND

FT. MEADE
• 1900-01 SD
(25-26)

WY

NB

UT

CO

FT. HAYS, 1885-89
• (10-14)
KS

AZ

NM

OK

FT. SILL, 1897-1900
• (21-24)

FT. GRANT
•
1901-02
(26-27)

TX

CP. DEL RIO
• 1890-91
(15-16)

FT. SAM HOUSTON
• 1894-98
FT. CLARK (19-21)
1889-90
(14-15)

(16-19)
FT. RINGGOLD
1891-94

Fort Assiniboine saw scant campaigning against hostile war parties. As hide hunters exterminated buffalo herds across the Great Plains, the way of life of the horse Indians became impossible, and they had to submit to confinement on reservations. With that development, tensions eased around Fort Assiniboine. Officers felt free to range far in pursuit of game. Hunting always was a favorite recreation on western outposts. At a young age, typical for frontier boys, Harry was taught to handle firearms. He became a crack shot, exercising marksmanship on a high level until the end of his life.

In 1885, after seven years at Fort Assiniboine, Lieutenant Wheeler was transferred to Fort Hays, Kansas. Dating from 1867, Fort Hays was a large post occupying a hill in north central Kansas. Below the hill, on the plains north of the fort, ramshackle Hays City offered soldiers a score of saloons and other recreational opportunities. "The carousing and lawlessness of Hays City were incessant," recalled Libbie Custer. "Pistol shots were heard so often it seemed a perpetual Fourth of July. . . ." George Armstrong Custer (along with his lovely wife) was stationed there, and from this fort Gen. Phil Sheridan had launched a winter campaign in 1868. Noted frontier gunman Wild Bill Hickok had worn a badge in Hays City, serving briefly as county sheriff in 1869. Sheriff Hickok killed a drunken soldier and a local troublemaker in separate gunfights, and the next year he shot two troopers during a saloon brawl. Harry Wheeler was ten to fourteen while he was at Hays, soaking up colorful local history during an impressionable stage of his life.[5]

For four and a half years Harry lived with his family on officers' row, the most impressive section of Fort Hays. In addition to the nine-room commanding officer's house, there were seven sets of two-story frame officers' quarters, aligned in a row facing north. Unlike most western "forts," Hays actually

Officers' row at Fort Hays, Kansas, where the Wheeler family lived from 1885 to 1889. Young Harry was ten through fourteen during the years he spent at the historic old post. (Courtesy National Archives)

Corporal Punishment

The Wheeler children were raised in a military family during an age of authoritarian parents, and corporal punishment was an accepted part of childhood. As the oldest child, Harry was a ready target for discipline, while the youngest child, William, often managed to elude punishment in the classic manner of the baby of the family. In 1917 Harry had occasion to reminisce about "how I once received the spanking of my life at the hands of my own dear mother" to an audience in Bisbee, Arizona.

"Well," said Harry, speaking about his brother, "every time he got into trouble over some boyish prank and mother started to spank him he would come forward with the most penitent air and take off his little jacket and roll his eyes and plead in a plaintive voice as he leaned over to take his medicine. And mother would forgive him every time. But I always got a licking. One time, when I was booked for punishment, my brother suggested to me that I adopt his style of tactics. I did, even to the point of leaning over to take my medicine. But it did not work. Mother laid on with a vengeance. And 15 minutes later I walloped that kid brother in the back yard, and when father came home he whipped me again." (Bisbee *Review,* December 6, 1917) boasted a fortification, a hexagonal stone blockhouse. Since Fort Hays was never attacked, the blockhouse was utilized as post headquarters.

Growing into his teen years at Fort Hays, Harry was trim and athletic, with blue eyes and thick brown hair. He loved to ride horseback, and he continued to hone his exceptional marksmanship at the firing range. Fascinated by guns, during his formative years at a series of western outposts, Harry was surrounded by rifles and pistols and men who were trained to use them.

In 1889, with Indian troubles in Kansas long ended, the army abandoned Fort Hays. The Eighteenth Infantry was sent to Texas, and Lieutenant Wheeler was assigned to Fort Clark in September 1889. Another large, historic post, Fort Clark had grown from a flimsy installation in the 1850s to a large station boasting substantial stone buildings surrounding a dry, rocky parade ground. Col. Robert E. Lee had served at Fort Clark before the Civil War, and in 1873 Col. Ranald Mackenzie led his Fourth Cavalry in a bold retaliatory raid into Mexico. Years later, Harry Wheeler of the Arizona Rangers would be authorized to make the same response across the border to pursue fleeing outlaws.

But for now, fourteen-year-old Harry Wheeler found himself in an isolated outpost only a short distance from the Mexican border. Las Moras River separated Fort Clark from the little frontier town of Brackettville to the north. Nothing but bare necessities could be obtained in Brackettville, and San Antonio was 135 miles to the east. There was a stagecoach connection with San Antonio, but transportation costs elevated the price of most items beyond the reach of a first lieutenant's pay.[6]

Parade ground bandstand in front of officer's quarters at Fort Clark, where the Wheelers transferred from Fort Hays in 1889. The music of military bands was part of Harry Wheeler's daily background for the first twenty-six years of his life. (Courtesy National Archives)

After a stay of only six months, Lieutenant Wheeler was transferred to a sub-post, Camp Del Rio. Del Rio was a raw border town. Although Del Rio became the seat of newly organized Val Verde County in 1885, it was no more than a dusty village beside the Rio Grande when the Wheelers arrived in April 1890. The happiest event of a dreary tenure was Wheeler's promotion to captain in February 1891, nearly two decades after he had received his commission.

A long year at Del Rio passed before the Wheelers learned that the little sub-post would be discontinued. In May 1891, Captain Wheeler, Annie, Harry, Sallie, and William moved nearly 250 miles down the Rio Grande to Fort Ringgold. Established in 1848 on a sandy bluff overlooking the Rio Grande,

From 1891 to 1894, beginning when he was sixteen, Harry Wheeler lived with his family on officers' row at Fort Ringgold on the Texas border. (Courtesy National Archives)

Fort Ringgold soon boasted a handsome collection of whitewashed buildings. But Ringgold proved to be a quiet post, and there was no action during the three years Captain Wheeler was on duty.[7]

Harry Wheeler may have spent little time with his family at Fort Ringgold. The Wheelers were at Fort Ringgold from May 1891 until May 1894, when Harry grew from sixteen to nineteen years of age. Inevitably it was hoped that Harry would follow his father to West Point. However, the schools at the outposts where he had grown up offered only elementary grades. Indeed, the Census of 1890 recorded 2,500 secondary schools in the United States, and fewer than seven percent of the population, aged fourteen through seventeen, attended these schools. Harry apparently attended a military school, most likely in San Antonio, about 240 miles to the north.[8]

The entire family moved to San Antonio in May 1894, when Captain Wheeler transferred with the Eighteenth to Fort Sam Houston. The United States Army had moved into San Antonio as soon as Texas became a state in 1846, renting the Alamo and other downtown buildings. During the 1850s, San Antonio supplied the frontier outposts of Texas, as the army battled Comanches and border raiders. After the Civil War, Reconstruction headquarters was established in Austin, but San Antonio civic leaders determined to bring back the army. Three parcels of land, totaling ninety-three acres centered around "Government Hill," were offered to the army, which accepted in 1875. A quartermaster depot was enclosed by four stone walls. Inside the "Quadrangle" was a landmark eighty-seven-foot tower, built as a water storage tank with an open lookout post for sentries. The water tank was converted into a clock tower in 1882. Fifteen sets of officers' quarters, known as the Staff Post, were erected just east of the Quadrangle during the mid-1880s. In 1886 the Infantry Post was constructed on additional land purchased by the army. Located two miles northeast of downtown, the post at San Antonio was renamed Fort Sam Houston in 1890.[9]

The Wheelers spent four years at this rapidly expanding installation. San Antonio also was expanding rapidly, boasting a population of 50,000 by the late 1890s. Trolley cars rolled past three-, four-, and five-story commercial buildings downtown, and prominent citizens lived in handsome Victorian homes in the King William neighborhood. Three years before the Wheelers moved to San Antonio, the plaza in front of the Alamo was turned into a park with sidewalks among shrubbery, trees, and rose bushes. For Harry Wheeler, a young military idealist, visiting the Alamo must have been a profoundly moving experience. For all of the Wheelers, who had lived near nothing larger than western villages since 1878, San Antonio in the 1890s must have provided countless small pleasures.

With frequent band concerts and military ceremonies, Fort Sam Houston was a popular spot for San Antonio citizens. Handsome young officers provided eager targets for matchmakers. The most famous of many such pairings involved Lt. Dwight David Eisenhower and Mamie Doud, at Fort Sam Houston in 1915. These matchings contin-

Above: Harry's sister Sallie in old age. (Courtesy Pam Hamlett) Below: Engraved gold watch presented to William B. Wheeler by men of the 18th Infantry, which he served as an officer for more than three decades, 1871-1903. (Courtesy Pam Hamlett, photo by Karon O'Neal)

Formation at Fort Sam Houston in San Antonio. Harry may have attended the nearby Texas Military Institute. (Courtesy National Archives)

ued with such consistency that San Antonio was dubbed the "Mother-in-law of the Army."

But there was no San Antonio marriage for Harry Wheeler. The young man seems to have sampled education beyond the elementary grades available at army posts, listing his occupation as "student" at the age of twenty-one. Whatever preparatory schooling he received, Harry never attained entry to West Point. In later years there was a reference that he had not reached the height requirement, which was five feet. By 1897, however, when he was twenty-one, Harry stood at five feet, six and a half inches, so it seems unlikely that a year or two earlier he was only five feet tall.[10]

If Harry could not follow his father into West Point, at least he could follow him into the army. By the time he reached his twenties, Harry was determined to serve his country. Reared on western outposts with traditions of recent frontier adventures involving hard-riding plains warriors and Mexican border raiders, Harry and his younger brother developed a need to perform military heroics. They admired their father and his fellow soldiers and the values they represented. Both of Captain Wheeler's sons would join the army, even though they had witnessed the gulf that existed between officers and enlisted men.

Harry Wheeler had grown up in an environment of patriotism, a compelling sense of duty, and a dogged devotion to the service. Ingrained in his makeup was the initiative and responsibility typical of a classic older brother. Intelligent and energetic, possessed of stamina and exceptional marksmanship skills, Harry would spend his life attempting to employ his best qualities on behalf of others. Although he sometimes was overzealous during his career, and inevitably manifested other human flaws on occasion, his upbringing instilled stern focus and a sense of purpose for the future.

By 1897 Harry Wheeler was ready to test himself in the military arena.

The MacArthurs at Fort Sam Houston

A few months before Captain Wheeler was posted to Fort Sam Houston, Maj. Arthur MacArthur transferred in after a four-year assignment in Washington, D.C. MacArthur, a Medal of Honor winner during the Civil War, brought his formidable wife, Pinky, and thirteen-year-old son, Douglas, to San Antonio (the older son, Arthur III, had just been appointed to the U.S. Naval Academy). Major MacArthur, like Captain Wheeler, spent four years at Fort Sam Houston.

Young Douglas MacArthur attended the West Texas Military Academy, which opened shortly after his arrival. Founded in 1893 by Episcopalian Bishop James S. Johnston, a former Confederate officer and combat veteran, the academy was located on Grayson Street, near Fort Sam Houston. Early enrollment records are unavailable, but it seems likely that Harry Wheeler also attended the new military school. Harry was five years older than Douglas MacArthur, who was a year older than William D. Wheeler. The boys must have known each other, at least around the post.

In 1897 Major MacArthur was promoted to lieutenant colonel and transferred to St. Paul, Minnesota. During the summer of 1898, with the United States at war with Spain, Captain Wheeler was ordered with the Eighteenth to the Philippines, where newly promoted Brig. Gen. Arthur MacArthur had just arrived with a command of 4,800 men. (Information from Manchester, *American Caesar*, 28-29)

CHAPTER TWO

Family Man and Cavalryman

"And still there was something—something about the murmur of leather, the soft jingling of bridles, the flashing of sabers and flying guidons—something about it all that made these days of glory."

—Former cavalryman James Warner Bellah, in *Reveille*

Although Harry Wheeler was frustrated in his efforts to be admitted to the U. S. Military Academy, when he was twenty-one he ventured north to Fort Sill, Oklahoma, and enlisted in the First Cavalry. An enthusiastic horseman, Wheeler was attracted to the cavalry by the traditional glamour of the mounted service. Certainly the cavalry units stationed at the outposts where he had grown up offered a dashing contrast to his father's pedestrian Eighteenth Infantry. His enlistment at Fort Sill perhaps was due to advice or a contact from his father, who had been on active duty for more than a quarter century and knew a great many officers. Filling out his enlistment papers on April 1, 1897, Harry C. Wheeler listed his occupation as "student." The examining surgeon noted a long scar on Harry's nose and a couple of raised moles on his torso. Private Wheeler was assigned to Company H.[1]

Like many of the western posts on which Harry had lived, Fort Sill had a rich frontier history. Located in southwestern Oklahoma, Sill began as an encampment early in 1869 during a winter campaign led by Gen. Phil Sheridan and featuring Lt. Col. George Armstrong Custer and the Seventh Cavalry. Two years later Fort Sill was visited by Gen. William T. Sherman, who was present during a dangerous scuffle with Kiowa war leaders on the front gallery of the commanding officer's quarters. In 1875 famed Comanche chief Quanah Parker brought his diehard band into Fort Sill, ending the Buffalo War. Until his death in 1911, Quanah was the acknowledged leader of the Comanche people, who were confined to the reservation headquartered by Fort Sill. Another famous war chieftan also spent the last years of his life near Fort Sill. The ferocious and wily Apache, Geronimo, had surrendered in Arizona in 1886. Geronimo and his followers were shipped to Florida, then to Alabama, and finally to Fort Sill in 1894. When Harry Wheeler reached Fort Sill in 1897, both men were celebrities in demand at public appearances; Quanah was in his early fifties, while the hard-drinking Geronimo was in his mid-seventies.

Fort Sill, where Harry Wheeler enlisted in the U.S. Cavalry. (Courtesy National Archives)

By the 1890s, Fort Sill boasted an impressive collection of stone buildings. Officers' quarters were neatly aligned on the north and east sides of the parade ground, while barracks were on the other two sides. On the west side of the parade were three sets of large barracks designed to accommodate two companies each. South of these structures was a stout guardhouse, in which drunken Geronimo was periodically confined. Southeast of the parade ground stood a large stone corral equipped with loopholes and built in 1872 to safeguard the horses from Indian theft. The cavalry stables were located behind the western line of barracks.[2]

Like most of the military posts on which Harry Wheeler had spent his life, Fort Sill was remote from the forces that were transforming the United States into the world's wealthiest nation. Aside from the past few years in San Antonio, Harry had rarely been around railroads, the country's most powerful industry during the late nineteenth century. Private Wheeler probably had never ridden an elevator, and such innovations as telephones, Coca-Cola, hot dogs, and toothpaste in a tube had played little part in his life. Isolated from the mainstream of modern America, Harry Wheeler had been conditioned to life in a West still close to its frontier heritage. Individualism and simple values and sweeping western vistas always would be of greater importance to him than the comforts and technology available in the urbanized, industrialized sections of America.

As a soldier, one technological innovation offered a great appeal for Private Wheeler. He was issued a Model 1896 Krag .30-40 magazine carbine.

Replacing the .45-70 single-shot Springfield adopted in 1873, this Krag-Jorgensen weapon of military design was the first United States military arm to utilize smokeless powder. Private Wheeler honed his extraordinary shooting skills on the firing range at Fort Sill. His sidearm may have been the famed .45-caliber Colt Model 1878 single-action revolver, but from 1892 to 1903 the War Department purchased 68,500 .38-caliber "New Double-Action Army Revolvers" to replace the older pistols. Harry had learned pistol marksmanship on a .45 single-action Colt, and after he left the cavalry he again took up that powerful, reliable old weapon. (During the Philippine insurrection, when the .38-caliber bullet proved to have inadequate stopping power against guerrilla jungle fighters, the army recalled the double-action revolvers and reissued the proven .45 single-action Colts from storage.)[3]

Private Wheeler's uniform had a different look from the soldierly appearance of his youth. In 1895 the longtime forage cap based on the French kepi was replaced by a rounded cap different from any previous headwear. In 1894 cavalry boots slowly began to be replaced by shoes and canvas leggings that were fastened by laces and hooks. The 1899 uniform regulations prescribed khaki trousers and blouses for field service. In the field all mounted men continued to wear leather gauntlets as well as felt fatigue hats.

During Private Wheeler's first year of service, garrison duty was tame and rather dull at Fort Sill. He was accustomed to the daily routine of drill and fatigue details. Off-duty he found romance with Mamie Olivia Stafford. A native of California, her background is unknown, but she and Harry were sufficiently congenial to produce a pregnancy. On February 14, 1898, they were married at Fort Sill, presumably at the stone chapel that was built in the 1870s. Harry was a twenty-two-year-old bridegroom, and less than six months later he became a father. William Allyn Wheeler was born on August 11, 1898. Although the boy bore the first name of Harry's father and brother, he would be called by his middle name.[4]

Allyn Wheeler late in 1898 at the age of three months. His father bragged that the baby had the "chest and arms and shoulders of a soldier." (Courtesy Pam Hamlett)

One day after Harry's marriage to Mamie, the USS *Maine* exploded in Havana harbor, killing 260 officers and men. Cuban revolutionaries were at war against Spanish authorities, and there was great sympathy for the rebels among Americans. The immediate assumption was that Spanish forces had sabotaged the *Maine* (today it is thought that the explosion was internal and accidental). Incited by the "yellow journalism" of the time, the American public was roused to fury by sensational newspaper stories. Less than one month after the sinking of the *Maine*, on March 8 Congress responded to rising public war hysteria by unanimously voting President William McKinley a $50 million emergency fund for national defense. On April 13 Congress overwhelmingly adopted resolutions that recognized Cuban independence, demanded the immediate withdrawal of Spain, and authorized President McKinley to employ U. S. armed forces to carry out these resolutions. Although Spain failed to enlist any European allies, the Spanish government felt honorbound to declare war on April 24.

At the beginning of 1898 there were only 28,000 officers and men in the regular army, and a substantial force would have to remain in the West to guard against a renewal of Indian problems. A call went out for volunteers, prompting tens of thousands of men to enlist. To outfit the newly organized volunteer units, government

The historic Commanding Officer's Quarters at the head of the parade ground at Fort Sill. (Photo by Karon O'Neal)

warehouses were emptied of uniforms, weapons, and equipment, including Civil War surplus. The War Department organized 182,000 volunteers into seven corps, providing rudimentary training in camps in the East, South, and in San Francisco. Regular army units began to be shipped to Tampa, Florida, soon to be joined by various volunteer regiments.

The First Cavalry was one of the regiments sent to Tampa to make up the expeditionary force to Cuba. The role of Private Wheeler is uncertain. Service records maintained for enlisted men were sketchy, and Wheeler's consists only of enlistment and discharge documents. In later years, after he became prominent in Arizona, newspapers mentioned that during the Spanish-American War "Wheeler was a member of the first U.S. regulars from Oklahoma" and that he "served in the regular army and in the volunteers during the Spanish-American war." An El Paso newspaper claimed that "as a Rough Rider he learned the elements of soldiering during the Spanish-American war." It is also possible that Private Wheeler, with a pregnant wife, might have remained at Fort Sill to help maintain order on the reservation. Indeed, he later stated that he served as chief of Indian scouts on the Fort Sill reservation, which may have been a police force of particular use while regulars were away at war. Action reports for the initial advance in Cuba, in late June, and the assault on the San Juan Heights, in early July, cite Companies A, B, C, D, E, G, I, and K of the First Cavalry. That left four troops, including Company H, to remain on reservation duty at Fort Sill. It seems probable that Harry Wheeler spent the "Splendid Little War" in Oklahoma.[5]

While 17,000 officers and men, including eight companies of the First Cavalry, campaigned in Cuba, military developments elsewhere affected Harry Wheeler's father and brother. To the surprise of the Spanish and almost everyone else, the first battle of the war was a naval assault by Commodore George Dewey against the inferior Spanish fleet in Manila Bay in the Philippines, on the other side of the world from Cuba. After destroying the Spanish fleet on May 1, Dewey made contract with Filipino *insurrectos* in rebellion against Spanish authority. While Dewey maintained a naval blockade, Filipino leader Emilio Aguinaldo declared himself president. But a U.S. ground force, totaling 11,000 regulars and volunteers, sailed for the Philippines in three contingents. The second contingent, which left San Francisco on June 16, carried 3,600 men on three transports. Aboard the *Colon* were elements of the Eighteenth Infantry, including Capt. William B. Wheeler and a youthful member of his company, Pvt. William Wheeler.

Harry's sixteen-year-old brother had been swept up in the clamor for war and became wild to enlist in the Rough Riders, the First Volunteer Cavalry Regiment which was being organized in San Antonio. Being underage, he had to have the consent of his parents, "which I got only after much pleading, begging and coaxing." Young Wheeler intended to enlist as a bugler, "thinking I had a better chance." But before he could approach recruiters from the Rough Riders, his father received orders to the Philippines, "and as I was resolute about going, he preferred me to go with him. Well that settled the whole thing." William enlisted in the Eighteenth Infantry on May 23, 1898, and was assigned to Company E, commanded by his father. Two days later the Eighteenth departed Fort Sam Houston for California. "After my sad farewells to my Mother, Sister and friends we left," he wrote in his journal.[6]

The trip west by train "was long, dirty, and tiresome" until reaching California, where "we were treated so well and had such beautiful scenery." In San Francisco they were in a tent camp at the "old race grounds" until boarding their ships. The trip took five weeks, with a stopover in Hawaii. On July 11 target practice was conducted aboard ship, with each man firing five rounds. "This was the first shots I fired as a soldier during the war," recorded young Private Wheeler in a journal. A few days later they sailed into Manila Bay and were cheered by Dewey's men, but the soldiers were still on the ship when Private Wheeler celebrated his seventeenth birthday on July 20.[7]

After landing, all three contingents assembled and marched to Manila. Victorious over Spain, the United States annexed the Philippines on July 7, 1898. But by early in 1899 the Filipinos decided they did not want merely a change of masters, and Emilio Aguinaldo led a guerrilla war against the

Americans. The jungle fighting was vicious, with casualties from combat and disease. Although the American army in the Philippines eventually totaled 70,000 men, resistance did not end until April 1902. Captain Wheeler missed the Philippine War. He was ill in his quarters at Jaro by August 25, 1898. During his illness he was promoted to major, but soon he was sent back to San Francisco and hospitalized at the Presidio. Throughout the remainder of his career he was forced to take lengthy sick leaves.

All three Wheeler men served simultaneously during the war with Spain,

Front and back of Wheeler's reenlistment card. (Courtesy National Archives)

Colonel Stewart's Elba

After Fort Grant was permanently abandoned, the post office closed in 1905. But in 1908 Col. William F. Stewart arrived as last commanding officer of Fort Grant. Although the colonel had served for four decades, his refusal to accept the customary retirement prompted President Theodore Roosevelt to assign him to exile at the vacated cavalry post. A caretaker and a cook comprised Colonel Stewart's entire garrison. He finally retired, and Fort Grant was converted to the Arizona State Industrial School.

and nearly two decades later the Wheeler brothers would reenter the service during America's next war. Harry and William had been raised alike, and they were conditioned to respond to call to service.

When Harry's three-year enlistment ended on March 31, 1900, he took his wife and little boy into civilian life—but only for three months. Now nearly twenty-five years old, he had spent his entire life on army posts. After time for a visit with his brother, now on recruiting duty in California, and other family members, Harry rejoined the First Cavalry, which had been transferred to Fort Meade in western South Dakota.[8]

Reenlisting on September 7, 1900, he was assigned either to his old troop, Company H, or to Company I (his enlistment papers offer conflicting assignments). But the War Department decided to expand the United States Cavalry from ten regiments to fifteen. Lt. Col. T. C. Lebo of the First Cavalry was selected for promotion so that he could organize the new Fourteenth Cavalry. Colonel Lebo, an old Indian fighter and Civil War veteran, had noticed Harry Wheeler's maturity, intelligence, and conscientiousness. Wheeler was recruited to serve as a sergeant of Company M of the Fourteenth Cavalry. Although he had served only briefly in his second tour with the First, his transfer to the Fourteenth was regarded officially as his third enlistment.[9]

Officers' row at Fort Grant, Arizona, Sergeant Wheeler's last duty station. (Courtesy National Archives)

The Fourteenth Cavalry was activated on February 2, 1901, and the new regiment was sent to Arizona, where Harry Wheeler would spend the rest of his life. Sergeant Wheeler and Company M were stationed at Fort Grant, located at the base of Mount Graham in 1873. The post was busy during the Apache War into the 1880s, but Fort Grant was abandoned in 1896. The post office stayed open, however, and when the army expanded during the war with Spain, Fort Grant was reactivated. When elements of the Fourteenth Cavalry arrived in 1901, they found an invigorating mountain climate. In the middle of the parade ground was a cement-lined lake, sixty by one hundred feet. "Lake Constance" was built in 1888, when a water and sewage system was installed, including water fountains throughout the post. Cavalry stables and quarters for the laundresses were located behind the barracks. Since housing was not provided for wives of enlisted men, Mamie Wheeler and little Allyn probably lived in laundress quarters, and she would have supplemented her husband's pay by washing for the troopers.[10]

On Wednesday afternoon, October 9, 1901, Sergeant Wheeler was on stable duty. While grooming a horse, suddenly he caught a vicious kick in the stomach. Wiry and tough, Wheeler expected to recover quickly. However, he had been injured internally, and he remained sore and weak. Capt. Charles Flagg, assistant surgeon assigned to Fort Grant, kept Sergeant Wheeler under observation. Dr. Flagg noted the position of the abdominal bruise and determined that Wheeler's left kidney and duodonem were injured, causing "inanition due to faulty digestion." In layman's terms, Wheeler was habitually exhausted from a lack of food or an inability to assimilate food. Sergeant Wheeler continued to suffer month after month. Finally, early in September 1902, eleven months after Wheeler was injured, Dr. Flagg recommended a medical discharge. Capt. W. R. Sedberg, commander of Company M, approved the recommendation, which then was endorsed by Colonel Lebo and the Medical Headquarters of the Department of the Colorado in Denver. Although certified as disabled, he waived admission to a soldiers' home. Sergeant Wheeler was discharged at Fort Grant on September 22, 1902.[11]

Harry Wheeler was twenty-seven. He had served in the U. S. Cavalry for more than five years, and military posts had been his home for his entire life. Now, with a wife and a four-year-old son, Wheeler would have to make his way in the civilian world.

CHAPTER THREE

Arizona Ranger

"Excellent service, honest and faithful—
gallant & intelligent, an officer of great ability."

—Ranger Capt. Tom Rynning, about Sgt. Harry Wheeler

Harry Wheeler liked his prospects in Arizona Territory. Still sparsely settled, Arizona retained as much frontier flavor as any territory or state in the United States, and there remained a distinct promise of adventure. In 1900 Arizona's largest town, Tucson, held only 7,531 people, and just 123,000 persons were scattered across the sweeping vastness of the territory. Early in the twentieth century, Arizona still offered far horizons and a sense of freedom and exuberance that radiated deep appeal for Harry Wheeler.

Following his discharge at Fort Grant, Wheeler brought his wife and son south to Willcox, where he found employment as a laborer. Located in southeastern Arizona along the Southern Pacific Railroad, Willcox was a growing town more than twenty years old when the Wheelers moved there in 1902. But Wheeler soon moved farther south to work as a miner in Tombstone.[1] The violent old boomtown had declined rapidly in the early 1890s, when water flooded the mines. Just after the turn of the century, however, the Development Company of America lowered water levels by sinking a shaft, then reopened some of the mines and offered employment to men like Harry Wheeler.

But Harry Wheeler was not cut out to be a miner or laborer. The need to serve was too deeply ingrained. Although he had to be discharged from the military, another opportunity for service presented itself. The Arizona Rangers, a law enforcement company organized with a distinctly military flavor, needed new recruits.

Harry Wheeler still sported his cavalryman's moustache when he joined the Arizona Rangers. (Courtesy Arizona State Archives)

While most of America embraced the modernity of a new and exciting century, Arizona was plagued by badmen who found other regions of the United States too settled for frontier outlawry. Bank and train robbers, rustlers, murderers, and other lawbreakers with fast horses stood a reasonable chance of remaining free in the enormous empty stretches of Arizona Territory. Therefore, individuals with the instincts of a manhunter could find a rare challenge remaining in Arizona. A man could pin on a badge, climb into the saddle and, in the righteous cause of justice and the territorial statutes, gallop into the mountains and canyons and deserts in pursuit of society's enemies. There still were plenty of wrongs to right in Arizona, where Harry Wheeler would find a fresh purpose in life.

By 1901, with outlaws seemingly gaining the upper hand in Arizona, cattlemen, mine owners, railroad officials, and newspaper editors pressured Territorial Governor Nathan Oakes Murphy to combat lawlessness with a special force modeled upon the famed Texas Rangers. Governor Murphy embraced the idea. While visiting with rancher-businessman (and fellow Republican) Burt Mossman in Phoenix, the governor stated, "What we need is a hard riding, sure shooting outfit something like the Texas Rangers or the Mexican Rurales."[2]

Mossman and Frank Cox, head attorney for the Southern Pacific Railroad, soon produced an eighteen-point document outlining a ranger organization, which they presented to Governor Murphy. Legislative opposition always could be expected to threaten public projects requiring tax money, and various county sheriffs and local officers would resent a police force with territorywide authority. But Governor Murphy skillfully worked behind the scenes in discreet cooperation with legislators who supported a ranger force. In March 1901 the ranger bill was quietly maneuvered through committees and was ultimately approved on March 21. Governor Murphy promptly added his signature.[3]

The legislation created a fourteen-man company: one captain, one sergeant, and twelve privates. Rangers were to be enrolled for twelve-month enlistments. The captain would be paid $120 per month; the sergeant $75 monthly; and the privates $55 each. The men were to provide their own arms, mounts, "and all necessary accoutrements and camp equipage," although the territory would provide ammunition, food, and forage for each Ranger, not to exceed one dollar for meals and fifty cents for horse feed per day. A tax of five cents on every $100 taxable property in the Territory was to be collected and placed in "the ranger fund," which could finance all necessary expenses. The force was to "be governed by the rules and regulations of the army of the United States, as far as the same would be applicable." Rangers were empowered to arrest law-breakers anywhere in the Territory, and were directed to deliver prisoners to the nearest peace officer in the county where the crime was committed. The governor was to appoint "competent persons as captain and sergeant."[4]

Governor Murphy appointed Burt Mossman as first captain of the Arizona Rangers, and in September 1901 he began to enlist charter members of the company. There was to be no uniform. Like the Texas Rangers, members of the company would outfit themselves in range clothes. Section 4 of the Ranger Act specified that the men were to use "the most effective and breech-loading cavalry arms." Each member of the company was expected to furnish his own "six shooting pistol (army size)." The Ranger sidearm thus would be the reliable Colt .45 single-action revolver.

Captain Mossman knew the rifle he wanted. A landmark in Winchester production, the Model 1895 was devised by John M. Browning, America's foremost genius in arms design. The 1895 Winchester was the first lever-action repeater to use a box magazine instead of the old tubular magazine. Five rounds nestled in the box, and the chamber could accommodate a sixth. One advantage of this rifle was that it used the same caliber as the army Krag, and "we could always be sure the commanding officers at Fort Huachuca and Fort Apache would load us up with plenty of ammunition whenever we ran low."[5]

Captain Mossman located company headquarters at Bisbee, a raucous copper mining town in southeastern Arizona. On October 8, 1901, a furious rifle duel between a posse and the Bill Smith gang of rustlers resulted in the first Ranger death, newly recruited Pvt. Carlos Tafolla.

Mossman served only one year as captain before returning to ranching. But just before leaving the Rangers he made a daring undercover arrest in Mexico, bringing back to Arizona the ruthless *bandido* and killer Augustín Chacon.

By the time of Mossman's resignation, Arizona Territory had a new governor, Alexander O. Brodie. During the Spanish-American War, Brodie served as a major in the famous Rough Riders. Wounded in action, he won promotion to lieutenant colonel and earned the admiration of Teddy Roosevelt, who appointed Brodie governor of Arizona after the resignation of Governor Murphy in 1902. Governor Brodie soon picked a Rough Rider comrade, Lt. Thomas H. Rynning, to take charge of the Arizona Rangers. A tall, lean frontier adventurer, Rynning would become a law enforcement mentor to Harry Wheeler.

Captain Rynning moved Ranger headquarters to Douglas, a border town which had been laid out by the Phelps Dodge Company in Douglas. Named after James Douglas, president of Phelps Dodge, the townsite was located to serve a vast new copper smelter. By 1902 saloons, bordellos, and gambling houses flourished in the dusty boomtown, and hoodlums from two countries gravitated to Douglas. Hoping to clean up the rowdy frontier community, Captain Rynning placed the Ranger base in a two-room adobe on Fifteenth Street, in the south end of town. The front room served as office, complete with bedrolls, guns, saddles, and tack. A plank corral was erected out back, and at least one horse stood saddled and bridled twenty-four hours a day for emergency calls.

Capt. Thomas H. Rynning of the Arizona Rangers had served an enlistment in the U.S. Cavalry and fought with the Rough Riders in Cuba. (Courtesy Arizona Historical Society)

Captain Rynning instituted training measures, and arrest totals escalated. During its initial year and a half of existence, the Ranger force had made noticeable inroads in outlawry around the Territory, and on March 19, 1903, the Twenty-second Legislative Assembly passed an act doubling the size of the company and substantially increasing Ranger pay. The captain's salary was raised to $175 per month, a lieutenant would be paid $130, four sergeants would receive $110 each month, and twenty privates would collect $100 apiece. Captain Rynning commenced a vigorous recruiting program.[6]

Harry Wheeler found himself attracted to the Ranger company. Out of uniform now for several months, law enforcement appealed to his stern sense of duty, and Ranger pay was far greater than army compensation. Wheeler knew he was a better shot with rifle or pistol than any lawbreaker he might encounter, and Captain Rynning, a combat veteran, stressed marksmanship. In addition to service with the Rough Riders, Rynning previously had spent five years as an enlisted man in the Eighth Cavalry, and he was pleased that Wheeler also was a former cavalryman.

On July 6, 1903, Wheeler's application was accepted by the Rangers; he was destined to become the most outstanding Ranger in the history of the force.

Service with the Rangers brought out his finest qualities—dedication, courage, intense commitment to public service. On an early personnel report, Captain Rynning wrote of Wheeler: "Excellent service, honest and faithful—gallant & intelligent, an officer of great ability." Just four months after enlisting, the twenty-seven-year-old Wheeler was promoted to sergeant.[7]

Stationed in Willcox, Sergeant Wheeler traveled by train to Tucson on Saturday, October 22, 1904. The following evening he was in Wanda's Restaurant on Congress Street when two holdup men approached the nearby Palace Saloon. One man positioned himself across the street as a lookout, while Joe Bostwick crept around to the rear of the saloon.[8] Inside the Palace four regulars were on duty: night bartender Decker; Lincoln, the craps dealer; Johnson, the roulette dealer; and a black porter. Half an hour before midnight, the only customers were "Policy Sam" Meadows, E. O. Smith, miner Matt Fayson, and carpenter M. D. Beede.

Bostwick slipped through the rear door of the Palace. He wore a slouch hat, a pair of coveralls, and a long, faded coat. He brandished a long-barreled .45, and his face was covered with a red bandanna, complete with eyeholes.

"Hands up!" he shouted.

Beede instantly darted out the front door, but everyone else was riveted to attention by the masked man and his gun. "Throw up your hands," Bostwick repeated nervously, "and march into that side room."

As the men moved toward the side room, the jittery bandit snapped, "Hold 'em up higher—hold up your digits."

Bartender Decker, with surprising jocularity, held up one finger, then another, and asked if that was enough. "Get a move on," growled the masked desperado, and Decker raised his hands and followed the others. Bostwick and Decker edged toward the craps table, where money was scattered near the dice.

Outside on Congress Street, the fleeing Beede ran into Sergeant Wheeler, who had just emerged from Wanda's Restaurant. Told by Beede that a robbery was taking place, Wheeler promptly turned toward the point of danger. Beede excitedly warned, "Don't go in there—there is a holdup going on."

Wheeler was cool and confident. "All right," he reassured Beede, "that's what I'm here for."

Drawing his single-action Colt .45, Wheeler quickly marched to the saloon entrance. Bostwick saw the lawman and turned to level his revolver, but Wheeler fired first, grazing the bandit's forehead. Bostwick snapped off a wild round, then groaned as Wheeler shot him in the chest. Mortally wounded, Bostwick sagged to the floor.

When the shooting started, the lookout man fired a round at Wheeler. The bullet imbedded itself harmlessly in the leg of the roulette table, and in the excitement of the fight Wheeler did not realize the source of the fourth shot until later.

The men in the saloon crowded around the fallen thief, and a physician named Olcott was summoned to the scene. Dr. Olcott ordered the wounded man be carried to the local hospital.

Wheeler telegraphed news of the shooting to Captain Rynning in Benson, and Rynning caught the first train to Tucson. The day after the shooting it was learned that the would-be bandit, calling himself "George Anderson," had checked into Tucson's San Augustin Hotel more than a week prior to the holdup attempt. "Anderson" disappeared after a couple of days, and the hotel manager entered his room and confiscated a traveling bag. Papers inside the luggage indicated that he was an advance man for the Independent Carnival Company and that his name was "Walter F. Stanley." The hotel manager recalled a man had complained about being bothered by people to whom he owed money.

On Monday night, word came that a hobo on an eastbound freight train had told other transients in his boxcar that he had a wounded partner in Tucson. Remembering the fourth shot in the fray, Wheeler promptly took a train to the east. On Tuesday night, however, Bostwick died, and orders were telegraphed to Wheeler to return for an inquest the next day. Wheeler reluctantly abandoned his pursuit of the alleged lookout man and headed back to Tucson.[9]

By the time he arrived, it had been learned that the dead man was from Locust Grove, Georgia, and that his wife was in Denver. Telegrams from the deceased's father revealed that his real name was Joe Bostwick, and the elder Bostwick directed that his son should be buried in Tucson. To a Tucson newspaper reporter, Sergeant Wheeler made a conventional statement of regret, but emphasized that "it was either his life or mine," then added pointedly, "if I had to do it over again I think I would do exactly the same thing."[10] Joe Bostwick, alias George Anderson, would not be the last badman to fall under Ranger Wheeler's guns.

Wheeler returned to his duty post in Willcox. The town had grown up beside railroad tracks when the Southern Pacific built westward through the Sulphur Spring Valley in 1880. Frame and adobe commercial structures lined the north side of Railroad Avenue for two blocks. There were a couple of two-story hotels, the Willcox House and the Macy Hotel, several saloons, general stores, a post office, a meat market, and the Willcox Drug Store. Willcox boasted an ice plant, a telephone connection, a volunteer fire department, and the *Arizona Range News*. The two-story frame depot, built in 1881, still dominates the business district, and several commercial buildings and residences remain from the turn of the century or earlier. In the northeast section of town a red-light district, dubbed "the alley," served cowboys and various saloon denizens. In 1900 a drunken Warren Earp, youngest of the famous gunfighter/lawman clan, was shot to death in the Palace Saloon.[11]

When the Wheeler family lived in Willcox, the population was about 800. There was a four-room brick school for little Allyn, who turned six in 1904. For Harry there was a sturdy jail, built of two-by-fours in 1897 and equipped with steel cells.

The Ranger's principal problem around his duty station was cattle rustling. The Sulphur Springs Valley was the center of one of the best grazing areas in Arizona, and Willcox had become an important shipping point. Twenty-two miles north of Willcox was Henry Hooker's vast Sierra Bonita Ranch. (Hooker had a house in Willcox, which still stands south of the railroad tracks, and he built an adobe church, the town's first place of worship.) There were other big ranches in the Sulphur Spring Valley, and rustlers haunted the open range. The plague of rustlers in Arizona was a major reason for creation of the Ranger company. During Wheeler's years in Willcox, rustling declined noticeably in the Sulphur Spring Valley, and ranchers began to fence in their spreads.

Indeed, by 1905 the Arizona Rangers had achieved their initial objective of curbing rustling activities in areas that had been afflicted by stock theft. A special trouble spot had been the Arizona-New Mexico line, where rustlers had slipped elusively from one jurisdiction to another, and where Sergeant Wheeler rode the ranges of southeastern Arizona. The diligent efforts of the Rangers had driven most stock thieves from eastern Arizona, which created a problem for New Mexico. So many rustlers now haunted New Mexico that officials decided to follow the Arizona solution. In 1905 the New Mexico Mounted Police was voted into existence, "identical in all but the name to . . . the Arizona Rangers," the Tucson *Citizen* proudly announced.[12]

All across Arizona Territory, Ranger arrest totals mounted at a record rate. During the fiscal year which ended June 30, 1905, the Rangers reported 1,052 arrests. Eight Rangers regularly worked with the Livestock Sanitary Board and the Arizona Cattle Growers' Association, and the force had begun to concentrate on assisting federal authorities in halting the flood of Chinese aliens being smuggled into Arizona. Rangers were arresting swindlers, forgers, army deserters, drunks, bunco artists, vagrants, and men who ran opium dens.

One Ranger arrest involved a fellow lawman, Lee Hobbs. Hobbs and his brothers were deputy sheriffs of Graham County, and they had been appointed by their uncle, Sheriff Jim Parks. In 1902 Lee Hobbs had worked aboard a British freighter in the Pacific. Becoming disgruntled, he led an uprising, shot the captain and first mate, then escaped in a small boat to an island. British officials posted a large reward, and in 1905 Arizona Ranger "Timberline Bill" Sparks identified Deputy Sheriff Lee Hobbs as the murderous mutineer. Realizing the explosive potential of arresting a fellow officer who had many influential relatives in the area, Sparks requested help from Ranger headquarters. Soon Sergeant Wheeler traveled from Willcox to Clifton, and Privates Jeff Kidder and Oscar Rountree arrived from their duty stations. When the four well-armed Rangers confronted Hobbs on Friday night, April 7, there was no trouble. Subsequent fears of a violent rescue proved groundless, at least in part because of the formidable Ranger presence, and Hobbs was extradited for trial.[13]

In 1905 Governor Brodie accepted an appointment as assistant chief of the Records and Pensions Bureau of the War Department. Arizona thereby lost the governor who was instrumental in creating the Rangers, at a time when the legislature was considering three separate bills to abolish the company. The cost of maintaining the Rangers was running close to $3,000 per month, giving thrift-minded legislators ammunition against the company. While some newspapers strongly supported the Rangers, others editorialized against the company—some clamoring for abolishment and some suggesting that the company be reduced by half. But the new territorial governor proved to be a champion of the Arizona Rangers. President Roosevelt selected Arizona's attorney general, Joseph H. Kibbey, and Governor Kibbey would battle persistent attacks against the Ranger company for the next four years.

Another change of leadership was rumored in 1905. Capt. Tom Rynning apparently was uneasy for a time after his Rough Rider companion-at-arms, Brodie, left the governor's office for Washington. Soon there was talk that Rynning would resign from the Ranger force, and that "Rangers Wheeler, Brooks, Sparks and Holmes are candidates for the captaincy."[14] Sergeant Wheeler was rated at the top of this speculation, ahead of even Lt. Johnny Brooks, second-in-command of the company.

Captain Rynning apparently had been told by Governor Brodie that he would be appointed superintendent of the territorial prison at Yuma when the position next became vacant. After Brodie left office, Rynning assumed that the new governor likewise intended to elevate him to the superintendency. When Superintendent Ben F. Daniels resigned, the Ranger captain did not even bother to make a formal application. Governor Kibbey, who had never been told that Rynning wanted the job, appointed another man to the position. An able politician, Rynning shrugged off his disappointment without public complaint. But soon he would become embroiled in a clash with Lieutenant Brooks, who resigned from the Rangers on July 6, 1905.

By this time Sgt. Harry Wheeler had impressed everyone with his efficiency and almost fanatical devotion to duty. Captain Rynning promptly appointed him to fill the lieutenant's post. Lieutenant Wheeler was stationed in Willcox, but he had been on the job only a few days when he accompanied Rynning by train to Yuma on official business. Shortly after his return, the new lieutenant was dispatched by rail to Prescott to help Pvt. Oscar Rountree smooth over a local difficulty.[15] Hardly had he again returned before Lieutenant Wheeler learned that a more demanding assignment awaited him in the weeks ahead. He would be filling in for Captain Rynning, who planned an extensive trek to inspect Ranger outposts across Arizona "and all the large cities of the Territory."[16]

In mid-August Rynning strapped his bedroll and ample provisions onto a packhorse, saddled his big gray, then mounted up and headed west for a marathon journey. Although Rynning kept in touch with headquarters, Harry Wheeler ran the company for the next six weeks. The experience would prove invaluable within a couple of years. Wheeler had to leave his home in Willcox to work at Ranger headquarters, and soon he would move his family to Douglas. When Captain Rynning finally made his way back to Douglas, "browned by the exposure to the wind and sun," he had ridden horseback a total of 1,300 miles. Having acquired a firsthand impression of conditions across much of the Territory, he hastened to Phoenix by rail to report to

Governor Kibbey. A man with keen political instincts, Rynning still had his eye on the prison superintendency or some other possible promotion, and he began to communicate cordially with Arizona's new governor.[17]

In the fall of 1905 Captain Rynning applied to Governor Kibbey for a thirty-day leave of absence to search for a party of men from Douglas who had disappeared during a trip to the Sonoran desert. There was widespread interest in the apparent tragedy, and editorials called for assistance by the Rangers. Kibbey gave permission to Rynning and three other Rangers to venture into Mexico as members of a private search party. Rynning and his men did not go in their official capacity as Rangers; a private subscription collected in Douglas provided them with traveling funds.[18] They would return empty-handed, but for a month Lieutenant Wheeler again commanded the company.

Late in 1905 Wheeler and three fellow Rangers performed a mission of heroic proportions, combining detective skills, selfless devotion to duty, and physical stamina in the face of incredible danger. Earlier that summer, a grisly homicide was committed at a small ranch on Pinto Creek one mile outside the village of Livingston. On the dark, rainy night of July 12, rancher Sam Plunkett and an elderly friend, Ed Kennedy, were slain in their beds. Their skulls were crushed with a piece of iron from a wagon tongue, and Plunkett was stabbed sixteen times. Kennedy was also stabbed repeatedly. They lay dead for two days before their corpses were discovered. Robbery was apparent; about $100 in cash was missing, as well as a gold watch and a revolver. Two Mexican employees—a big man named Gonzalez and a youth named Ascension—could not be found and were presumed guilty of the crime.[19]

From 1903 to 1906 the headquarters desk usually was managed by Sgt. Arthur Hopkins, an ex-soldier from Colorado. Wheeler and Hopkins later would reunite in Cochise County. (Courtesy Arizona State Archives)

Pvt. William S. Peterson, a Texan who had been in the Rangers since 1902, headed the immediate investigation. Aided by Indian trailers and Al Sieber, the noted army scout of Indian war fame, Peterson followed the tracks of the suspects for twenty miles in the direction of Globe. The two Indians circled in opposite directions until they cut trail.

The killers had been on foot, but ten miles from Globe, they apparently were picked up and rode away on horseback. Although the trail disappeared in Globe, a blood-stained knife was found, along with a bloody shirt which had been discarded.

Soon it was learned that Pantaleon Ortega, who tended bar at Mark Cheever's boardinghouse in Globe, had helped the two criminals escape. Evidently he brought his two friends to the boardinghouse, tended to three knife cuts suffered by one of the men in his leg, cashed a paycheck for them, and bought them new clothing. Ortega secluded Gonzalez and Ascension for two or three days before helping them to leave the vicinity.

Law officers, apparently including Lt. Harry Wheeler, noted that whenever a man with a badge was present, Ortega was noticeably uneasy. Mrs. Cheever was asked why the bartender was so nervous around lawmen, and she went to Ortega. He confessed to her about assisting his two friends, whom she remembered from several meals at her boarding table. Ortega also told her that he had received letters from them from Minas Prietas in Sonora. Mrs. Cheever related the conversation and stated that she was certain she could recognize the men. Harry Wheeler had Ortega arrested and placed in the Gila County jail in Globe. It was learned there that one of the suspects had been confined overnight for vagrancy after the murder, but he was released routinely the next morning.

Months passed with no further progress in the case. However, even as the crime faded from public attention, Lieutenant Wheeler and a few other law officers never stopped probing for a lead. At last Wheeler heard from an informant that the two suspects were in Sonora, going from one mining camp to another and never staying more than two weeks in one place. Wheeler, Sgt. Billy Old, and new Ranger recruits Dick Hickey and Eugene Shute determined to go into Sonora in search of the killers. Shute was related to one of the victims, Plunkett, and he may have joined the Rangers for the sole purpose of seeking his kinsman's killers in Mexico. Hickey, too, may have enlisted primarily to go on this manhunt, perhaps in hopes of reward money, which by this time totaled $1,050.[20]

In Magdelena there was no sign of the fugitives, but Wheeler and his men paid a visit to Col. Emilio Kosterlitzky, asking the *Rurales* commander for aid in finding the murderers. The *Rurales* had no men to spare; the Yaqui Indians were engaged in a typically ferocious uprising, and Kosterlitzky warned the Rangers to be wary of these murderous tribesmen during their search.

Wheeler, Old, Hickey, and Shute took a train to nearby Santa Ana, then traveled by stagecoach to a remote mining camp. The fugitives were not there, so the Rangers returned to Santa Ana and boarded a train for a 150-mile trip south to Ortiz. In Ortiz the Rangers bought supplies and acquired a wagon and team, intending to proceed to La Dura, ninety miles distant and located in the heart of Yaqui country. But as they were preparing to leave the next morning, a Mexican army officer arrived and forbade their journey. He stated that a Yaqui war party was within ten miles of Ortiz and the roads were unsafe. A cavalry squadron was camped nearby, however, and he promised to provide them with a military escort.

The day passed with no sign of an escort. Late that night the Rangers quietly hitched up their horses and headed for La Dura, where they hoped to find Gonzalez and Ascension. After driving about twenty miles, they encountered a battered cavalry troop whose commander described a vicious fight the day before, with severe losses to the Yaquis. He detailed the dangers of the country ahead and tried to dissuade the Americans from proceeding. Wheeler, however, called him aside, and with his characteristic sense of obligation explained that he and his little squad also were soldiers, as loath to turn back from their duty as soldiers in Mexico. The Mexican leader gravely saluted Wheeler, and the two bands of men went their separate ways.

After making good progress, the Rangers camped for a night in a cluster of mesquite trees. In late December on the western approach to the Sierra Madres, nighttime temperatures plunged to chilling levels, but the danger of discovery by Yaqui warriors made a campfire too great a risk. The Rangers, who had no blankets, spent a miserable night shivering and stamping and waiting for the dawn so they could again be on the move.

At daybreak, however, another cavalry troop rode up and took them into custody: They would be guests of the military for their own protection. Wheeler protested, explaining why they were in Mexico and that they would assume all responsibility for their actions. Nevertheless, they were escorted to a blockhouse five miles away, where a small garrison provided them with beds and food.

After four days at the blockhouse, letters from Ortiz ordered the release of the Rangers and the protection of an escort. Wheeler and his men traveled to La Dura, where a search for the Plunkett-Kennedy murderers proved fruitless. They returned with their escort to the blockhouse after a round trip of ten days, then proceeded east a short distance to Guaymas. The fugitives were not spotted in Guaymas, nor in Empalme, a few miles to the west.

Doggedly the Rangers decided the murderers might be working with crews constructing a railroad across one of the most deserted stretches of Sonora. They rode a train twenty miles to the end of the completed track, after which they set out on foot. The Rangers trudged far into the night, then spent a few miserable hours trying to sleep through the cold. The next morning they ate the last of their provisions, put themselves on short water rations, and struck out along the right-of-way. During the day's trek, Hickey became so footsore that he removed his shoes, tied the laces together, and slung them around his neck. His three companions laughed at him, but the next day they had to resort to the same technique.

By this time their canteens were empty, and thirst was added to the misery of hunger and fatigue. On the third day afoot the four Rangers stumbled ahead without speaking, carrying empty canteens and stopping to rest every ten minutes.

For three days they had encountered no one and had seen no houses. Wheeler, realizing how desperate their situation was, ordered his men to push

Gunrunners, Mexican revolutionaries, and smugglers kept large numbers of Rangers near the border in 1906. Congregated in front of the Bank of Bisbee are, left to right: Constable Jack White of Bisbee, Capt. Tom Rynning, unknown, Ranger Billy Speed, Ranger John Greenwood, Ranger Ray Thompson, Ranger Porter McDonald, Ranger Rube Burnett, Sgt. Arthur A. Hopkins, Lt. Harry Wheeler. (Courtesy Arizona State Archives)

on through the night. They staggered wearily onward in silence that finally, gloriously, was broken by an excited cry from Hickey: "That's a house!"

A hint of light flickered through the darkness. The Rangers plunged toward the light, soon coming to a one-room adobe shanty. The only openings were a door and a few portholes. When the Rangers knocked on the door, feet scurried inside and a high-pitched voice dubiously proclaimed in Spanish: "Get your pistols, boys. Kill the Yaquis." Shouted explanations from the Rangers only produced such a cacophony of screams, curses, and prayers from inside that the desperate Americans could not make themselves understood. Braving the possibility of gunfire, the Americans burst into the now darkened room and struck a match.

Seven men, three women, and half a dozen children cowered in a corner. The men, although terror-stricken and without a single gun, had knelt in front of the women and children, intending to be the first to be slain by the dreaded Yaquis.

Wheeler and the others tried to explain that they were not the Yaquis, but it was difficult to penetrate the panic of the Mexicans. At last, however, the Mexicans realized that the intruders meant them no harm, and the Rangers made clear their identity and plight. The relieved Mexicans became perfect hosts, placing the Rangers on their own pallets, then carefully allotting them water in gradual quantities. The *norteamericanos* had their battered feet washed and bandaged, after which the women served tortillas, beans, goat's milk cheese, and coffee. The exhausted Rangers then fell into a deep slumber, not awakening until the middle of the next afternoon.

The Mexicans continued to tend to the Rangers, explaining that the main road crew was ten miles farther on but would return within a few days. The Anglos availed themselves of their hosts' hospitality for three days, as their feet and bodies recovered from the recent ordeal. When the construction crew came back, Gonzalez and Ascension were not among them, so the Rangers made their way back to Empalme.

Next they decided to try their luck at Minas Prietas, where a solid clue finally emerged. As the Rangers searched the camp, they were told that two men fitting the description of Gonzalez and Ascension had left Minas Prietas just a few days earlier. They had announced their destination as Nogales. The Rangers immediately headed north.

The suspects could not be located in Nogales, but the entire Ranger force was alerted that the murderers probably were back in Arizona. Mining camps throughout the Territory were scoured in vain. Wheeler returned to his duties in Willcox—and happened upon the very men he had trailed back and forth across Sonora.

It was raining hard in Willcox, but despite the deluge two Mexicans sat on the railroad tracks outside town, refusing to come in for shelter. Wheeler's suspicions were aroused, and he went out to confront the two drenched men. When Wheeler approached, the two men stood up and began to move away. The Ranger lieutenant called out that they were under arrest. The larger of the two men, Gonzalez, whipped out a wicked-looking knife, and his *compañero*, Ascension, opened up a pocketknife. Wheeler pulled a gun and easily took them into custody.

Gonzalez and Ascension were jailed in Willcox, and they nervously paced in their cells throughout the night. Gonzalez was overheard repeating, "We will be hung in Globe." But Ascension always replied, "No. They will hang you but not me." Ascension later stated that Gonzalez had slain both Kennedy and Plunkett. Gonzalez had forced Ascension to watch while he stabbed and battered their employers, then the two thieves seized the money and divided their plunder before fleeing on foot. When the two were bound over to the Gila County grand jury,

Lt. Harry Wheeler holding his 1895 Winchester. Note the fringed buckskin gloves. (Courtesy Arizona State Archives)

Ascension confessed willingly and wangled a release. Gonzalez managed to escape, but later committed suicide.

Harry Wheeler was understandably disgusted at these developments. He and his three companions had not only braved enormous hazards to search a foreign, hostile land for the murderers but also had received no travel allowance from the Territory. Relatives of the dead men provided some of the expense money; otherwise, the Rangers paid their own way.

Recruits Hickey and Shute quit the Rangers shortly after returning from Sonora. Hickey resigned on January 20, 1906, and Shute left the force eleven days later.[21]

Harry Wheeler, reflecting in 1910 on the mammoth manhunt, marveled at the dedication of his men: "Every conceivable hardship and danger had been endured uncomplainingly. Rangers drawing $100 per month, with absolutely no expense allowance, had readily and willingly spent their own wages . . . in the performance of their duty." With a trace of rueful enlightenment, he asked rhetorically: "Were the Arizona Rangers patriots or fools? I leave it to the questioner."[22]

Harry Wheeler found himself unusually busy during the early weeks of 1906. As the new year began, a criminal gang exerted such a grip on Douglas that it became dangerous to go out at night. It was an embarrassing reflection on the Rangers, since headquarters was at Douglas, but Tom Rynning simply turned the problem over to his capable lieutenant.

Wheeler characteristically met the criminal challenge head-on. He brought six Rangers into Douglas, then led them in patrolling the city streets after dark. While catching some sleep during the day, Harry Wheeler and his men rode horseback for ten consecutive nights through the streets of Douglas from dusk to dawn. The "yeggmen" (slang of the day for criminals) were completely cowed by the imposing presence of the heavily armed Rangers astride their horses. The Ranger patrol "put the thieves and thugs to flight," intimidating the yeggmen so thoroughly that Wheeler and his men could find no one to arrest. A newspaper trumpeted: "RANGERS RESCUED DOUGLAS FROM BAND OF YEGGMEN."[23]

Within days of taming Douglas, Lieutenant Wheeler was in Tucson, where he arrested a fugitive named Harry Howard. Howard, still a teenager, had been incarcerated for burglary in what Los Angeles boasted as the finest jail in the Southwest. But Howard and another inmate found escape easy, crawling through a hole in the wall of the second floor and lowering themselves with a rope. Howard's description was widely circulated, and a $100 reward was offered.

The escapee slipped into Tucson aboard a train on Sunday afternoon, January 28. After dark he wandered from the railroad yards uptown, hoping to find food. At about 8:00 he was at Congress and Church streets, where he was noticed by Harry Wheeler. Wheeler, already searching for the prisoner, thought he recognized Howard and took him to jail. Los Angeles authorities were notified, and Wheeler picked up $100 in "Pin Money."[24]

Another 1906 incident involving Wheeler occurred when an American wool grower whose ranch was near Naco discovered that several of his goats had strayed across the line into Mexico. He crossed over into Naco, Sonora, and asked a Mexican customs official named Jiminez for permission to search for his goats. Jiminez granted his request, but while that rancher hunted his goats, Jiminez turned up and placed him under arrest. The luckless wool grower was tossed into Naco's *juzgado local.*

Lieutenant Wheeler was in Naco, and the rancher had informed the Ranger of his little foray into Mexico. When Wheeler learned of the rancher's arrest, he confronted Jiminez in the Mexican customs office. Jiminez told the Ranger to remove his hat. Wheeler refused unless Jiminez would remove his headwear. There was a tense standoff before Wheeler stalked out of the office—with his hat still settled squarely on his head.

Wheeler promptly notified Captain Rynning in Douglas about the incident. Rynning contacted Gen. Luis E. Torres in Mexico, who wrote the Ranger captain. Torres first expressed gratitude for the recent help of the Rangers in watching the border for a gang of *bandidos* reportedly heading toward Arizona. Then Torres stated: "I deeply regret the lack of courtesy shown by the administrator of the customs service in Naco toward my friend, Lieutenant Wheeler, and I have reported the case to the proper officials. I wish to apologize myself for the lack of good behavior on the part of Mr. Jiminez, and I wish to say further that I work at all times to keep the best of relations between the people of our two countries."[25]

The upper ranks of the Ranger company remained in stable hands in 1906. Tom Rynning began his fifth year as captain and Harry Wheeler, a Ranger since 1903, was still the lieutenant. But in October, Sgt. James McGee resigned, and on the last day of 1906 Sgt. Arthur Hopkins, who had presided over the headquarters desk since 1903, left the company to become the undersheriff of Cochise County.

Throughout the history of the Rangers there were periodic accusations of brutality. In August 1906, Pvt. Charles Eperson, a Ranger since 1903, had to defend himself against a charge of cruelty while making an arrest. At Gila Bend, Eperson took into custody a young man named James Williams, who had stolen a ride on a freight train from Tucson to Los Angeles. Williams decided that he was treated with undue harshness, and he filed a complaint. He claimed that when he tried to run away, the Ranger had fired seven shots at him. His face was bruised and both eyes had been blackened by a brutal beating, and he alleged that Eperson had confined him in the Gila County jail without food and water for an entire day. However, Lt. Harry Wheeler journeyed from Douglas to Gila Bend and conducted a local investigation which showed Williams's accusations to be groundless. When the hearing was held in Phoenix, Wheeler presented his findings and won exoneration for Eperson.[26]

Lieutenant Wheeler, meantime, made his way back to Douglas with a stop at Tucson, where he was interviewed by a reporter for the *Star.* After commenting on the Eperson-Williams incident, the *Star* renewed speculation that

Wheeler might soon succeed to the captaincy. It was thought that Tom Rynning might become sheriff of Cochise County in November, in which case Wheeler would likely fill the resulting vacancy of Ranger captain. But once more rumors of Rynning's resignation proved groundless, although he continued to be alert for promising opportunities.[27]

At this point Wheeler became aware of a robbery being planned by holdup artist Willis Wood. Wood had several confederates, including James Alexander, a bigamist and counterfeiter, and Burt Alvord, a former peace officer turned outlaw who recently had been released from Yuma Territorial Prison. The gang apparently intended to steal a load of bullion from the King of Arizona Mine when it was brought to Mohawk for shipment, although it is possible that they intended to rob a Southern Pacific train near Mohawk. Mohawk lies fifty miles east of Yuma, and the outlaws meant to head south through the Mohawk Valley, then across the Tule Desert and into Mexico. Most of the thirty-mile ride to the border is through arid land so barren that scarcely any vegetation grows. The gang, however, went to the trouble of filling and placing twenty water barrels along their escape route. Barrels were located every five miles, and the outlaws planned to water their horses and then empty the remaining water so that any pursuers would have to proceed at a slower pace.

The plot was uncovered by Lieutenant Wheeler. Shortly after traveling to Gila Bend and Phoenix to clear up the charges against Private Eperson, Wheeler was dispatched to Yuma on official business. In Yuma he recognized and arrested James Alexander, who was wanted in Graham County for various charges. Before sending Alexander to jail at Solomonville, Wheeler extracted

There was an explosive confrontation in Benson when Harry Wheeler, Tom Rynning, and three members of a lovers' triangle converged on the town in February 1907. The depot may be seen behind railroad cars at far right. (Courtesy Arizona Historical Society)

part of the story of the robbery scheme. He was told about the water barrels and about Wood and Alvord, although Alexander refused to divulge the identity of other gang members.

Wheeler assembled Sgt. James McGee, Lew Mickey, and Charles Eperson to ride along the planned escape route. They found the freshly filled water barrels but no robbers. The Rangers, now reinforced by a few area officers, set a trap, but the outlaws apparently sensed danger and abandoned the scheme. After a few days the Rangers rode to the Mexican border and back, destroying the water barrels, now warped in the blazing August heat. They could find no out-laws, but the plot was successfully foiled by the Rangers.[28]

Early in 1907 Lieutenant Wheeler became involved in a gunfight which be-came one of the classic *mano a mano* duels in all of frontier history. The gun-play occurred on Thursday, February 28, in Benson, where a lovers' triangle ex-ploded into violence. J. A. Tracy, agent for the Helvetia Copper Company at Vail's Station, traveled thirty miles by rail east to Benson for a murderous con-frontation with Mr. and "Mrs." D. W. Silverton. Silverton, member of a promi-nent Kentucky family, had studied mining engineering in college and had trav-eled west "to see the practical side of mining." To satisfy his romantic side he was staying in Tucson with a tall, shapely brunette in her mid-twenties. The couple claimed to have been married six weeks earlier in Phoenix by an evan-gelist named McComa, but later no one could recall a traveling preacher by that name, and no marriage license could be located.

The woman apparently met both men in Nevada; Silverton late in 1905, and Tracy early the next year. Tracy evidently had been married to her (Arcus Reddoch called him "her estranged husband," and she had lived in Vail's Station with Tracy), and when he learned that she was in Tucson he paid her a visit to offer her a diamond ring. She declined, and Tracy returned to Vail's Station without comment. The next day, however, she received four threatening letters from her frustrated suitor.[29]

"Mr. and Mrs. Silverton" decided to tour Douglas, Bisbee, and Cananea, and they boarded a train Wednesday afternoon. En route to Benson, where they planned to spend the night, the train made a stop at Vail's Station. Looking out of her window, the woman caught sight of Tracy standing on the depot plat-form. When she pointed out Tracy to Silverton, he bounded out of the car and the two men exchanged heated words. As the train pulled out of Vail's Station, Tracy angrily tried to catch the platform of the rear car.

An hour later the train arrived in Benson and the couple checked into Room 14 of the Virginia Hotel, across the street from the depot. Silverton engaged a porter to tell him if Tracy showed up, and early the next morning he received word that Tracy was indeed in Benson.

Tracy had come by freight train during the night, armed with a Colt .45 and muttering that he was "going to Benson to get a couple of people." When Silverton emerged onto the hotel porch on Thursday morning, he spotted Tracy standing beside the train for Bisbee. Ducking back inside, Silverton told the

The Southern Pacific Railroad Station, site of the classic gunfight between Harry Wheeler and J.A. Tracy. (Courtesy Arizona Historical Society)

hotel proprietor, Eduardo Castañeda, that he needed a gun for protection against Tracy. Castañeda opined that he should seek a law officer instead of procuring a firearm.

The nearest lawmen happened to be the two highest-ranking officers in the Arizona Rangers, who were staying in the Virginia Hotel. Captain Rynning had recently taken a fall from a horse, badly injuring his back and hip. He had holed up in the Virginia Hotel to take massage treatments from a Benson physician and had wired Lieutenant Wheeler, who was stationed in Willcox, to take charge of the company. Wheeler arrived and checked into the hotel to receive further instructions from Rynning. Castañeda, knowing that Rynning was crippled, sent for Wheeler, who was eating breakfast.

Wheeler listened to Silverton's story and was shown a photograph of Tracy by the brunette. Wheeler searched Silverton for any concealed weapon, then headed for the depot to disarm Tracy. The man was sitting on the steps of the dining car, but as Wheeler approached, Tracy saw Silverton and his paramour come out of the hotel. Tracy jumped up, cursing, and pulled his revolver from his pocket.

"Hold on there," barked Wheeler, "I arrest you. Give me that gun."[30]

Relentlessly stalking his foe, Wheeler advanced, firing methodically and ordering Tracy to surrender. Tracy's third shot wounded Wheeler in the upper left thigh near the groin, but the Ranger drilled his opponent four times, tumbling him onto his back. Tracy was hit under the heart, in the neck, arm, and thigh, and he gasped, "I am all in. My gun is empty."

Wheeler dropped his Colt, having fired all five rounds, and limped forward to secure his prisoner. But Tracy had two bullets left, and he treacherously opened fire again, striking Wheeler in the left heel. Gamely, Wheeler began hurling rocks at Tracy, whose gun finally clicked on an empty cylinder.

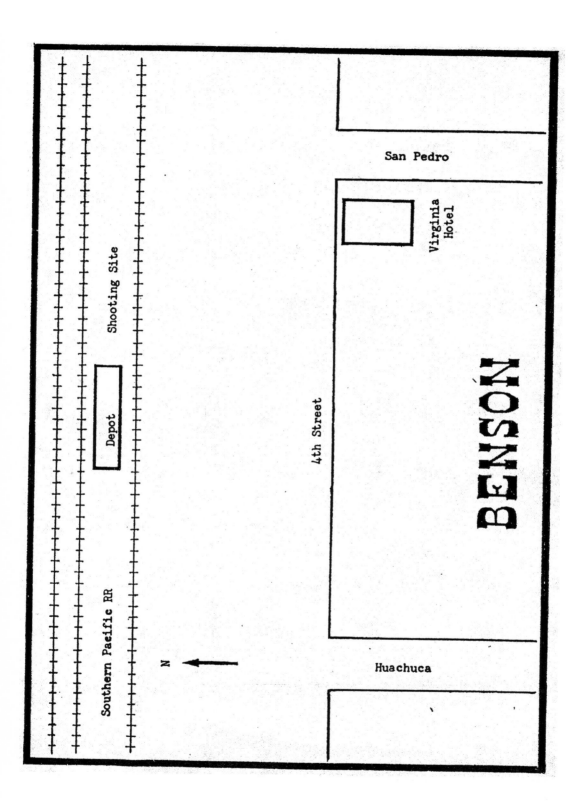

"I am all in," he repeated. "My gun is empty."[31]

Wheeler limped to him, but Tracy refused to give up his gun (later several cartridges were found in his pocket). At that point the porter ran up flourishing a small pistol, which Silverton tried to seize from him. Both men intended to pump more lead into Tracy.

The bleeding Wheeler managed to calm them as other onlookers crowded around. Wheeler finally disarmed Tracy, and someone brought a chair for the wounded officer.

"Give it to him," said Wheeler. "He needs it more than I do."

Wheeler relinquished responsibility for Tracy to a Benson peace officer, then extended his right hand. "Well," said Wheeler, "it was a great fight while it lasted, wasn't it, old man?"

"I'll get you yet," muttered Tracy with a hint of a smile.

The two men shook hands, then Wheeler retrieved his own six-gun and, with assistance, headed for the hotel. Captain Rynning hobbled outside and took a statement from Tracy. The scorned suitor asked to be sent to a Tucson hospital, and he was placed on a cot in the baggage car. But by the time the train reached Muscal Station, just ten miles west of Benson, the thirty-eight-year-old Tracy breathed his last. His final words were: "There is a woman in the case." His remains were shipped to Chicago.[32]

A reporter from the Bisbee *Review* asked for a statement from Wheeler, who replied that he was sorry Tracy had died.

Rynning's doctor tended Wheeler's wounds and suggested he seek treatment at the hospital in Tombstone. Rynning accompanied his lieutenant by rail thirty-five miles to Tombstone, where Wheeler was hospitalized for two weeks. But the wound near the groin never ceased to trouble him, especially on long horseback rides.

In June it was learned that J. A. Tracy had been wanted for two separate murders in Nevada, with a $500 reward on his head. One of his victims was the brother of former Ranger Dick Hickey, now a justice of the peace in Pinal County. Nevada officials offered Wheeler the reward, but he immediately turned it down. Although he was "a poor man," Wheeler would have no part of blood money, instead urging that the $500 be given to the widowed Mrs. Hickey.[33]

Within less than four years as an Arizona Ranger, Harry Wheeler had pursued and arrested a seedy diversity of lawbreakers, and he had shot dead two gunmen in face-to-face shootouts. He had advanced from private to sergeant to lieutenant, and as second-in-command of the company for nearly two years he had been placed in charge of the Rangers on several occasions. Harry Wheeler had earned the right to command the Arizona Rangers.

CHAPTER FOUR

Ranger Captain

"As a peace officer Mr. Wheeler is most competent, ... highly intelli-gent, a man of splendid jugdement, cool—skillful, daring, and the right man in the right place at all times."

—Sheriff John White

In March 1907 Capt. Tom Rynning finally received the promotion he long had sought. Jerry Millay, superintendent of the Yuma Territorial Prison, resigned because of ill health, and the position was offered to Rynning. "Of course it was some wrench to leave the Rangers," reminisced Rynning, who had captained the company for all but the first year of its five and one-half years of existence. But Rynning considered the hardest work of the Rangers to have been accom-plished, and he was a politically oriented man with administrative gifts who was eager for a fresh challenge. A new prison was being established at Florence, using convict labor to build the complex. Rynning would conduct the move from the adobe pile along the Colorado to the new facility, where he intended "to make decent citizens" out of many of the same lawbreakers his Rangers had apprehended. Rynning resigned his commission on March 20, 1907, and ten days later he arrived in Yuma.[1]

On previous occasions when Rynning's resignation had been rumored, it had been speculated that Harry Wheeler would be promoted to captain. There was considerable public interest about who would become the new captain of the Rangers, but any suspense over the matter would be of brief duration. Harry Wheeler had impressed everyone with his bravery and skills as an offi-cer and with his intense devotion to duty. One supporter, Sheriff John White of Cochise County, wrote Governor Kibbey praising Wheeler in ways typical of those who knew the man: "He is one of the finest, and most honorable gentle-men that it has ever been my good fortune to know, his character is without blemish ... As a peace officer Mr. Wheeler is most competent ... highly intel-ligent, a man of splendid judgement, cool—skillful, daring, and the right man in the right place at all times."[2]

Governor Kibbey promptly contacted Wheeler about the position, and Harry just as promptly accepted. Indeed, Arizona newspapers had predicted Wheeler's promotion even as his gunfight with J.A. Tracy made front-page head-lines. The legislature confirmed his appointment on March 22, and on Saturday, March 25, Harry Wheeler took the oath as third captain of the Arizona Rangers.[3]

Two days later, Sgt. Billy Old was promoted to lieutenant. His close friend, Sgt. Jeff Kidder, had been mentioned for the lieutenancy. Both men were highly capable officers and crack shots, but Kidder, despite a year's seniority over Old as Ranger, used the authority of his badge with a heavy hand and seemed to at-tract trouble. Billy Old proved to be a diplomatic and capable choice as the Ranger second-in-command. Old had been stationed for years in Nogales, but Wheeler sent him to Prescott so that he could direct Ranger activities in the northern part of the territory.

One of Wheeler's first moves was to transfer headquarters from Douglas to Naco. Douglas had built up quickly, and the Ranger presence there had exerted a taming influence. The Phelps-Dodge Company had made a determined effort to improve the moral climate of the town; for example, so much money had been spent (primarily by the company) on religious edifices that Douglas was now called "the City of Churches."[4] But twenty-five miles to the west, just across the border from Naco, Sonora, the raw American community of Naco, Arizona, had become a pesthole.

Just after the turn of the century, the Phelps-Dodge Company considered building a smelter at Naco. When the owners of the townsite refused to donate land, the smelter was erected at Douglas, and Naco was condemned to a sec-ondary existence. However, W.C. Greene owned a residence at Naco, and the freight activity stimulated by his massive operation at Cananea in Mexico caused a certain amount of economic progress. Freight cars loaded with mining equipment and supplies rumbled south through the big opening in the border fence, and great slabs of copper were shipped north through Naco. A brick bank was constructed on the 100-foot-wide main thoroughfare, "D Street," which runs north and south. The Copper Queen mercantile building also was brick, and the Hotel Naco was a two-story adobe which still looms on the east side of the street. Greene kept a dozen employees busy in an office building, several warehouses lined the railroad tracks, and a $30,000 customshouse was erected. John Baker moved his Owl Restaurant from Benson to Naco on a flat-car. The town maintained a steady, if small, economy. The Naco *Budget* offered a daily diet of boosterism to newspaper readers. For years trained hounds had coursed at the Naco Amusement Park. Naco even had a baseball team; so many

A dismounted Ranger patrol late in 1907. At left is Capt. Harry Wheeler. Next to him is Rye Miles, and standing fourth from the left is Oscar McAda. (Courtesy Arizona Historical Society)

Captain Wheeler, at right, leads a patrol. (Courtesy Arizona Historical Society)

Captain Wheeler was a conscientious administrator at Ranger headquarters, but he liked nothing better than leading men in the field. (Courtesy Arizona Historical Society)

Rudolph Gunner, highly regarded by Harry Wheeler, is mounted at far left in this 1908 photo. Other Rangers who can be identified are Captain Wheeler (third from left), Rye Miles (fourth from left), and John McK. Redmond (far left). (Courtesy Arizona State Archives)

Wheeler and the patrol head toward a settlement. (Courtesy Arizona Historical Society)

Ranger Fund Warrant	No._____	$_____
	To the Territorial Treasurer of Arizona Territory	
	Phoenix, Arizona,	
	*Pay to the order of*_____	
	_____ *Dollars,*	
	Account of _____	
	COUNTERSIGNED:	

Captain Wheeler regularly submitted expenses to be paid through Ranger Fund Warrants. (Author's collection) nationalities were represented on the roster that one Arizona newspaper termed them "a Congress of Nations." On a trip to Tucson, Wheeler, aware that Tucson was a baseball hotbed, bragged on the Naco club. He tauntingly claimed that the Naco manager would not allow his team to play in Tucson, since such a match "would only be a practice game for the Naco crowd."[5]

The population of Naco, Arizona, was only 600 or so when Harry Wheeler brought Ranger headquarters to town. Naco, Sonora, had more people, and the nearby presence of Mexican dives added to the potential for outlawry on the Arizona side of the border. Located on the major route from Cananea to Bisbee, the Arizona side of the border town became the scene of massive smuggling activity and a general congregating point for men of criminal inclinations. Local officials were in league with outlaws, and acts of violence were commonplace. By 1907 Naco was a corrupt community crying for the permanent presence of the Arizona Rangers.

Captain Wheeler imprinted a forceful stamp on his men. Wheeler had been in the company for nearly four years, and he was the only Ranger who had served at every rank: private, sergeant, lieutenant, and captain. The product of a nineteenth-century military upbringing, he brought patriotic fervor as well as up-from-the-ranks experience to the command post of the Ranger. He came to the captaincy with strong ideas about the mission and methods of the company, and with an iron will he endeavored to compel each Ranger to meet the highest standards.

On June 1 Captain Wheeler issued a set of exacting expectations:

GENERAL ORDER # 1

Rangers will not congregate in saloons; nor in any bawdy house, for the purpose of amusement, or out of idleness. This is not intended to interfere with any Ranger acting in his official capacity; nor to prevent his taking a drink if so inclined; nor the exercise of any right or privilege in which any gentleman would feel safe.

GENERAL ORDER # 2

It being a well established fact that men of honor, will meet their just, financial obligations on time and according to promise, the attention of all Rangers is called to the evil of going beyond their means, and for any reason borrowing or contracting loans they will be unable to meet.

The reputation of this company has been *very* high, but of late one or two incidents, which have come to my notice, have caused me much embarrassment and humiliation. All Rangers must meet their obligations.

Every man is a guardian of the honor and reputation, not only of himself, but the entire organization. It is every man's duty to aid in perpetuating the integrity of the service, by unmasking any undesirable member, who by accident may be among us.

GENERAL ORDER # 3

Every man is hereby prohibited from entering Mexico in any *official capacity* whatsoever, armed or unarmed. Unless by special request or permission of the Mexican Authorities, and being accompanied by some Mexican Official. Even under such conditions, Rangers will remember they go *unofficially,* and simply as any other private citizen.

GENERAL ORDER # 4

All Rangers will enforce strictly and impartially, the laws which prevent gambling, women and minors in saloons, etc. All laws will be enforced, but I desire extreme vigilance and precaution upon the part of Rangers, in preventing the violation of the laws above mentioned.

We all know that Gambling has caused more suffering and crime, serious crime, than any other dozen causes combined. In my opinion, the complete suppression of this evil, will result in a falling off, of at least 50% of the arrests for Felonies. Consequently lessening the needs of hundreds of women and children, who have known want and privation heretofore.

I consider it an honor to any man, or organization, who aids in suppressing this evil.

GENERAL ORDER # 5

In all cases where prisoners are taken, the greatest humanity will be shown, and each Ranger is instructed to mentally place himself in the others place and act, legally, accordingly.

I want no man to needlessly endanger his life by taking foolish chances with desperate criminals, and if any one must be hurt, I do not want it to be the Ranger, at the same time I want every precaution taken to insure a peaceful arrest, and in all cases, when an arrest has been consummated [sic] the prisoner must be shown the courtesy due an unfortunate, and the kindness a helpless man deserves and gets from a brave officer.

GENERAL ORDER # 6

The new monthly reports will be made out the first day of each new month and sent in to Headquarters. Every item must be filled out and the report certified to on the back.

In addition that I may keep in constant touch with all members, a postal card will be sent in to headquarters, each Saturday, telling where you are and where you may be reached for the next few days, as nearly as possible.[6]

The word "honor" recurs throughout Wheeler's directives, along with other terms meaningful to the man: "duty," "integrity," "gentleman." The company would war against gambling, shun saloons, and avoid personal indebtedness. Scrupulously, Wheeler insisted that his men avoid the casual entries into Mexico that had been common throughout the Rangers' existence. Within a few days of these general orders, Wheeler and some of his men chased four fugitives across the border, but the captain would not allow pursuit south of the line.[7]

The Ranger company was composed of men whose characters contained strong doses of frontier individualism, and many of them resented new regulations, which smacked of Puritanism and bureaucratic red tape. There was to be a new precision to arrest reports, and a *weekly* postcard report to headquarters. "Of course, some men are high spirited," commented Wheeler, "to the extent that any restriction whatever, placed upon them causes them to feel injured."[8] Many of the tough, pragmatic adventurers who made up the company felt injured, and a clash with their idealistic, strong-willed new captain was inevitable.

Wheeler explained to Governor Kibbey: "I do not wish to trample upon the liberties of the men under me, nor take advantage of my position in any way," but he regarded these orders as necessary "for the good of the service in general." It should not have surprised Wheeler that the new mandates "have met cordial reception by some of the men, but I intend they must be obeyed even to the extent if necessary, of letting those go, who feel they are unable to abide by them."[9]

True to his word, Wheeler began "letting those go" who would not comply with his Ranger ideal, and during his tenure as captain he discharged numerous men for one transgression or another. Throughout the history of the force there were enlistees who served only briefly before deciding they did not like the service, and each captain was forced to deal with recruits who demonstrated undesirable qualities. While the turnover rate under Wheeler was only slightly higher than the rate under Captains Mossman and Rynning, there can be no doubt that Wheeler exerted a stern pressure upon his men. During Wheeler's less than two years as captain, twenty-six men left the force: many resigned for undetermined reasons ("I wish a few more would quit," remarked Wheeler after weeding out one or two undesirables),[10] but several were forced out because of drinking problems or insubordination.

In 1907 the Rangers enlisted fourteen men, including nine who hailed from Texas. Four had previously served as peace officers, while seven listed "stockman" as their occupation. Frank A. Ford, at twenty-two the youngest recruit of the year, listed his occupation as stenographer; he served as headquarters clerk for less than four months before he resigned on the first day of August. W.F. Bates, a July recruit, also lasted not quite four months before Wheeler decided that he was unsatisfactory as a Ranger. George L. Mayer enlisted in August and resigned three months later, and in November Travis Poole, another August recruit, was discharged for "leaving Territory without permission." James Smith signed up in June, but despite an "Excellent" rating by Wheeler he chose to leave the company in October.[11]

Late in 1907 James Emett, a rancher from Lees Ferry near the Utah border, applied for a Ranger position, using his personal influence with Territorial Attorney General E.S. Clark and circulating a petition to ensure his appointment. But information soon came to the governor's office that Emett wanted a Ranger badge solely as a license to pursue a feud with the cowboys on a neighboring ranch owned by B.F. Saunders. It was discovered that Emett had a shady reputation; he had been defended in Utah by Clark in a case involving embezzlements and suspected homicide, and it was expected that if Emett became a Ranger he would try to kill Saunders's foreman. The controversy over Emett doomed his chances, and Wheeler never accepted him into the company.[12]

Wheeler did not continue Rynning's practice of enlisting former Rough Riders as Rangers. He found "Teddy's fighters" inadequate for his purposes "because not one soldier in 100 can either rope or read a brand, and Rangers must have these accomplishments . . . as their duties are most frequently along the lines of the livestock business."[13]

Wheeler's most interesting recruit of 1907 was William A. Larn, a thirty-three-year-old cattleman originally from Fort Griffin, Texas. Larn signed his enlistment papers on October 1, 1907, in Williams, but his enrollment as a Ranger was not made public. Larn was to work undercover to break up a band of cattle rustlers in northern Arizona. The gang had "successfully defied all efforts . . . to capture them for years," but Lieutenant Old expected to land the thieves with Larn's help. "We expect great things from this man Larn," exulted Wheeler to the governor's secretary, adding, "no one at all knows that he is a Ranger."[14]

Arizona Ranger Billy Speed challenged drunken bad-man William F. Downing in the streets of Willcox, killing the town bully with a Winchester shot. (Courtesy Arizona Historical Society)

Yet great things from Larn did not materialize. Ranger arrest records do not indicate the incarceration of any rustlers in northern Arizona during this period, and on the last day of the year Larn resigned. The reasons were vague, but on his personnel file Wheeler wrote, "Service unsatisfactory."[15]

A few Rangers had been designated "inspectors." This was never a rank established officially by the legislature, but rather an informal designation of Rangers who worked regularly as livestock inspectors. The role of inspector had evolved under Rynning, but

Captain Wheeler decided that inspectors should perform all functions of a Ranger. Soon he found it necessary to write a critical letter to Pvt. Ben Olney, a thirty-five-year-old Texan who lived near Safford and who had enlisted in February 1906.

Olney responded with a mixture of resentment and repentance: "I will say that I was very angry when I read [your letter] and I felt pretty sore for I never knew I was to go every time . . . a Mexican killed another in Clifton or Morenci or Globe. . . . My understanding when I first enlisted under Mr. Rynning was that I did not have much to do being an Inspector, but . . . if I have not done enough to suit you I am sorry and I am willing to do better." Olney was married and emphasized to Wheeler: "I would like to hold the job if I can because I need the money. . . . I have worked for wages nearly all my life and I never got discharged yet. I have always been a good friend to you and all the Boys and I don't know any ranger in the company now that I don't like."

Olney, who lived more than three miles outside town, told Wheeler that he would have a telephone placed in his home so that he would be more accessible, and he outlined a program of law enforcement activities he hoped to pursue if permitted. Wheeler decided to give Olney, whom he regarded as "very honest," another chance, and Ben's work proved satisfactory. Although he never saw any action as a Ranger, he served until the company was disbanded.[16]

Another Texan, Porter McDonald, had enlisted in June 1905 and was designated an inspector by Rynning. McDonald worked out of Tombstone, doubling as a Cochise County deputy sheriff under Sheriff John White. Although Rangers were prohibited from serving in other law enforcement capacities, McDonald accepted fees from Cochise County. He also used a railroad mileage book given to him by Sheriff White, which permitted the holder to free passage. Governor Kibbey had directed Wheeler to take up any such books held by Rangers. Everyone complied except McDonald, who wrote Wheeler protesting that White had given him the mileage book: "I did not get it from the assistance of the Ranger Force or by request of the Gov. nor by a request of my own." Threatening to send Wheeler *"the star,"* upon request, McDonald defiantly stated: "I absolutely refuse to turn this mileage book over to any one except those that gave it to me."[17]

Wheeler, of course, was furious when he read McDonald's letter. The captain immediately wired McDonald to submit his resignation, which was dated November 26, and he forwarded the offensive letter from "ex-Ranger" McDonald to the governor. Wheeler explained the situation involving Ben Olney as well as McDonald, pointing out that "they have the idea that when they are inspectors, that they are removed from all jurisdiction of the Ranger Company." Wheeler commented that McDonald "has peculiar ideas and is insubordinate and the only way to get along with him is to let him do as he pleases; I have a couple more in the Company who are troublesome at times, but I am going to be the Captain. . . ." Wheeler asked Sgt. Lew Mickey to assume McDonald's livestock inspecting activities, in addition to his other duties. There would be no more "special" Rangers.[18]

Not only was Harry Wheeler a firm leader of men and an expert field officer, he rapidly proved to be a meticulous master of office detail, corresponding voluminously with his men and the governor's office. Indeed, Governor Kibbey specifically praised his administrative qualities, concluding: "Rarely has an officer been so efficient in both field and office work."[19]

After Wheeler submitted his first annual report, to his obvious chagrin he learned that at least 100 arrests had not been recorded on paper. Inquiry among his men revealed that many reports had been lost, and Wheeler instructed his lieutenants and sergeants to try to compile a list of unrecorded arrests his men could recall. He also took steps to ensure that all future arrests would be precisely documented.[20]

Wheeler himself handled an unusual 1907 arrest which gave the stern Ranger leader a rare moment of amusement. On Saturday, May 18, Wheeler was in the countryside near Naco when he was approached by two deserters from Fort Huachuca. "We have avoided Naco," they confided "because of the d——d Rangers." They asked the exact location of the Mexican border, which Wheeler pointed out while they continued to curse the Rangers. Then Wheeler, enjoying himself hugely, politely mentioned that they could not proceed into Mexico. When they asked why, "I told them that they had avoided the rangers alright but had come to the rangers Captain for information." Wheeler, of course, took the pair into custody and held them for the military authorities.[21]

In August, Captain Wheeler reported a total of only twenty-seven arrests—felonies and misdemeanors combined—by the Rangers, but travel reached 9,000 miles. The Rangers rode 7,500 miles on horseback, more than eleven miles per man per day, as well as 1,500 miles by rail. In November the Rangers rode 8,493 miles, more than twelve miles per man daily. Wheeler had directed his men to change emphasis and disregard arrest totals: "the men have been instructed to do more riding . . . , and pay more attention to the serious crimes and less to the small trivial things easily taken care of by the local officers. This policy is sure to improve the conditions of any section where Rangers are stationed, constantly riding the country in sections not usually traveled by other officers."[22]

Wheeler preferred, wherever possible, to station his men in pairs. Chapo Beaty recalled that "Rangers always traveled by two's," a simple precaution followed by modern policemen who cruise in pairs in patrol cars. Aside from the obvious safety factor, Wheeler knew that two Rangers could corroborate each other's testimony on a witness stand.[23]

Captain Wheeler felt that a machine gun would prove useful during strikes or other situations which promised mob action. He requested a .30-caliber Colt machine gun, but apparently the governor, sensitive to complaints about the expense of the company, never authorized purchase of such a weapon for the Rangers.[24]

In a direct move to keep expenses down, the governor decided to maintain the roster below authorized strength. Earlier in the year there had been a strong movement in the legislature to reduce the company by more than half. In February a bill was defeated to abolish the company, but Ranger opponents countered by pushing through committee an amendment to the existing Ranger bill that would limit the force to a captain, a lieutenant, and ten privates. Although this resolution was tabled by a convincing vote a week later, Governor Kibbey seemed to feel that Ranger opponents might be appeased if the roster and payroll were reduced. As vacancies occurred during the year the departing men were not replaced, so that by June there were just twenty men in the company, six fewer than maximum strength. Numerous requests for Ranger assistance from across the territory caused the addition of a couple of men, but by the end of the year the roster totaled only twenty-two Rangers. "They work in the utmost harmony with the sheriffs and other peace officers of the several counties," optimistically stated the governor at the close of his report to the secretary of the interior. [25]

Captain Wheeler did not flinch from enforcing unpopular laws, which found passage during this period as Arizona's response to the Progressive reform movement. One of those laws involved rodeos. Arizonans were enthusiastic rodeo fans: Prescott claims to have the oldest *continuous* annual rodeo (commencing in 1888), while Payson claims the oldest *consecutive* annual rodeo (early 1880s), despite rival claims from such western communities as Pecos, Texas (1884) and Caldwell, Kansas (1885). By the early twentieth century, rodeos and Wild West shows were popular throughout Arizona, but in 1907 the Twenty-fourth Legislature—"in response to a great wave of reform that swept before it licensed gambling and kindred immoral practices"—passed an act to prevent "steer tying contests."[26]

Clay McGonagill, O.C. Nations, and Bill Pickett, famous early-day rodeo performers, had been touring the Territory, astounding large crowds with feats of bronc busting, roping, and Pickett's specialty, "steer throwing." Pickett, a black cowboy from Texas known to rodeo fans as the "Dusky Demon," would gallop alongside a running steer, jump onto its back, and wrestle its head upward by grasping the horns. Pickett then would sink his teeth into the steer's upper lip and throw the animal easily. Bulldogs, when working cattle, controlled the beasts by biting their lips, and Pickett's technique became known among the rodeo crowd as "bulldogging"—the only event in modern rodeoing that can be traced back to a specific individual. An Arizona newspaper commented huffily: "To the morbid this has proven a most interesting feat and crowds have gathered expressly to see this part of the performance."[27]

The spoilsport law against steer tying contests went into effect on April 1, 1907, but for a couple of weeks Pickett and his fellow performers continued to tour Arizona with no interference. On Saturday, April 12, there was a performance at Don Luis, just south of Bisbee. A large number of "the morbid" gathered, but someone complained. Another performance was scheduled for Sunday at Don Luis, but Capt. Harry Wheeler came up from Naco, and, assisted by several other officers, halted the fun by threatening to arrest anyone who threw or roped any steers. The management had the foresight to gather "a large number of unbroken broncos," and the crowd had to be satisfied with an exhibition of bronco riding. The public had been protected from "cruelty to animals in the guise of feats of skill," and the Bisbee *Review* smugly concluded: "There will be no more of it wherever there is an Arizona Ranger."[28]

In 1907 the Rangers also were forced to clamp down on gambling, certainly a popular pastime for many Arizonans. For years there had been a movement by "the better class of citizens" in the Territory to do away with professional gamblers "and women who, while not always directly associated with the gamblers, are by that far reaching term 'sports,' indissolubly linked with the men of the green table."[29]

The legislature finally decided to curb gambling activities by prohibiting all of the traditional games of chance, except poker, in public places, and saloons were to be cleaned up by forbidding the admittance of women and minors. The new laws immediately caused a rash of enforcement problems for Rangers throughout Arizona. In Nogales, for example, Jeff Kidder reported that the "saloon men here seem to think the women and minors in saloons Law is all a joke." He made an arrest in a saloon where a thirteen-year-old boy worked, and while talking with a local justice of the peace in another saloon the judge himself called a twelve-year-old bootblack inside to shine his shoes. "It has always been a custom for minors to hang around in saloons in this town," complained the exasperated Kidder.

One Nogales "resort" was operated by three women who served liquor in one room. It was customary in Nogales for women to eat at saloon lunch counters, and the prosecuting attorney feared that he would have to prosecute the wives of his friends. Saloonkeepers in Douglas, angry that they could not even employ female singers to attract customers, began collecting funds to finance a legal challenge.[30]

By August, Wheeler was able to report to the governor that public gambling "is not indulged in anywhere" except for a few underground faro and roulette games that the Rangers would have "one chance in ten thousand" of finding. In Douglas he could not even locate a craps game. But Wheeler pointed out that there was widespread abuse of the poker exemption; since poker could be played with no obvious percentage going to a house gambler, men congregated in the most popular saloons and legally played poker among themselves. "There is no doubt the law is abused in this respect," grumbled Wheeler, who was certain that a percentage rakeoff still was practiced, "but in such manner that no conviction could be obtained." He pointed out that unless the "Legislature passes an act forbidding *all Gambling* as in Texas, these lesser abuses will continue."[31] The recent Texas law had caused an exodus of professional gamblers from the Lone Star State; many El Paso high rollers had migrated to southeastern Arizona.

Frank Wheeler complained to his captain in November that in Yuma "the Women are increasing in number and the Poker Games are getting bolder and gaining in Number." The district attorney of Yuma County, Peter Robertson, had requested special help from a Ranger in gambling matters, but Wheeler felt "he wants me to make a fool of myself." Also in November, Privates Cy Byrne and Owen Wilson arrested a woman for drinking in a Winslow saloon, but they lost this and two similar cases due to efforts of the mayor, constable, and justice of the peace. Captain Wheeler was appalled that the justice who handled the case said "he had a mind to arrest our men for carrying a gun—Said Rangers had no right to be in town and make arrests nor even carry a gun." In his December report Wheeler pointed out to the governor "that in every case of an arrest for 'Women' being in saloons [sic], the Defendant comes clear." Despite varying degrees of noncompliance, Captain Wheeler still was satisfied that the curtailment of gambling activities "has had a great tendency to lessen crime of all degrees, serious or otherwise, I should say, at least 40% if not more."[32]

One Ranger incident in 1907 involved a noted rabble-rouser of the day, Mary Harris Jones, and provided a portent of future trouble for Harry Wheeler. Mother Jones was a chubby, white-haired older woman with spectacles and chipmunk cheeks—and a crafty, determined glint in her eyes that suggested why she was called "the most dangerous woman in America." Since the 1870s, Mother Jones had ventured around the United States issuing socialist harangues at coalmines, train yards, factories, and logging camps on behalf of the growing labor movement. In 1907 strikes and anti-union repression brought the controversial seventy-five-year-old agitator to Arizona Territory.[33]

Arriving in Arizona early in the year, she spent time with laborers in Globe, Bisbee, and other mining camps. Late in June "The Miners' Angel" established headquarters at a hotel in Douglas and lined up a series of meetings.[34] On Sunday, June 30, she was introduced to Manuel Sarabia, outspoken opponent of President Porfirio Diaz and a leader of the revolutionary *Junta Liberal Mejicana*. Sarabia, a small man (five-foot-three, 130 pounds) in his mid-twenties, sported a black mustache and was a natty dresser. Charged in Mexico with inciting revolution, he fled to Texas in 1904, eventually making his way to Chicago, St. Louis, and other points. About June 1, 1907, he arrived in Douglas, hiring on at the *International-American* under the alias Sam Moret. Throughout his travels Sarabia had continued long-range insurrectionary activities against the heavy-handed *presidente,* and when he met Mother Jones he boasted that he had fought Porfirio Diaz and was in the United States seeking refuge. That night, as Mother Jones addressed a crowd of smelter workers gathered in the street, Sarabia, who for some reason did not attend the meeting, walked to the depot on the west side of town intending to mail a letter. But on the way, Ranger Sam Hayhurst leveled a gun at him and told him he was under arrest.

The previous day, while traveling by train from Bisbee to Douglas, Hayhurst and Captain Wheeler encountered Ramos Bareras, captain of a newly organized Mexican border force. Bareras told the Rangers about Sarabia, claiming that he was a murderer as well as a revolutionary, and giving Wheeler Sarabia's description and Douglas address. In the customary spirit of cooperation between border officers, Wheeler agreed to arrest Sarabia and hold him until extradition papers were received. After apprehending Sarabia, Hayhurst took his prisoner to city hall. Local officials held Sarabia incommunicado through the next day, then spirited him away into Mexico in an automobile on the first night of July. By July 4 he was in Hermosillo, where he was jailed for several days.[35]

When Mother Jones learned that Sarabia had been arrested and secretly returned to Mexico, she immediately responded to the plight of her fellow agitator. A mass meeting was held in Douglas, the resignation of the Mexican consul at Douglas (who had aided in abducting Sarabia) was called for, and complaints were filed against Hayhurst and four other officers. More than a hundred telegrams were fired off to Washington, and Arizona officials also were bombarded with protests and demands for intervention. Governor Kibbey notified Harry Wheeler to do what he could to resolve the Sarabia "kidnapping," which was attracting a great deal of adverse criticism. Mother Jones was impressed when she met Wheeler; she regarded him as "a pretty fine fellow to be captain."[36]

Wheeler contacted Gen. Rafael Torres, and both men journeyed to Hermosillo. On July 11 Torres secured the release of Sarabia, who traveled by rail back to Nogales, accompanied by Wheeler. Sarabia soon found himself back in a cell, however, incarcerated in Tucson's Pima County jail alongside three compatriots. All four men were charged with violation of United States neutrality laws. They were convicted in May 1909 and sentenced to eighteen months in the territorial prison, but by then Sarabia had jumped bail and had disappeared, rumored to have fled to Canada.[37]

In 1907 Wheeler was called upon to lead a Ranger expedition into barren desert terrain of Pima County. On August 30, in the Papago village of El Cubo, Lariano Alvarez was murdered by an Indian named John Johns. El Cubo was surrounded by a forest of organ pipe cacti and situated beside a large water hole in the high country twenty-five miles south of Ajo. Mescal frequently was smuggled into the isolated village from Mexico, and the men in El Cubo and other nearby communities spent much time in a drunken state. Alvarez died five days later.

Tom Childs, Alvarez's brother-in-law who lived in Ten Miles Well, wrote Sheriff Nabor Pacheco about the murder. Pacheco sent an arrest warrant to Childs, deputized him by mail, and instructed him to bring John Johns to Tuscon. Childs and several friends rode to El Cubo, but the Indians throughout the area were murderously hostile to the intrusion. Childs prudently led his men out of El Cubo without trying to seize Johns and returned the warrant to Pacheco with the warning that "the Indians are up in arms, and threaten to kill the first white man that attempts to travel the Cubo trail."[38]

Sheriff Pacheco determined to exercise his authority in this remote part of his county. He frequently had worked with Rangers, and in this situation he contacted Capt. Harry Wheeler. There were at least 2,000 Indians in the area, and the two officers agreed that an expedition in force would be necessary. Wheeler quickly assembled nine Rangers: Sergeants Jeff Kidder, Billy Speed, and Rye Miles, and Privates W.F. Bates, J.A. Fraser, Travis Poole, John Rhodes, James Smith, and Tip Stanford. Wheeler himself would lead the large Ranger contingent, which meant that nearly half of the company (only twenty-two men were currently on duty) would be committed to a two-week expedition. From Pacheco's office Wheeler wrote the governor about this situation, telling him where the remaining twelve Rangers were stationed and that Lieutenant Old would command in his absence from Prescott.[39] Sheriff Pacheco brought along one deputy, as well as a wagon and team.

The twelve-man posse, armed to the teeth, rode out of Tucson at 5:00 A.M. on Sunday, September 15. On Thursday morning, their fifth day of travel, they encountered an old Indian about eighteen miles from their remote destination. Sheriff Pacheco asked him to guide the party to Gunsight, a mountain mining camp. The Indian agreed, stating that the best trail would lead through a *rancheria* called El Cubo. Pacheco replied his assent with a straight face, and at about 1:30 in the afternoon the posse rode into El Cubo, deserted except for several women and children. Pacheco then innocently asked the guide to find a man named John Johns, but the Indian suddenly realized the purpose of the posse and refused to look for the murderer.

Within a few minutes several Papago men returned to the village. They were arrested and questioned, and an old man revealed that Johns was in a nearby field. Pacheco and Wheeler rode out, and as they neared the field they saw a man hurrying away through the weeds. Wheeler galloped after him, quickly seized his prey, and brought him back. The captive admitted that he was John Johns, but he accused another Indian, named Citiano, of the murder. Both Johns and Citiano were placed in the wagon and shackled into leg irons.

Many of the Indians were armed with rifles, but the twelve-man posse proved sufficiently intimidating to avert any resistance by the villagers. Six more Indians were rounded up as witnesses, and the party headed toward Tucson. Johns eventually was convicted of murder in the second degree and, in February 1908, sentenced to ten years in the territorial prison.

During the past year, Captain Wheeler had been aggravated by an underground roulette game in Naco. About once a week, usually when most of the Rangers were out of town, the roulette table would be set up late at night down an alley adjacent to the Caw Ranch Saloon, which earned at least $199 per month in profits from this regular game. E.P. Ells, the local constable and a Cochise County deputy sheriff, provided cover for the game, presumably for a payoff. Wheeler was especially irritated that this game was carried on in the town that housed Ranger headquarters.

At last Wheeler developed an elaborate scheme to close the game. On Thursday, February 6, the headquarters detachment (consisting of Wheeler and three other men) rode out of Naco on one of Wheeler's frequent scouts. After dark, however, Wheeler and his men, reinforced by two Bisbee policemen, sneaked back into town and concealed themselves at an outhouse overlooking the presumed site of the game. There were "several fast women" present; Wheeler had paid them $40 to drive down from Bisbee in an automobile and encourage the roulette gamesters to open play. Wheeler crept close enough to hear the girls ask the men to "roll the ball," but for some reason they would not start a game. The lawmen waited all night, but they could not catch the gamblers in the act of playing. When Wheeler disgustedly wrote the governor about his unsuccessful scheme, he had not slept in forty-eight hours. He concluded the report by stating his determination to stay on the case: "Public sentiment here apparently is in favor of these people, but we are not influenced by the sentiment at all." A few days later, Wheeler directly confronted the proprietors of the saloon, informing them that he knew the roulette game was being conducted and virtually daring them to continue their illegal activities.[40]

Wheeler was as conscientious as ever of administrative responsibilities, but he continued to ride into the field in search of rustlers and fugitives. A January scout had to be postponed when a Bisbee police officer was slain and Wheeler assisted with the investigation. A March scout would have been delayed when each of the Rangers assigned to headquarters had to be sent to various trouble spots. But Wheeler simply rode into the field alone. Another solitary mission was performed by Pvt. Sam Hayhurst, who left early in the year for West Texas in search of George Mabry, who had committed a brutal murder in Douglas in 1905.[41]

By 1908 there was widespread corruption in Yuma. District Attorney Peter Robertson urgently requested Ranger assistance. Frank Wheeler was stationed in Yuma, but it was felt that someone was needed who was unknown to the lawless element. Capt. Harry Wheeler had to travel to California on official business late in January, and on his return he stopped in Yuma. He met with Frank Wheeler, who had just caught a Tucson diamond thief and recovered $2,000 worth of jewelry, and then he conferred with District Attorney Robertson, who convinced the head Ranger of the need for undercover help.[42]

Wheeler dispatched Rudolph Gunner and R.D. Horne, who both had enlisted late in 1907. Despite their brief service, they had impressed Captain Wheeler. "I don't know what I would do without these two men," said Wheeler in a January letter to the governor. "I have worked them day and night, yet they are always willing, agreeable and full of ambition, and absolutely obedient. I want to secure more like them."[43]

Gunner went out first, posing as a representative of *Everybody's Magazine*. Robertson had been so careful of the lawmen's hidden identity that when he advanced Gunner $45 for expenses, he asked Wheeler not to mention his name on the reimbursement voucher "because I don't want him 'tipped' off." Gunner returned to Naco late in February, having collected considerable evidence against saloonkeepers who had been violating the laws against gambling and women. He reported to Wheeler that he had been in Yuma dives that he would not have left alive had his identity been known. Wheeler sent him back to continue the investigation, accompanied this time by Horne, who had just returned from official duties in Cananea.[44]

Finally, Gunner revealed his identity. He and Horne were given an office, and, assisted by Frank Wheeler, began issuing warrants to men and women who had flaunted the saloon laws. More than one citizen was angry at having been taken in by a Ranger, and Gunner wisely ignored the request of an indicted saloonkeeper named Dutton who wanted him to come to the dive for a talk. "The feeling in town against us is very strong," wrote Gunner to Wheeler, "more so against me than H[orne]." Robertson offered his thanks to Wheeler for sending "such good men."[45]

A few days later, however, Gunner despondently reported that the "cases came up to-day and we were properly Kangarooed." Both the sheriff and presiding judge acted against Robertson and the Rangers. "The Dist. Atty don't know a damn thing!" jeered the sheriff, and the judge slapped the defendants on the wrist after ruling "that the evidence is not sufficient to convict." Gunner even felt that Frank Wheeler's performance had been half-hearted, because he was hoping to be elected sheriff.[46]

Saloonkeeper Dutton bragged around town "that he was going to get that little kid," a reference to Horne, who was slight of stature. But later in the day Gunner and Horne encountered Dutton with another man in front of the Rangers' hotel.

"Say, Dutton," challenged Horne, "I understand you intend to beat me up. I'll bet if you do, you'll never do it on the Main Street."[47]

Dutton and his friend visibly became "very uncomfortable." At this point Frank Wheeler appeared on the scene, and Dutton hastily "squared matters." That evening a newspaper reporter stopped Gunner, who said that the writer "shook hands with me and said that he was sorry we lost out in the 'first inning,' but that the good element was with us.—I am afraid the good element is in the minority."[48]

The next day Gunner spoke with Tom Rynning, who now was warden at the Yuma prison. The former Ranger captain told Gunner that they probably would not get a jury to convict, and in succeeding days Rynning sadly saw his prediction come true. P.J. Sullivan, deputy U.S. customs collector at Yuma, drunkenly abused a prosecution witness in a saloon, attacked the man, and abruptly was walloped to the floor. District Attorney Robertson told Captain Wheeler that his life had been threatened: "I think the condition here now is about the worst I ever saw." Robertson asked Wheeler and the attorney general of Arizona to come to Yuma, and requested that Gunner be left at his side for a few weeks longer. Gunner seethed under the insults of the prosecuting attorney, while growling to his captain: "The riffraff is rejoicing and we have to stand a good deal."[49]

Mail service was excellent early in the century, thanks to a multitude of trains which delivered letters across the Territory by the next day. The day after Robertson and Gunner wrote the above letters to Wheeler, the captain telegraphed that Gunner could stay in Yuma as long as needed. Gunner reported that Robertson "was jubilant; he says as long as that man stays with me I'll fight them to the bitter end."[50] Wheeler, incensed, sent a bitter letter to the governor and enclosed reports from Gunner and Robertson. Wheeler left for Yuma on the next train, pleading with the governor: "If you order me to do it, in 29 minutes I'll take possession of that town and in a day or two at most I'll establish law and order."[51]

But nine days later, on March 16, Wheeler returned to headquarters.[52] He had not been permitted to establish Ranger law in Yuma, and trial results had been predictably disappointing. Wheeler decided to find relief in the field. He planned a far ranging scout, and by the end of the month he was riding through the mountains and desert at the head of a Ranger patrol.

Sergeants Jeff Kidder (right) and Rye Miles, bound for field duty with mounts and pack horses. Kidder was the only Ranger who was in Wheeler's class as a gun artist. (Courtesy Arizona Historical Society)

Sgt. Jeff Kidder was the only Arizona Ranger who was considered to be in Harry Wheeler's class as a gunhand. Kidder joined the Rangers in April 1903, three months before Wheeler. Kidder and Wheeler were born in the same year, and Jeff was reared on a frontier farm in Dakota Territory. Jeff handled firearms throughout his boyhood, practicing incessantly with a Colt .45 and becoming a crack shot with either hand. A graduate of Vermillion High School in South Dakota, Jeff never married and eventually gravitated to Arizona in search of adventure. He pinned on a badge in Nogales, then enlisted in the Ranger company at the age of twenty-eight. Stationed at Nogales, he later won promotion to sergeant. Although Sergeant Kidder had likable qualities, even his friends agreed that "he did not have a bit of sense when he was drunk." Often pugnacious and heavy-handed with prisoners, Kidder had many enemies.[53]

Jeff Kidder's father died in 1905, leaving Jeff a handsome inheritance. Kidder bought a new single-action Colt .45, an engraved, silverplated weapon with pearl grips and a five-and-one-half-inch barrel. He continued his ceaseless pistol practice, firing off so many rounds that in 1907 he had to send the Colt back to the factory for replating and other repairs. Kidder came to be regarded as the quickest draw in the Ranger force. Although there were a number of crack marksmen in the company, Jeff also was con-

In 1905 Jeff Kidder bought an engraved, silver-plated Colt .45 with a five-and-a-half-inch barrel. He fired so many practice rounds that in 1907 he had to send the Colt back to the factory for replating and other repairs. (Courtesy Arizona Historical Society)

sidered "one of the best shots of the Rangers. At 30 steps he demonstrated repeatedly that he could hit a playing card three times out of six on an average. He could shoot equally well with either hand."[54] In Douglas after dawn on New Year's Eve, 1906, Sergeant Kidder was fired upon while he was in the vicinity of the railroad roundhouse. Kidder drew his Colt and blasted out three rounds. One slug slammed into the right eye of his assailant, filling him with a mortal wound.[55]

When Sergeant Kidder returned to Nogales in February 1908 from a solitary border patrol, the newspaper welcomed him back: "Jeff is a mighty efficient, experienced officer; where he is, there reigns peace and quiet."[56] By March the Nogales peace and quiet was threatened by "a number of undesirables," but Sergeant Kidder simply ran them out of town.[57]

Soon Kidder again was in the field, returning to Nogales on Wednesday, April 1. He stabled his horse at Al Peck's Livery and walked up Grand Avenue to the post office for his mail. A letter from Captain Wheeler, currently leading a sweep for outlaws through the Chiricahua Mountains, reminded Kidder that his enlistment expired each April 1, and the veteran Ranger was invited to meet Wheeler at headquarters in Naco to be sworn-in for another year. Kidder, always rough with lawbreakers, was under "some minor charges preferred by the criminal element," but there had been complaints against him before and he had every intention of remaining a Ranger.[58]

On Thursday Kidder scooped up his little dog, Jip, and placed the ever-present mutt across his saddle. The sergeant rode east out of Nogales with a pack animal in tow and headed across the Patagonia Mountains. He made it to John Sutherland's Bootjack Ranch, where he spent the night with the old bachelor. Kidder finished his journey on Friday, April 3, riding into Naco during the afternoon. He checked in at headquarters, spent some time there with Sgt. Tip Stanford, then announced that he was going to cross into Mexican Naco to meet a friend coming up from Cananea. Stanford surmised that the "friend" was one of Kidder's numerous informants.[59]

There had been malignant resentment against *gringos* in Naco, Sonora, since the 1906 troubles in Cananea. Wheeler told his men they would most likely be killed over there and had ordered them not to cross the line. Kidder, intending to go anyway, wanted to appear inoffensive while still keeping a means of self-defense. He stripped off his gun rig, concealing the silver-plated .45 in his waistband beneath his coat, and punched six cartridges out of his ammunition belt into a pocket. Then he headed on foot toward the border entrance. Kidder crossed into Sonora accompanied by friends and by Jip, bouncing along at his master's heels.[60]

Kidder may or may not have encountered his friend, but he made a valiant effort to find him. He investigated several *cantinas,* visited with various bartenders, and fandangoed with a number of dancehall girls. By midnight he was in a *cantina* where an American had been shot three months earlier. Kidder retreated to a back room with "Chia," a new girl in Naco. (Later he stated that he was asking Chia where to locate a fugitive.) After a while Kidder was ready to leave, but when he checked his vest pocket he found that his last silver dollar was missing. With a certain lack of chivalry, he accused Chia of stealing his dollar. Infuriated, she hit Kidder, screamed for the *policia,* and jerked open the door. Immediately two officers, Tomas Amador and Dolores Quias, burst into the room, revolvers in their fists.

Amador squeezed off a round and the bullet punched into Kidder's middle, entering just to the left of his navel and ripping out his back. The impact of the heavy slug hurled Kidder off his feet, but even as he crumpled to the floor he palmed his Colt. Sitting on the floor, he opened fire and dropped both policemen with bullets in the knee and thigh. Neither officer had any fight left, and Jeff crawled to the door and struggled to his feet, followed by Jip.

Stunned and bleeding, Sergeant Kidder stumbled outside and tottered shakily toward the border, a quarter of a mile away. Several Mexican line riders blocked his way, triggering Winchester bullets at him. He cocked his .45 and pulled the trigger, but the gun was empty. Under heavy fire, Jeff cut to his left and made the fence.

Too weak to struggle through the wire, he reloaded his pistol with his last six cartridges. Victoriano Amador, chief of police and brother of the officer who had drilled Kidder, headed the attack. Jeff nicked him in the side, then held the others at bay until he ran out of ammunition. Finally, he shouted out that he was "all in."

Chief Amador led nearly a score of men to the sergeant, who stood unsteadily until one of his adversaries clubbed him with a revolver. The wounded Kidder toppled to the ground, and was dragged about fifty yards away from the fence, where he was again pistol-whipped. One angry officer wanted to "blow Kidder's brains out," but the wounded police chief halted this final brutality. At last Kidder was dragged all the way to the *juzgado local* and dumped into a cell. The vindictive officers rifled Kidder's pockets, taking his badge, a pocketwatch he had received for graduation from high school, his Masonic key, and, of course, his fancy Colt. Kidder was offered no medical attention and was not even given a blanket. Shot in the gut and bleeding, he spent the next two hours alone in a cold cell.

When word of the fight reached the American side, Mexican officials were quickly contacted. A judge named Garcia permitted the removal of Kidder to a private home, although Jeff was not released from Mexican custody. A Mexican officer armed with a Winchester was stationed near his cot as a doctor tended Kidder's wound. At dawn on Saturday, another physician from Bisbee crossed the line to aid Kidder. Their diagnosis was grim: Kidder's intestines apparently had been perforated, and the most optimistic opinion they would venture was that he might recover.

Throughout the day Kidder was visited by friends and fellow officers as Tip Stanford telegraphed several points in a vain effort to contact Captain Wheeler. A reporter from the Bisbee *Review* interviewed Kidder, who talked freely with the journalist and his other visitors while his dog faithfully lay by the cot.

"I know that a great many people think I am quick-tempered and without looking into the details will form the opinion that I precipitated this trouble. It is probable that I may die, and I would like the public to hear my side of the affair," he said.

While relating the story of the shooting and of his treatment after surrendering, the wounded Kidder commented bitterly, "If anybody had told me that one human being could be as brutal to another as they were to me I would not have believed it." He concluded, "It's too bad such an unfortunate thing occurred, but if I am fatally wounded, I can die with the knowledge that I did my best in a hard situation."

Deputy U.S. Marshal John Foster, who had been the Ranger lieutenant when Kidder enlisted five years earlier, was by Jeff's side. "You know, Jack," said Kidder, "that I would have no object in telling what is untrue. They got me, but if my ammunition had not given out, I might have served them the same way."[61]

Kidder seemed to hold his own throughout Saturday, but during the night he weakened noticeably. He repeatedly left word for Wheeler that he had disobeyed orders by going into Mexican Naco only because he was searching for a fugitive. A little after 6:00 Sunday morning, thirty hours after he was shot, Jeff Kidder died at the age of thirty-three.

Mexican authorities at first refused to release Kidder's body. The shooting aroused violent feelings on both sides of the line, and reportedly as many as

1,000 Americans were ready to march across the border to retrieve Kidder's remains. American fury was fanned by rumors that Kidder had been deliberately lured into a fatal trap, perhaps because of his overbearing manner or perhaps because Mexican officers were jealous of his successful actions against border lawbreakers.[62] Officials were trying hard to keep a lid on the explosive situation, but the right leadership would have triggered an armed invasion. Wisely, Judge Garcia granted permission to release Kidder, and the body was taken to the Palace Funeral Parlor in Bisbee.[63]

The dead man's skull was so badly battered that embalming fluid ran from his eyes and nose. "Kidder's head must have been almost jelly," announced the undertaker. One three-inch laceration had gone to the bone in his forehead, and another swollen wound was clotted with blood on the right side of his neck. Several ribs had been broken by kicks, while the backs of his hands were torn, apparently from trying to ward off blows to his head and body.[64]

Captain Wheeler still could not be located. Since March 18 he had been absent from Naco on one of his periodic sweeps. He was accompanied by Sgt. Arthur Chase and Privates Rudolph Gunner and R.D. Horne, leaving Sergeant Stanford alone at headquarters. Wheeler and his detachment rode through Santa Cruz, Pima, Pinal, and Cochise counties, as well as southwestern New Mexico. For weeks the Rangers combed some of the wildest and most barren portions of Arizona, searching for rustlers and, on the day Jeff Kidder died, arresting a Mexican wanted for murder in Sonora. Early Tuesday morning, riding back through the broad Sulphur Spring Valley east of Tombstone, the Rangers encountered two cowboys who told them about Kidder. It was twenty-eight miles to Bisbee, and both men and horses were fatigued from their long trek through rough country, but Wheeler led out immediately. Before noon the Rangers and their prisoner arrived in Bisbee on jaded mounts.[65]

Wheeler and his men went directly to the undertaking parlor. Kidder lay in an open coffin, his face plainly showing the effects of a beating despite the ministrations of the undertaker. None of the four Rangers spoke, but their expressions were bitter. Tears came to Wheeler's eyes. After the funeral services he said: "Jeff Kidder was one of the best officers who ever stepped foot in this section of the country. He did not know what fear was . . . and was hated by the criminal classes because of his unceasing activity in bringing them to justice."[66]

Sergeant Stanford had wired Kidder's mother in San Jacinto, California, on Sunday, then wrote a letter giving details. Mrs. Kidder asked that Jeff's body be shipped to California for burial. On Wednesday, April 8, 259 members of the Bisbee lodge of Elks escorted Kidder's coffin to the depot, and one of the Elks accompanied the body to San Jacinto. Jip followed his master's coffin to the depot, where Sam Hayhurst picked up the little dog with the idea that it would become the Ranger mascot. But Jip mourned and continually ran away, trying to find Kidder. Captain Wheeler passed a hat and raised more than enough money to send Jip on a train to California.[67]

Wheeler wasted no time in going to Naco, Sonora, to investigate Kidder's death. The Bisbee *Review* reporter already had interviewed the Mexican policemen and other principals through a translator. Wheeler now spoke with the three wounded officers directly, as well as the numerous eyewitnesses. The stories conflicted wildly, and, of course, put Kidder in an unfavorable light. In one account, a bartender in the *cantina* stated that Jeff "had taken at least fifty drinks."[68]

It took a trip to Cananea, but Wheeler managed to recover Kidder's revolver and badge, the latter which was found in a pawn shop. Mexican authorities, trying to smooth over the explosive border situation, helped Wheeler locate Kidder's effects.[69] The saloons of Naco, Sonora—about fifteen in number—were ordered closed, and twenty policemen and line riders were dismissed, including the wounded chief. A Tucson *Citizen* headline melodramatically announced: "RANGER'S BLOOD WASHES AWAY A REIGN OF VICE."[70]

One of the other wounded policemen suffered complications and died,[71] but Wheeler was irked to learn that some of the discharged officers soon were reinstated. The Ranger captain immediately requested Mexican officers to "refrain from coming over here armed"; they were to send him a note asking his assistance in legal matters. Wheeler again forbade his men to cross into Mexico. Then he sent Kidder's gun and discharge papers to the family in California.[72]

Kidder's discharge became a source of controversy. Mexican authorities had inquired if Kidder was an officer in good standing on April 3, the date of the shooting, and the Ranger captain had replied affirmatively. However, Kidder's enlistment had run out three days before the gunfight. He had gone to headquarters in Naco to reenlist, but he could not complete the process until the captain returned. Ranger reenlistment procedure was to submit discharge papers to the governor for his signature after each year's service; at the same time the governor would sign an enlistment for another year, if the Ranger wanted to stay in the service. It was intended that service would be continuous, and Wheeler pointed out that in the military, if a brief interval occurred between discharge and reenlistment, customarily the soldier's service was extended until he was actually discharged. Wheeler grudgingly conceded, however: "Strictly speaking, I would feel he was not in the service . . . the day of his wounding."[73]

Technically, therefore, Jeff Kidder was not regarded as a member of the company when he was slain. Carlos Tafolla, shot during the second month of the company's existence, retained the dubious distinction of being the only man slain as an Arizona Ranger.

In May, Captain Wheeler closed in on a horse thief named George Arnett. Arnett, a thirty-seven-year-old hard-case who sometimes used the alias George Wood, had been stealing horses for several months in Cochise County and disposing of them across the border in Mexico. Suspected of robbing two Chinese men near Tombstone, Arnett also had bragged about looting a gambler in Lowell, and he had served a penitentiary term for horse theft. Wheeler had arrested him in March for robbing the Chinese men, and he considered Arnett "the worst man in Cochise [County]."[74]

Arnett blamed Mrs. Edward Payne of Lowell for revealing the robbery, and when he threatened to shoot her and her husband, she asked area lawmen for help. Acting on a tip from an Arnett accomplice, Wheeler and Deputy Sheriff George Humm, who was regarded as an expert marksman, set a trap for the suspected horse thief in a canyon about a mile east of Lowell, which is just a mile east of Bisbee. For four nights in a row, Wheeler and Humm held a fruitless vigil. On the fifth night the two lawmen left Lowell at about 2:00 A.M., Wednesday, May 6, and rode toward a rendezvous along different trails. Each man tied his horse in the mountains and walked to the canyon, carrying "bull's eye" lamps. When they met, Wheeler concealed himself behind a big saguaro cactus, while Humm ducked behind a bush.[75]

About an hour later, the officers heard someone approaching. A horseman topped a rise, leading a saddled mount. (Wheeler later testified his unconfirmed impression that a second thief was present, but vanished when the shooting started.) When the rider and his two animals were less than twenty feet away, Wheeler and Humm beamed their lamps at him, ordering him to throw up his hands. Instead he shouted, wheeled and spurred his horse, and snapped off a shot which clipped a bush between the lawmen. Wheeler already had leveled his revolver, and he held his lamp in his left hand at arm's length to distract the outlaw's aim. When the fugitive fired, Wheeler instantly triggered his .45, and he heard Humm's revolver go off beside him.

The retreating outlaw fired a second pistol shot from about fifty feet away. Humm scrambled for his rifle and squeezed off one round as the outlaw galloped up the mountainside and disappeared over a ridge.

The lawmen believed their prey had escaped unscathed. Their horses were secluded at some distance, so they hurried on foot back to their mounts and met in Lowell. The two officers rode back to the canyon, and as they crossed the ridge they spotted the outlaw's two horses, one of which had been wounded in the hind legs.

Realizing that the horse thief must have been injured, they carefully began to search the surrounding area. About 4:00, by the light of their lamps, the officers located Arnett's corpse no more than a quarter of a mile from the site of the shooting. He had been shot twice: one slug passed through his left arm below the elbow, while the fatal bullet raged through his left shoulder, into the left side of his neck, and emerged from his right ear. A coroner's jury was quickly brought to the canyon, and after they viewed the remains, Arnett was hauled into town by the Palace Undertaking Company.

That afternoon the inquest was conducted at the coroner's office, and Wheeler testified: "I have heard a relative state that Arnett had said he would never submit to arrest." Wheeler and Humm, of course, were exonerated since it was "the general opinion of the public that a dangerous man has met his end."[76]

Wheeler and Humm had received inside information about Arnett's activities from a gang member known as Charles Coleman. The stoolie's real name was Charles W. Heflin, a thirty-year-old criminal from Navarro County, Texas.

Captain Wheeler standing behind his men. (Courtesy Arizona Historical Society)

Heflin evidently was willing to trade outlaw secrets for legal clemency. Wheeler and Sheriff John White had contacted "Coleman" about doing undercover work, and after proving himself by helping to trap Arnett, Heflin seemed to be a candidate for further undercover work.[77]

Wheeler planned a sweep into Sonora, where Arnett and his confederates had taken several hundred horses that were stolen in Arizona. Heflin's services as a guide were imperative, and Wheeler temporarily placed the outlaw on the Ranger rolls in May. "He is not a man I would for one instant have in my Company," explained Wheeler, who commanded Heflin to sign an agreement specifying the limitations of his enlistment. Ranger Heflin was to be "shorn of all authority to act as an officer." His Ranger papers were to read "C.W. Heflin," and his identity was to be kept a strict secret.[78]

Heflin revealed that Constable Ells of Naco, with whom Wheeler had clashed before, had been associated with Arnett, and that the two had planned a payroll robbery, aborted because of Arnett's death. Wheeler also learned that Arnett had been protected by a high Mexican official who owned a rancho near Moctezuma, 150 miles south of the Arizona-Sonora border. Arnett had personally delivered many stolen horses to this official, and Heflin promised that the animals could be found in the man's pastures.

Soon area badmen began to sense that the authorities were receiving inside information, and various outlaws deserted the Bisbee-Naco vicinity for Sonora. Pleased at this exodus of so many "tough characters," Wheeler commented that "Heflin is safe."[79]

Wheeler had almost completed his preparations for the expedition into Sonora when Mexican officials notified him that it would be necessary to delay his entry until June 10. Disappointed, he rode into the mountains for a few days on a scout, and then returned to receive the pleas of Mrs. Fikes, who had just learned that her stolen horses were pastured near Moctezuma. Armed with a personal letter from Gen. Rafael Torres and accompanied by Mrs. Fikes's son, Wheeler eagerly traveled to Douglas to meet a Mexican major and several enlisted men across the border. Local sportsmen, knowing that Wheeler was an expert marksman, tried to persuade him to stay over for the day to bolster the Douglas Rifle Club in a shooting contest against the Fort Huachuca team. But Wheeler, impatient of further delays, insisted upon leaving that night, Friday, May 29. "It was a wild and dangerous country down there—no law—no officers—little known and a favorite resort of renegades—I hear a dozen Mexicans down there are wearing crepe on their hats over George Arnett being killed. . . ." The fearless captain of the Arizona Rangers found this lawless, threatening environment an irresistible challenge.[80]

Within a week, Wheeler had traveled to Moctezuma, secured a number of horses, and started north with five stolen animals. Exhilarated, he was convinced that the thieves were frightened. Stopping at Nacozari to rest his mounts, he wrote to the governor's office that "you should see the looks I get sometimes of the tough element, which to me, is a matter of pride."[81]

Wheeler obtained twenty days' leave of absence from the Ranger service for himself and Sgt. Rudolph Gunner, as well as C.W. Heflin and George Humm. Impressed by Humm during the fight with George Arnett, Wheeler had arranged for the deputy to be placed on the Ranger rolls from June 10 to June 20, 1908. Heflin, serving as guide, was not allowed to carry firearms.[82]

Wheeler, Gunner, Humm, and Heflin rode out of Naco into Mexico on Thursday morning, June 11. They were accompanied by a Mexican army escort, including a major and a lieutenant. Averaging fifty miles a day, they plodded through sizzling summer heat across mountain trails. Rising each day at 3:30, they were in the saddle by 4:30 and did not pitch camp until 8:00 P.M. After nine days of hard riding, penetrating mountain hideouts, and crisscrossing rustlers' haunts, the exhausted party entered Moctezuma. Three of Arnett's rustling accomplices were captured, along with four stolen horses; the rustlers were wanted on Mexican charges, and Wheeler sent them to Hermosillo.[83]

Wheeler never really seemed to mind the hardships, and he always relished a head-on challenge with outlaws. With a glint of triumph he reported: "The

Arnett gang is now broken up and the criminal element is badly frightened."[84] Harry Wheeler genuinely enjoyed intimidating badmen.

One of Arizona's most belligerent badmen was William F. Downing, who was an intimidating presence in Willcox, after serving seven years in the Yuma Territorial Prison. The Ranger who had replaced Harry Wheeler in Willcox was a Texan named Billy Speed, who was threatened on more than one occasion by the bellicose Downing.[85] Speed had been with the Rangers since 1906, but neither Wheeler nor Rynning had been impressed with his performance. Both Ranger leaders put up with him because he was an expert cowman who provided excellent service to the Livestock Sanitary Board. Curiously, Captain Wheeler promoted Speed to sergeant in the hope that higher rank would improve his qualities as a Ranger. This experiment proved unsuccessful, and the thirty-seven-year-old Ranger was demoted to private.[86]

Despite his unsatisfactory two-year tenure as a Ranger, within a few months Speed proved to be one of the few men in Willcox who would not be cowed by the reputation and threats of William Downing. Billy Speed remained mindful of Captain Wheeler's admonition that "if anyone must be hurt, I do not want it to be the Ranger."[87]

The festering predicament with Downing finally came to a head in the summer of 1908. In July the local justice of the peace wired Captain Wheeler twice in one day, stating that Speed and Constable Bud Snow were absent on duty elsewhere and that Downing was drunk and terrorizing the town. Wheeler immediately dispatched Sgt. Rudolph Gunner and Pvt. John McKittrick Redmond to Willcox, ordering them to shoot Downing at the first flicker of trouble. By the time they arrived, Downing had settled down. Gunner and Redmond decided to stay in town for several days until the badman promised to behave. Nevertheless, Wheeler wrote Speed with emphatic instructions "to take no chance with this man in any official dealing you may have with him." Wheeler left no doubt as to his meaning: "I hearby direct you to prepare yourself to meet this man, and upon his least of slightest attempt to do you harm I want you to kill him."[88]

Speed followed his captain's advice on August 5, 1908. Downing was drunk and issuing profane threats against Speed, who stalked the badman through the dusty streets. When the men sighted each other, Downing drunkenly reached for a pistol he had forgotten to bring. Speed dropped him with a single Winchester bullet, and Downing died moments later. A coroner's jury concluded that Speed "was perfectly justified in the act and therefore we exonerate him from all blame in the matter."[89]

Wheeler was telegraphed about the killing. He wired the governor's office, then left on the first train for Willcox. In his report he praised Speed and emphasized that everyone in town was afraid of Downing. Wheeler remarked that "this is the first time I have ever known a dead man to be without a single friend and the first time I have known a killing to meet absolute general rejoicing [sic]."[90]

In December 1908 Wheeler proved that, despite his deadly expertise with firearms, he was not trigger happy. Following a good piece of detective work, Wheeler and another officer arrested a murderer named Christo Davlandos. Davlandos was a Greek who lived in Cananea, but the arrest apparently was made in Naco. After Davlandos was handcuffed, the lawmen began to walk their prisoner toward jail. Suddenly, Davlandos broke away, and even though his hands were cuffed behind his back, he outdistanced his pursuers. "I could easily have shot him," said Wheeler, "but I couldn't do it."[91] Wheeler, who often had fought head-on duels with outlaws, refused to shoot the fleeing Davlandos in the back because he was handcuffed and because he was afraid the man might be innocent. When it came down to it, the deadly Harry Wheeler demonstrated ultimate respect for the American legal system.

During 1908 Captain Wheeler feared that he would lose key men to other law enforcement jobs. Several ex-Rangers had already filled various officers' positions around the Territory, and as respect for the Rangers grew there were efforts to secure the services of members of the company for numerous lawmen's offices. Wheeler wrote to the governor's secretary stating that many citizens of Santa Cruz County were trying to persuade Lieutenant Old to run for sheriff. He also thought "it extremely probable that [Frank] Wheeler will be the next Sheriff of Yuma County," and there was talk of making Tip Stanford constable of Naco, Rye Miles constable of Benson, Bob Anderson city marshal of Globe, and Sam Hayhurst constable of Douglas.[92]

Harry Wheeler himself was approached by numerous citizens, both Democrats and Republicans, to run for sheriff of Cochise County. "I have no time to run around playing the [political] game," wrote Wheeler. "I cannot pay attention to my business and work for my political interests at the same time but I know that I could win this next election." Despite his protests, Wheeler discussed at length his election possibilities.[93] Clearly, the political bug had bitten Wheeler, but he stayed with the force, and so did Billy Old and Tip Stanford and Sam Hayhurst. There was a mystique about the Rangers that bound many of the best men to their five-pointed stars.

To save money and thereby allay critics of the Rangers, the approved strength of the force during the year was a maximum of twenty-three officers and men. Even though outlawry was noticeably declining in Arizona, Harry Wheeler continued to be barraged with petitions for Rangers. "As you know, Sir," wrote Wheeler to the governor in June, "the demands made upon the Ranger service are constantly becoming more numerous, and I am unable to comply with many requests made upon me."[94] The surviving Ranger correspondence for 1908 is filled with pleas for Rangers. In August Wheeler reported, "I have thirty requests for Rangers, or more, that I cannot honor, until some of the boys finish present work."[95] Wheeler himself was often in the field, and not infrequently he had to scatter his headquarters squad to various points in response to pleas for Rangers. When the Rangers were forced to abandon Naco for any length of time, invariably "some depredation" was committed by local criminals.[96]

Captain Wheeler returned to Naco in October from a long scout and was shocked to discover his headquarters clerk, Pvt. A.F. Chase, "under the influence of liquor, and upon the Mexican side, contrary to my strict orders." Wheeler was fond of the thirty-year-old Chase, regarding him as "worth two ordinary men" and stating that he was "my favorite ranger, of all I have ever had." But even though the captain was grieved over the situation, he reported the incident to the governor and called for Chase's discharge.

For once, however, the rigid captain had second thoughts. Numerous citizens and fellow Rangers pleaded with Wheeler not to fire the big, likable Chase, and it took little intercession to save him. "I fought down some personal habits years ago," wrote Wheeler to the governor. Wheeler recounted Chase's assets: "He has experience both as a soldier and as a handler of stock, is well educated and comes of an excellent family." Wheeler proposed to suspend Chase's pay for a month, "and have him do all the extra work around the quarters and Camp." Throughout the history of the Rangers, the governor had permitted the captain final say on personnel matters, and Kibbey gave his permission for Chase to remain in the company.[97]

The next month Wheeler was further disappointed to learn that fondness for the bottle had caused Sgt. Rudolph Gunner to neglect his duties. Wheeler abruptly broke his straying protégé to private, although Gunner reenlisted the next month.[98] November revealed another Ranger who had a drinking problem. Samuel Black, a forty-five-year-old West Virginian who had served as city marshal of Flagstaff, was enlisted by Lieutenant Old in April 1908. Although Black was a promising Ranger (Wheeler was especially impressed when Black arrested his own brother-in-law), late in November Old reported to Captain Wheeler that the man had been discovered drunk. Wheeler had not yet met the new private, who could not be reduced in rank, but the captain immediately discharged Black from the force.[99]

A.E. Ehle, who had been a Ranger private for less than nine months, left the company on May 1. He had received a cash inheritance and decided to raise oranges in California rather than chase criminals in Arizona. Wheeler was sorry to lose Ehle, as well as veteran Bob Anderson, who tendered his resignation at the same time. Anderson had been enlisted in October 1902, and only Frank Wheeler, who had signed up one month earlier, had served longer than the forty-two-year-old Tennessean. Harry Wheeler managed to talk Anderson into serving out his sixth enlistment, but in October, Bob turned in his badge.[100]

A more welcome departure was that of Pvt. J.A. Fraser. A native of San Antonio, Fraser came to the end of his enlistment in July. Wheeler liked Fraser no better than he liked most Texans: "I have had difficulty in compelling him to pay his debts, and in general I do not approve of his character." The rigid Wheeler had spoken, and the Ranger was terminated on July 19. Fraser, along with another Texan who had fallen from grace with the Rangers, W.F. Bates, tried to stir up trouble for Wheeler. They had little success.[101]

By this time Wheeler had developed a strong dislike for "Texans who have not been away from Texas very long." After firing Travis Poole in November

1907, he wrote the governor's secretary: "You will note all our unsatisfactory men are from Texas, . . . they seem to desire to be tough and without exception are hard to get along with." He made a similar complaint to the governor, and while he was having problems with Billy Speed, Wheeler blamed "his Texan disposition." Wheeler stated that his lieutenant concurred with his anti-Texan bias, but Old was from Texas himself, along with more than four of every ten Rangers. Texans always had been regarded by commanding officers as superb fighting men but terrible soldiers between battles, unruly and disobedient, and the commander of the Arizona Rangers clearly concurred.[102]

The exit of Pvt. R.D. Horne caused resentment among the Rangers. In April, after less than six months as a Ranger, Horne planned to return to the East as a member of a theatrical troupe, probably one of the Wild West shows on tour. He evidently intended to use his Ranger experience on his billing. Learning of this plan, Harry Wheeler was predictably irked. Horne had served occasionally at the headquarters desk in Naco, and Wheeler prominently marked on his discharge papers that he had been a clerk. Wheeler commented to the governor: "some of the romance of the Discharge, being thus eliminated, he will be less likely to make improper use of it, by sticking it up at some stage entrance." The other Rangers were equally insulted at the cheapening of their commissions by the theatrical designs of Horne. "His comrades are all offended with him," wrote Wheeler, "as they consider their Discharge a Sacred document."[103]

In 1907 Harry Wheeler had requested a machine gun for the Ranger Company, and in 1908 he asked Governor Kibbey to replace the Ranger issue 1895 Winchester with the army's weapon, the 1903 Springfield. Wheeler considered the Springfield "far above any arm," and the Rangers could obtain ammunition at half price from military posts. Wheeler also asked for a pair of bloodhounds, regarding them as a necessity in tracking down fugitives in the wilds of Arizona. Trained bloodhounds of the type Wheeler wanted could be purchased in Texas for $300, and the Ranger captain pointed out that they could be shipped rapidly by train wherever they were needed in the Territory.[104]

Another request resulted from the fact that many Rangers were stationed so far from headquarters that Wheeler never got to visit with them and consult with the citizens about area conditions and their relations with the Rangers. But considering the press of his other duties, inspection trips across the Territory could be made only by train, and funds were unavailable for such journeys. "This is really my duty but it would cost me more than I would receive in an entire Months salary," he said.[105] Wheeler asked Governor Kibbey to authorize funding for inspection trips, but opposition to Ranger expenditures was accelerating. The governor reduced the payroll by keeping the authorized roster below strength, and he did not approve expenditures for inspection trips or bloodhounds or Springfield rifles or a machine gun.

The rejections did not discourage the captain, who continued to enjoy his work. Harry Wheeler loved to ride the open country in search of outlaws. During 1908 he ranged far and wide, repeatedly penetrating Arizona's wild mountain and desert country. He rode on long scouts and short ones; he rode at the head of Ranger detachments and he rode alone; he headed into Mexico at least three times, and he squeezed in a trip to Mexico on official business. He spent the first twenty-five days of October on a 600-mile sweep through Cochise, Santa Cruz, and Graham counties, and after a few days to rest the horses, he planned another patrol to last most of November.[106]

Like modern policemen who cruise through troubled neighborhoods, hoping to deter crime by their presence, Wheeler and his men observed "that hardly any crime ever occurs in the sections over which we ride and patrol."[107] On the long October patrol, Wheeler and his men caught only one malefactor, a horse thief who escaped jail a few days after the Rangers turned him over to local authorities.[108] Outlaws plainly were intimidated by the Rangers, but there was mounting evidence that the company had put a permanent crimp in criminal activities throughout the Territory. After Billy Speed killed William Downing in Willcox, Wheeler informed the governor that Downing was "the last of the professional bad men in this section."[109]

Wheeler's report for the month of August revealed that the Rangers had made less than two dozen arrests: "The whole country seems remarkably quiet and scarcely any crimes are being committed anywhere."[110] And following the death of George Arnett and the breakup of his horse-stealing ring, Wheeler reported with obvious disappointment that "there has been absolutely no trouble of any kind and I am getting tired of so much goodness as are all the men."[111]

Throughout Arizona, the Rangers rapidly were working themselves out of a job.

CHAPTER FIVE

The Last Ranger

"The pride of my life has been my Company."

—Capt. Harry Wheeler

By 1909 the Arizona Rangers had been in existence for more than seven years. Over one hundred men had worn a Ranger badge, but only one had held every rank. Harry Wheeler had commanded the Rangers for nearly two years, hounding lawbreakers relentlessly while administering the company with conscientious efficiency.

With the Rangers operating smoothly, Captain Wheeler decided that he could leave his duties for an overdue trip to Gainesville, Florida, the retirement home of his parents. Col. and Mrs. Wheeler both were afflicted with cancer, and in the spring of 1908 Harry had requested a leave of absence from Governor Kibbey. Although Kibbey granted this petition, the Ranger captain had second thoughts. Harry reasoned that since a trip to Florida would cost at least $300, he would forego the journey and apply the travel funds to the needs of his parents. Besides, his brother William was in Florida with Colonel and Mrs. Wheeler.[1]

While still a major, the elder Wheeler had been granted an extended sick leave from November 15, 1901, until June 15, 1902. Promoted to lieutenant colonel in 1903, by 1904 he again was placed on extended leave. Although the ailing Wheeler was only fifty-eight, he was placed on the retirement list in 1905. Following the army's customary practice, Wheeler was promoted to colonel just before leaving the service, which provided additional pension pay. Colonel Wheeler and Annie made their new home at 700 East Main Street in Gainesville, and he was awarded the Order of the Indian Wars in 1907. But

Colonel Wheeler's health continued to fail. He went blind, and then died on November 28, 1908, at the age of sixty-one.[2]

Harry did not travel to Florida, but within a month his mother reached the verge of death. On the first day of 1909, Harry again sent a request to Governor Kibbey for a leave of absence, which was granted immediately.[3]

Lieutenant Old, stationed now in Winslow, would command the Rangers in Wheeler's absence. Sgt. Tip Stanford would take over at headquarters in Naco, a familiar role for him because Wheeler was so often in the field. Before he left, Wheeler finalized the discharge of Luke Short, who had resigned after merely a few months' service to become a mine foreman at Sylvanite. He also said good-bye to Rudolph Gunner. Gunner, an intelligent and experienced peace officer, had so impressed Wheeler that he won promotion to sergeant only a few months after his enlistment in December 1907. But when Gunner's drinking problem worsened, a disappointed Wheeler demanded Gunner's resignation. "I cannot keep a drinking Ranger," stated Wheeler, pointing out that "a man who carries a gun and the Authority of the Territory must of necessity remain sober."[4] At the same time Wheeler enlisted O.F. Hicks, a thirty-six-year-old married man who had been a peace officer since he was twenty.

Wheeler finished up last-minute business on Sunday, January 3, and prepared to board a train that night. Before departing, however, he and a few other officers arrested a highwayman who had killed a woman in Cananea and fled to Arizona. Wheeler extracted a confession from the murderer, sent him across the line to waiting Mexican officers, typed out a brief report to the governor, and still had half an hour to catch his train.[5]

Sadly, Wheeler would not reach Florida in time to see his mother alive. Annie Cornwall Wheeler died on Monday, January 4. Like her recently deceased husband, she was only sixty-one. At least Harry was able to visit with his siblings, William and Sallie. The Wheeler will was executed, but the estate was modest. Harry returned to Arizona with his father's U.S. Military Academy degree—a framed sheepskin—along with his army commission and his promotions. Harry also claimed possession of two prints of English coats of arms: Wheeler and Cornwall.[6]

The Wheelers were away from Arizona for three weeks. Perhaps Harry vacationed briefly with Mamie and ten-year-old Allyn. When he returned to Ranger headquarters in Naco on Monday, January 25, 1909, his most immediate problem involved two troublesome privates, E.S. McGee and Orrie King. McGee, a two-year veteran from Texas, was stationed in Bouse in Yuma County, but since his marriage he had become uninterested in Ranger duties. Just before leaving for Florida, Wheeler had sent him an order, which he ignored. Wheeler was so furious that he would not even permit McGee to resign, instead insisting that he receive a dishonorable discharge from the company. The next day, January 27, Wheeler disposed of Texan Orrie King in the same way. King, who had enlisted in August 1908, came highly recommended by citizens of Douglas, but Wheeler learned unforgivable facts about his background.

Immediately, Wheeler turned in a dishonorable discharge for King, who would prove to be the last man dismissed from the force by Harry Wheeler.[7]

A far more threatening problem than personal foibles had materialized during Wheeler's absence: the most serous anti-Ranger effort was in progress. He returned from Florida to find that supportive letters from seven county sheriffs and a number of district attorneys had reached his headquarters desk. On January 26 Wheeler wrote the governor's office, describing these letters and asking to whom they might be forwarded for the greatest benefit.[8]

Wheeler was able to do nothing further about the political hazard to his company. The governor's office wired him on January 27 that serious trouble was about to erupt in Globe: "Go there at once with available men." The message reached Wheeler at 10:30 P.M., and immediately he began to wire and telephone his men at their various stations. The captain and his headquarters squad boarded the first northbound train. There was no direct rail route, however, and Wheeler did not alight in Globe until thirty-six hours after his departure.[9]

By that time several Rangers already had arrived. Although in January the mountain weather was frigid, the Rangers ignored the rain and biting cold, forded swollen streams, and struggled toward Globe. Sgt. Lew Mickey rode more than a hundred miles, "crossed a torrent," and arrived within twenty-four hours. Several other men rode horseback eighty or ninety miles in a day's time to get to Globe, and by the end of the week fourteen well-armed men wearing silver stars were patrolling the streets of the mining town.

On the night of January 28, Captain Wheeler telegraphed the governor's office that all was quiet. Unhappy miners who had been threatening disturbances were talking with mine owners, and work was expected to resume in the morning. On the next day, Friday, Wheeler sent another telegram with the information that the miners indeed were returning to work, and the atmosphere was so "quiet and promising" that he was beginning to release his men to return to their duty stations. Wheeler and a few of his men stayed over a couple days, but the crisis clearly had passed, and on Sunday all Rangers left town. The governor's secretary stated that he felt from the beginning that the threat of trouble was "somewhat exaggerated," but the presence of fourteen Arizona Rangers doubtless had an immediate quieting effect upon disgruntled parties in Globe.[10]

On Monday, after his return to headquarters, Captain Wheeler enlisted Tom Gadberry. Despite Wheeler's stated dislike for recent residents of the Lone Star State, he nevertheless signed onto the roster a number of native Texans. Gadberry was a forty-year-old Texan who was destined to wear his Ranger badge a total of fifteen days. He was the last man enlisted as an Arizona Ranger.[11]

In 1907, when the Twenty-fourth Legislative Assembly met in biennial session, two anti-Ranger bills had been introduced. One bill, severely reducing the Ranger company, passed the legislature but was vetoed by Governor Kibbey. As the next regular legislative session approached in January 1909, it was a foregone conclusion that a determined attempt would be mustered to abolish the Rangers.

Seated in front of the Arizona capitol at far right, with a big hat on his knee, is Thomas Weedin. A Democratic councilman from Pinal County, Weedin introduced the 1909 bill to abolish the Rangers. He was strongly supported by fellow councilman Eugene Brady O'Neill, seated at far left. Seated third from left is newspaperman Kean St. Charles, a member of the Assembly in 1901 who was the only legislator to express opposition to the creation of the Rangers. (Courtesy Arizona Historical Society)

The Ranger question became a political punching bag. Since its creation by a Republican administration in 1901, the Rangers had always been regarded by Democrats as a Republican instrument. The citizens of Arizona vigorously supported party politics during the early 1900s, as a reading of editorial pages of the period plainly reveals. Republican Governor Joseph Kibbey had aroused strong Democratic opposition throughout his four-year tenure, and by 1909 Democratic politicians recognized the abolishment of the Rangers as an obvious partisan ploy against the governor. Ominously, in the two-house Arizona legislature, Democrats outnumbered Republicans in the Council ten to two, and in the House of Representatives eighteen to six.

Campaigning for legislative seats had focused upon the Ranger question in many counties, and was especially intense in Maricopa County.[12] Elected to the Council from Maricopa County was Democrat Eugene Brady O'Neill, a bitter enemy of Governor Kibbey, and the House delegation was composed of one Republican and three Democrats, including Sam F. Webb, who was elected Speaker. Soon after the November elections, several Democratic legislators, including O'Neill and Thomas Weedin, met in Phoenix "to map out plans."[13] One of their stated aims was to do away with the Rangers. A few days later Captain Wheeler was interviewed by a newspaper reporter and asked about the anti-Ranger movement. "I have heard very little objection to maintaining the Ranger force," he said hopefully, "but it comes up in the legislature at regular intervals and has some following from certain sources."[14]

The sixty-day session was scheduled to open on Monday, January 18. By Sunday the legislators had assembled in Phoenix and met informally "to discuss proposed measures."[15] A Democratic caucus was organized, pledging, among other things, to repeal the 1901 bill which had created the Rangers. On Monday the legislature filled the speakerships, approved various appointments, and attended to other introductory business.[16]

Both houses convened on Tuesday afternoon to hear Governor Kibbey's long and carefully prepared message to the legislature.[17] Fully aware of the anti-Ranger movement, Kibbey attempted to mollify arguments against the company. He emphasized that "the Arizona Rangers have proved so often their usefulness that it seems impossible to recommend the repeal of the law authorizing the force." Indirectly addressing the jealousy of local law officers, he stressed that Rangers patrolled the "many remote sections in which the county peace officers do not ordinarily travel," but which, of course, were haunts of lawbreakers. Knowing that Captain Wheeler had made a specific effort to avoid conflict with county lawmen, the governor pointed out "that the Rangers to a large extent per-form functions which can not well be performed at all by sheriffs or their deputies." Kibbey spoke of the high quality of the enlisted men, and he detailed the number of arrests and mileage traveled during the past two fiscal years, as well as expenses incurred. In the interest of the economy, he also stated that "it is my purpose to keep the number of enlisted men as low as possible." (At that point Captain Wheeler had only nineteen men under his command.)

By the end of the week, however, Governor Kibbey was on an eastbound train for Washington, D.C., to push for Arizona statehood in Congress. On Saturday, January 23, Thomas Weedin, a Democratic councilman from Pinal County who edited the Florence *Blade*, introduced bills to abolish the Rangers and the office of public examiner. As a part of the anti-Ranger package, a bill was proposed—and passed—creating "Deputy Rangers," who could be ap-pointed by county governments at a monthly wage not to exceed $125.[18]

The county supervisors also were in annual session at Phoenix, and a reso-lution was introduced to do away with the Rangers. The resolution caused "a lively discussion," but when the supervisors deadlocked ten to ten over the matter, it was decided to table the resolution and offer no recommendation about the Rangers to the legislature.[19]

Across the Territory there were strong feelings about the Rangers. Since the fall elections of 1908, Democratic newspapers had called for abolition of the force.[20] There was considerable opposition to the company in the northern coun-ties, since just one-third of the men were stationed in the "Northern Detachment" under the direction of Lieutenant Old. In earlier years the Rangers had almost completely neglected the northern counties, mainly because there was far more crime in the south. Now that the Rangers' presence was being felt in such communities as Winslow and Williams, their no-nonsense crackdowns may have been resented. Although some resentment existed in the south among those who had felt Ranger heavy-handedness, for the most part southern Arizona enthusiastically supported the company of peace officers which had imposed order upon their unruly area. It long had been rumored that many sheriffs were jealous of the Rangers, particularly since Ranger arrests often cost local officers fees and rewards. But many sheriffs had cooperated successfully with the Rangers, and Wheeler had collected letters of support from eight Arizona sheriffs and several district attorneys. Mulford Winsor, a keen observer of Arizona events of the day and a knowledgeable Ranger historian, felt that "quite likely a majority" of Arizona citizens supported the Rangers.[21]

On Thursday, January 28, Captain Wheeler's report for December reached the governor's office. Newspapers supportive of the Rangers trumpeted that the company had made fifty-eight arrests during the month, fifty-five of which had resulted in convictions. It was emphasized that two Rangers had been sent to the mining camp of Courtland and promptly had enforced order upon the lawless population. The Tucson *Citizen* concluded that the work of the Rangers "has not conflicted with that of other peace officers but has been supplemental to it. The arrests made by them have been those which would not have been made but for them."[22]

However, on Friday afternoon the Council voted to pass the bill to repeal the Rangers. The next day there was a joint caucus of the House and Council. The caucus vote to abolish the office of public examiner received no opposition even though Governor Kibbey had supported continuation of the office. On the Ranger issue, however, legislators from Cochise, Graham, and Pinal counties were outspoken in their arguments that the company was "a necessity in the Territory."[23] Still, the large Democratic majority held firm, and the Council voted to abolish the Rangers. It was regarded as certain that the Council vote ensured that the House would support the anti-Ranger bill when it went before them the next week.

Captain Wheeler had called the Rangers to Globe, but all were painfully aware of the legislative threat to their force. Ranger morale, of course, began to suffer, and there was a noticeable increase in criminal activities as lawbreakers opportunistically sensed the demise of their formidable adversaries. Captain Wheeler returned to Ranger headquarters from Globe, but almost immediately he had to ride into the field to search for horse rustlers. He instructed his headquarters clerk, Pvt. Emil Lenz, to write the governor's office that the respectable citizens of Naco supported the Rangers, and that Neill Bailey, one of three Cochise County representatives, had worked with Thomas Weedin to undermine the Rangers. Bailey, a Democrat from Naco, supposedly had supported the Rangers until the most recent elections, when Wheeler had interfered with some highly questionable practices. His ire thus aroused, Bailey now had become a leader of the anti-Ranger movement.[24]

On the day the letter was written, February 3, the House of Representatives voted its approval of the anti-Ranger bill. Two days later, Captain Wheeler rode in from his wilderness pursuit to Douglas, where he learned of the House vote. He wrote a long letter to the governor, expressing "the general and violent opposition" to the pending abolishment of the company. Wheeler was understandably dismayed that he had not been called to testify before the legislature about the Rangers. Complaining about the "false and malicious tactics [that] have been resorted to by Neil Bailey, among the Democratic members of the House and Council," Wheeler stated that he had telegraphed Ben Goodrich, a council member from Tombstone, to have himself "summoned before any Committee." Wheeler asked the governor's aid in having him brought to Phoenix so that he could "answer freely and willingly, each and every question" that might occur to the legislators about the Rangers.[25]

Wheeler then made a startling proposal. So that no one could attribute his defense of the Rangers to a selfish desire to perpetuate his captaincy, he intended to resign his commission. "The pride of my life has been my Company," he said. But he felt that his resignation, following an impassioned testimony before the legislature, might persuade enough "fair minded men to turn the tide in favor of the service." Wheeler was willing to make this personal sacrifice for the good of the Rangers and the people of Arizona. The sacrificial offer was publicized in Arizona newspapers, and on Thursday, February 11, the governor's office asked the captain to come to Phoenix. Even though he was on the scene, no invitation to testify was sent from either house.[26]

Letters of protest began to pour into the governor's office and into Ranger headquarters. Ranchers, mining executives, law officers, government officials, merchants, and Rangers themselves decried abolishment of the company. The Tucson Chamber of Commerce sent letters to the Pima County delegation and to other legislators denouncing the abolishment of the force. The Rangers were widely praised as the most important element in subduing outlawry in Arizona, and the governor was urged to "do all in your power to retain our ranger force."[27]

John H. Slaughter, owner of the San Bernardino Ranch and legendary sheriff of Cochise County during the 1880s, issued a newspaper statement praising the Rangers in enthusiastic detail. Another lengthy newspaper endorsement came from the first captain of the Rangers, Burt Mossman, who pled for continuation of the force he had founded, even if economy demanded reduction to the original thirteen men. Harry Wheeler himself, despairing of not being called to testify, contributed a long interview to the newspaper skirmish. He detailed Ranger services to Arizona, commented upon the relatively inexpensive cost of the force, emphasized the support he had received from various Arizona sheriffs and other citizens, and otherwise stated his case before the public.[28]

There also was considerable editorial support for continuation of the Rangers. Responding to journalistic criticism in the *Citizen*, Democratic Councilman James Finley of Tucson defended his anti-Ranger vote in a letter to the editor, denying that the caucus had influenced him and offering standard arguments as his justification. Finley objected to Rangers serving as livestock inspectors, insisting that such expenses should be borne by cattlemen rather than taxpayers. Finley also pointed out that the Rangers "have been devoting much of their time to looking after smuggling on the border, the expense of which should have been borne by the Federal government." Rangers had indeed been active as livestock inspectors, and for years they had patrolled the border to assist line riders of Mexico and the United States in controlling smugglers, although much of this effort had curtailed rustling as well. The *Citizen* fired back that since opinion in favor of retaining the Rangers was "almost unanimous" among his constituents, then Finley was duty-bound to reverse his position and "represent the large majority of the people he was elected to represent."[29]

It was anticipated that Governor Kibbey, upon return from Washington, would veto the bills abolishing the Rangers and the office of public examiner. Everyone expected the legislature to override the governor's veto regarding the public examiner, but the avalanche of public protest raised hope in some quarters that the Democratic caucus might relent on behalf of the Rangers.[30]

Kibbey was back in Phoenix by the end of the week, and he prepared a lengthy message to the assembly. On Monday morning, February 15, the governor vetoed the bills that abolished the Rangers and the office of public examiner. The bills were returned to the legislature along with the veto message, arriving in the Council chamber a little after 10:00 A.M.

Captain Wheeler vainly hoped to testify at Arizona's State Capitol, where his beloved Rangers were discontinued on February 15, 1909. (Courtesy Arizona Historical Society)

The Council had just convened, and only a small crowd was looking down from the ornate, three-sided gallery. As soon as the reading of the minutes was completed, the message regarding the Ranger bill was deliberated. It took more than half an hour to read this message. In his carefully worded communication, Kibbey repeated the arguments he had stated in support of the Rangers at the opening session of the legislature. Then he stated that he had received letters endorsing the Rangers from numerous sheriffs and district attorneys, and he quoted long passages from two letters. Next he took up the various criticisms proffered by Ranger opponents and refuted them, point by point. His message concluded with a long attack upon the political bias that had made the Rangers a Democratic target.[31]

At one point during the message, as Kibbey criticized the "inconsistent attitude" of legislators who once had supported the Rangers, the reading was interrupted by Brady O'Neill, a strong critic of the governor. He moved that the further reading of the message be dispensed with, and a few fellow Democrats clapped their hands in support. But the presiding officer, George Hunt, ruled against the motion. Hunt stated that if the Council intended to vote upon the governor's veto, they should have the courtesy to hear his remarks.

The reading continued, and when the veto message finally was finished Hunt pronounced the customary questions: "Shall the bill pass the governor's objections thereto, notwithstanding?" The Council members had expected the vetoes, and the caucus had determined to remain firm. All ten Democrats voted against the veto, leaving only two Republicans to support the governor.

Thomas Weedin, who had originated the anti-Ranger bill, asked to be heard on a question of personal privilege. Granted the floor, Weedin launched a thinly disguised attack upon the governor. He recalled that two years earlier he had introduced a similar bill, and he reiterated his anti-Ranger arguments of 1907. Referring to the governor's assertion that the Rangers were necessary to preserve law and order, Weedin claimed that this was a reflection upon other Arizona peace officers—indeed, upon Arizona itself. "I resent the slander," declared Weedin vehemently.[32]

Vigorous applause erupted. Weedin then charged that each Ranger had been forced to contribute ten percent of his salary to Republican campaign chests. This erroneous claim was followed by an illusory excursion into mathematics: Weedin stated that the Rangers had cost Arizona $66,000 per year (during the previous fiscal year Ranger expenses totaled $28,476.31),[33] while there had been 1,100 arrests, and each arrest supposedly had cost the Territory more than $3,000.

William J. Morgan, Democrat from Navajo County, claimed that every man, woman, and child in his county supported his anti-Ranger vote. Morgan went on to praise the stellar qualities of the local peace officers of Navajo County. Brady O'Neill then blurted out a coarse insult against the governor. Several people in the gallery hissed their disapproval, and Hunt pounded his desk. But O'Neill continued to snarl vituperation against Kibbey. His remarks became personal as he criticized Kibbey's record "and flayed him unmercifully."[34]

Captain Wheeler, still hoping in vain to be asked to testify on behalf of his beloved company, looked on with suppressed anger as the Rangers were vilified. The steel-nerved man of action watched helplessly as the Rangers met doom at the hands of partisan politicians.

The Council finally returned to business and overrode the governor's veto of the bill abolishing the public examiner's office. Word quickly spread that in the Council the necessary two-thirds majority had been reached to abolish the Rangers and the public examiner, and when the House convened at 1:00 a large crowd had gathered in the gallery. The messages were immediately read, and one after another the two vetoes were voted down. One Democrat strayed from the fold on the Ranger bill, but the 17 to 7 vote was more than Ranger opponents needed to abolish the force. Speaker of the House Sam F. Webb added his signature to that of George W.P. Hunt. Section 3 of the anti-Ranger bill stated: "This act shall be in force and effect from and after its passage." There was to be no transition period.[35]

Early in the afternoon of February 15, 1909, the Arizona Rangers abruptly ceased to exist. That day Rangers apprehended horse thief Peter Morris in the Chiricahua Mountains, and on a ranch in the Dragoon Mountains Pvt. Emil Lenz traded shots with Allen Rose before the robber would submit to arrest.[36]

Harry Wheeler returned to Naco, still seething with resentment. Each of the Rangers had to be notified that the company no longer existed, but several of the men were still in the field and could not be reached for a time. Pvt. John McK. Redmond, searching remote country for horse thieves, tried to close with outlaws for five days after the Rangers had been abolished. The rustlers, trying to stay ahead of Redmond, were captured by another officer. "It would have been a pretty 'how-dy-do'," growled Redmond, "if I had been killed or had killed one of them after my commission had been taken from me."[37]

On February 17 Wheeler forwarded to the governor's office the discharge papers, in duplicate, of the members of the final roster. He awarded "Excellent Discharge" to seventeen of his men. Typically, Wheeler downgraded the discharge of Tom Gadberry, "too recent in the force for me to know him intimately," and that of H.E. Woods, who, when summoned to Globe, "allowed himself to be detained by such a thing as a swollen stream of water." But the next day Wheeler relented, stating in a follow-up letter that he felt that it would be an "injustice" to the long faithful Woods to grant him less than an excellent discharge.[38]

The following day Wheeler accumulated the materials his men had sent in, and he compiled the monthly report for January 1909. Before detailing the arrests, the captain described the heroic way in which his men had overcome obstacles of water and distance in hurrying to Globe to avert labor difficulties. He mentioned that Billy Speed once had patrolled 754 miles horseback during one month, the all-time Ranger total, and Wheeler otherwise praised the efforts of his "faithful and loyal body of Public Servants." The seventeen-page report is handwritten; the ribbon on the headquarters' Oliver typewriter had worn out, and Wheeler could find no replacement.[39] All of Wheeler's remaining correspondence was composed in his bold handwriting. Although Wheeler now was off the territorial payroll, his sense of duty and deep affection for his job kept him at headquarters to finish the tasks necessary to tie up the loose ends of his company.

During the latter half of February, a few letters arrived at the governor's office offering support if some method could be found to reinstate the company. Wheeler released a letter refuting the criticisms of Thomas Weedin and other Ranger opponents, and he expressed the gratitude of the Rangers to citizens who had supported the company.[40]

On Thursday, March 5, Harry Wheeler wrote the report of Ranger operations during the first fifteen days of February. The men in the field had ridden an average of thirteen and one-half miles per day, and forty-one arrests had been made. Wheeler proudly pointed out that not one arrest "was acquitted, compromised nor dismissed." He reported that sixteen head of cattle and three horses and saddles were recovered from a hideout in the Huachuca Mountains. Rangers had been working on this case for months, and arrests would have followed if the company had not been repealed.[41]

Harry Wheeler could linger at his beloved occupation no longer. Although his discharge would not be sent by the governor (accompanied by a highly complimentary letter of gratitude) until March 25,[42] Captain Wheeler had no further functions to perform. The last Ranger left his post.

CHAPTER SIX

Sheriff of Cochise County

"The Cochise sheriff's office was the best conducted in Arizona."

—Arizona State Examiner

By the time the Ranger company disbanded in March 1909, Harry Wheeler was the best-known law officer in Arizona Territory. He quickly pinned on another badge, as a deputy sheriff of Cochise County. Deputy Wheeler was assigned to patrol the road between Douglas and Rodeo, New Mexico, with the primary duty of intercepting bootleggers. Even though the deputy's position represented a professional demotion, at least he would draw a paycheck, and again his wife and son could live in growing Douglas. But soon he applied to the federal border service. On December 22, 1909, he became a mounted inspector in the U.S. Customs Service. Wheeler rode the border for more than a year, resigning on January 3, 1911, in order to run for an office which once again would place him in the public eye.[1]

Thanks in large part to the Ranger company, which had rid the Territory of its worst outlaws and its raw frontier image, Arizona at last was proceeding to statehood. In 1910 Congress permitted Arizona Territory to write a constitution and apply for statehood. Although there were delays, the constitution eventually was accepted, and Arizona would become the forty-eighth state on February 14, 1912. Throughout Arizona there would be elections late in 1911 to elect a new roster of state officials.

As early as 1908 Harry Wheeler had been urged to run for sheriff of Cochise County. The political bug had bitten him, but his position as Ranger captain was too important to relinquish.[2] In 1911, however, Wheeler presented himself as a Democratic candidate for county sheriff.

The position was attractive to a number of men. In September the county seat newspaper, the Tombstone *Prospector,* published a list of candidates for the various offices, men who "are among the prominently mentioned who are said to be getting out their petitions." The men intending to run for sheriff included C. A. McDonald of Tombstone, Harry Wheeler of Douglas, and Jack Bolan, W. J. Needham and William White, all of Bisbee. The primary elections for the Democratic, Republican, and Socialist parties would be held on October 11, while the general election would follow on December 12. W. J. Needham withdrew from the race, and John Larrieu entered the race as the Socialist candidate. William White ran for the Republicans, while Wheeler, C. A. McDonald, and Jack Bolan vied for the Democratic nomination.[3]

During the October primary, the well-known Wheeler won the Democratic nomination by 254 votes. Wheeler totaled 823 votes, McDonald collected 569 votes, and Bolan finished third with 408 votes. The victorious Wheeler was showered with the "congratulations of friends," and he launched an effort to win the general election. "The genial candidate is still busy campaigning," reported the *Prospector* when Wheeler visited Tombstone, "and expects to be busy until Dec. 12th."[4]

Harry Wheeler, dapper in a bow tie, was elected sheriff of Cochise County three times. (Courtesy Arizona Historical Society)

For a week in early December, the Democratic candidates campaigned together around Cochise County, visiting one community each day. They began in Bisbee on Saturday, December 2, then proceeded to nearby Lowell on Sunday. The candidates spent Monday in the county seat. On Monday night, at Tombstone's ornate 1882 courthouse, enthusiastic Democratic supporters crowded into the courtroom. "Harry Wheeler spoke of prevention of crime and methods of obtaining the best practical results, making several illustrations and pledging his best efforts in conduct of the office." The next day the candidates went to Benson. They were in Willcox on Wednesday, Courtland on Thursday, and finished the tour in Douglas on Friday, December 8. The Tombstone *Prospector* remarked that "Harry Wheeler comes before the voters with an excellent record as a seasoned peace officer and a studied policy of preventive [sic] measures to lessen criminality with its attendant economic and moral benefits."[5]

The general election was a triumph for Democrats. Their victories included George W. P. Hunt for governor, both U. S. Senate seats, Arizona's single representative to Congress, and most other offices. Harry Wheeler defeated his Republican opponent by a margin of 612 votes out of more than 3,000 cast. Sheriff Wheeler appointed Guy Welch as his undersheriff, or office deputy, and he graciously appointed one of his opponents, Jack Bolan, as deputy sheriff on duty at Bisbee. He would appoint an undersheriff and five deputies, as well as jailers in more than a dozen communities around the county. Sheriff Wheeler's $10,000 bond was posted by five prominent citizens, including noted rancher John Slaughter, who had served two terms as Cochise County sheriff during territorial days.[6]

An Arizona sheriff was the chief peace officer of a county, charged with arresting any person who committed or attempted to commit a public offense. The sheriff was required to attend all courts, except justice and police courts. As agent of the superior court, the sheriff was required to serve all legal processes and notices; summoned jurors had to be contacted in person or by leaving a written notice at their place of residence. Sheriff Wheeler was allowed a salary of $5,000 per year, although the legislature soon reduced the amount to $4,000 annually (sheriffs in the smallest Arizona counties received only $1,300, but the average American worker earned less than $600 yearly). The sheriff was granted travel expenses by his county board of supervisors, as well as numerous fees that were stipulated by the legislature (serving each original summoms in a civil suit, $1.50; posting any notice required by law, $2.00; levying each writ of attachment, $2.00; etc.).[7]

On Wednesday, February 14, 1912, Harry Wheeler and the other newly elected county officials gathered in Tombstone to be sworn in after President Taft in Washington signed legislation granting statehood to Arizona. When a telegram arrived with confirmation of President Taft's signing, the new Cochise County officials assembled in the courtroom. They were administered the oath of office in a group by Justice of the Peace Daniel W. McFarland. Harry Wheeler now took over the sheriff's office from John F. White, who had served for the previous five years.[8]

The new sheriff moved into the corner office just to the right of the entrance to the courthouse. Tombstone had declined severely since its violent heyday as a mining boomtown during the 1880s, and the county had acquired several houses along Toughnut Street near the courthouse. In addition to his $5,000 annual salary and a travel allowance, Sheriff Wheeler was permitted to use "the cottage on the corner of 3rd [and Toughnut] opposite the courthouse, formerly occupied by" the county treasurer. The day after he was sworn into office, Sheriff Wheeler headed south to Douglas to pack up his household and move his family to Tombstone.[9]

Above: The Cochise County Courthouse was built on Toughnut Street in Tombstone in 1882. When Harry Wheeler became sheriff, his office was on the ground floor in the front to the right of the entrance. (Author's collection) Below: Interior of the sheriff's office at the Tombstone Courthouse. (Photo by Karon O'Neal)

On Friday, March 1, more than 100 cattlemen congregated in the courtroom. Notified by mail and newspaper announcement and word of mouth, Cochise County ranchers met to organize a stockman's association. "The cattle industry in the county is next to mining and the supervisors think it best to consult stockmen in matters pertaining to their industry," announced the Tombstone *Prospector*. County officials welcomed the ranchers to the courthouse. "Sheriff Wheeler was called upon to express his ideas . . . and made a good talk for protection of the industry, the good results to be obtained by co-operation and appealed to the cattlemen to assist his office in keeping a watch on thieves and fugitives." Wheeler discussed the concept of a small force of county rangers, whereupon a motion was made and enthusiastically approved that four rangers be appointed by the sheriff "from various sections of the county." Soon the Cochise County Stock Growers Association was officially formed. Following a break for supper, the ranchers returned to the courtroom for organizational details. A couple of days later, Sheriff Wheeler appointed four county rangers. (By the end of the year, the ranger experiment would be ended by the county as an unnecessary expense.)[10]

As county sheriff, Harry Wheeler was a prominent figure in Tombstone, and so were his wife and son. On Saturday, March 23, thirteen-year-old Allyn Wheeler was surprised at his home by about "twenty-five young friends." His birthday was not until August, but he was a good-looking and sociable youngster. While Harry and Mamie served refreshments, Tombstone's younger set welcomed Allyn to town. "Various games were played until a late hour and a jolly good time is reported by those who were there." A few months later, on November 9, Allyn again "was the recipient of a pleasant surprise party

Saturday evening. The merry crowd assembled at the Wheeler home about 7:30, and many games were participated in by all present. Delicious refreshments were served and the merry-making continued until midnight, when all departed for their respective homes, voting the evening as most enjoyably spent."[11]

Sheriff Wheeler traveled frequently, picking up or delivering prisoners and investigating crimes. As often as possible, he used the automobile that had been purchased by Cochise County. In June he presented to the board of supervisors "a report on savings to the county in railroad fares, time and hotel expenses by the use of the county automobile." Wheeler noted that in April the sheriff's department traveled 2,298 miles, along with 2,184 miles in May. "For the month of May is shown a total saving to the county on account of the machine of $329.75. ... The average daily saving to the county was $11.75."[12] Throughout his law enforcement career, Wheeler eagerly embraced new developments in technology and weaponry. In July he requested that every man who owned a horse and gun register with the sheriff's office. "This force could be used as an emergency posse when needed," he wrote. In November Wheeler made a hurried auto trip to the site of a murder. The *Prospector* reported that "the sheriff in the county automobile made a record-breaking trip to Huachuca Siding following the receipt of news of the killing and obtained first-hand evidence from the eye-witnesses which he turned over to the county attorney's office."[13] In December the sheriff swung into the saddle again for an old-fashioned cross-country pursuit. He led a mounted posse 300 miles, arresting two fugitives near the border of Mexico, and delivering them to jail in Tombstone.[14]

In December 1912, Mamie Wheeler took Allyn to Berkeley, California, to enroll their fourteen-year-old son in a better school than Tombstone could provide. Mamie then visited her sister in Oakland for a few weeks. But shortly after returning to Tombstone in January, Mamie received a message that her sister had suddenly died, and she immediately departed again for Oakland. Harry felt too busy to accompany his bereaved wife, but when Mamie returned by train, he met her on January 17 in Tucson. Mamie's deceased sister left a daughter, called Sunshine, and Harry and Mamie decided to take the little girl into their home. Sunshine regularly was referred to in the newspapers as the "daughter" of Harry and Mamie.[15]

In April 1913 two baseball games were arranged in Tombstone between "Tombstone" and the "Jurors." In the second decade of the twentieth century baseball was the national pastime, and if a community was not large enough to support a professional team, there were local nines. Pitching for Tombstone was the popular lawman, thirty-seven-year-old Harry Wheeler. Games were scheduled for a weekday afternoon at 4:00 and for Sunday at 2:30. The first game ended in a 5-5 tie, while the Jurors won on Sunday, 11-10. But Wheeler, perhaps out of town on business, did not pitch in either game.[16] A couple of weeks later Allyn returned from school in California, permanently, and began representing the family in local baseball games. By summer, Allyn was mentioned for his "good work" as a second baseman.[17]

The Town Too Tough To Die

Tombstone was long past its violent heyday when Sheriff Harry Wheeler lived among its decaying adobe buildings in the second decade of the twentieth century. But during the early 1880s, Tombstone became a legendary community of the Wild West. The most famous of all western shootouts, the Gunfight at the OK Corral, exploded beside a Tombstone livery stable in 1881. Gamblers, gunmen, and outlaws gravitated to the silver mining boomtown, and so did 10,000 somewhat more orderly people. The most colorful and lethal inhabitants included Wyatt Earp and his brothers, Doc Holliday, Buckskin Frank Leslie, Johnny Ringo, Curly Bill Brocius, Luke Short, and Sheriff John Slaughter. Victims of gunplay were deposited in Boot Hill, which became one of the West's most famous bone orchards, while more respectable citizens were placed in the City Cemetery.

The most imposing structures in town were the ornate 1882 courthouse on Toughnut Street and, on Fremont Street, Schieffelin Hall, the largest adobe building in the United States, with a seating capacity of 700 and a forty-foot-wide stage. The principal commercial thoroughfare was Allen Street, featuring the Oriental Saloon, the Crystal Palace, and the Bird Cage Theatre, which stayed open twenty-four hours a day for nine years. Newspapers included the Tombstone *Epitaph,* the West's most cleverly titled periodical, along with the *Prospector* and the *Nugget.*

Although the Tombstone Mining District eventually produced more than $36 billion in bullion, all too soon water flooded the shafts. For a time after the turn of the century the water level was lowered and some of the mines reopened. In 1902 Tombstone's first railroad, the El Paso and Southwestern, reached town. But the population declined precipitously, and legislative efforts were launched to move the seat of Cochise County to thriving Bisbee (legislation finally passed in 1929). When Sheriff Harry Wheeler took office in 1911, there were many abandoned and dilapidated structures in historic Tombstone.

On Friday, August 1, Sheriff Wheeler was in Douglas, implementing "a systematic scheme to round up suspicious characters and drive them from the city." He appointed a force of deputies, then arranged for the Douglas police chief to have "his men ready for co-operation." Wheeler continued to travel in the county automobile, sometimes in company with other officials. At this point Cochise County decided to purchase a new auto, and the Ford dealer in Douglas submitted the most acceptable bid. Sheriff Wheeler now could travel around Cochise County in a brand-new Ford.[18]

Early in September the Wheelers, probably needing more room because of Sunshine, moved half a block east, "into the Staunton residence on Toughnut Hill." Harry then departed with a deputy on a business trip to El Paso, traveling in the sheriff's big Overland. Sheriff Wheeler now was prosperous enough to move to a larger house and to buy a car. But Harry was impressed by the county's new Ford. He sold the Overland, and in October he went to Douglas and bought a Ford roadster. "The Sheriff is stuck on the new car," reported the Tombstone *Prospector,* "and while not exceeding the speed limit, is trying her out."[19]

After having spent six weeks in California visiting her now-deceased sister, Mamie Wheeler restlessly began to find other trip opportunities. Two months after returning from her sister's funeral, Mamie traveled to Naco to visit friends "for a fortnight." She stayed in Tombstone only five days before boarding a train to return to Naco. In November, she and Allyn traveled to Bisbee to attend a "big ball game," then in June 1914 Mamie, Allyn, and Sunshine departed "for Bisbee, where they will remain for several weeks."[20] This pattern of extended visits continued, indicating strongly that Mamie was not content at her home in Tombstone. Harry was absent from Tombstone a great deal of the time, and Mamie was justified in feeling neglected. Perhaps the presence of the orphaned Sunshine added to the problems of an already troubled marriage. The prominence and comparative prosperity of Sheriff Wheeler was not enough to maintain the devotion of his wife.

Harry sometimes took his teenaged son along with him on trips. In March 1914, for example, Allyn accompanied his father to Douglas, "where they went to take the Sheriff's auto for repairs." In September the Wheeler men again traveled together to Douglas. In December Allyn, now sixteen, went to Fairbank, east of Tombstone, to work for a time "as chauffeur for the Boquillas Land and Cattle Co."[21]

From time to time Sheriff Wheeler enjoyed encounters with former Ranger comrades. Several were constables or policemen in Cochise County communities, whose jobs necessitated occasional visits to the county seat. Billy Old, Luke Short, Arthur Hopkins, and Porter McDonald were among the ex-Rangers who were in and out of Tombstone. Constable Old, who had served as Wheeler's Ranger lieutenant, was shot to death by his wife in 1914. Sheriff Wheeler probably attended the funeral in Pearce, and it is likely he contributed to the large monument erected by friends of Old at the Pearce Cemetery.[22]

Wheeler also had the chance to see Dayton Graham, the first sergeant of the Arizona Rangers. Another legendary Arizona peace officer, Jeff Milton, regularly visited Tombstone and eventually retired in the old mining town.

Sheriff Wheeler, still in his thirties, took every opportunity to make criminal arrests. Early in October, Tombstone miner Jim Felkner shot his father-in-law to death after a family dispute. Felkner headed south toward Mexico, but Sheriff Wheeler "immediately" went in pursuit. An experienced and resourceful manhunter, Wheeler apprehended Felkner in the vicinity of Douglas and brought him to the Tombstone jail. Two months later, a Mexican soldier murdered a comrade, then fled across the border into Cochise County. Sheriff Wheeler and Deputy Percy Bowden soon found the fugitive in broken country near Hereford, and in short time the lawmen induced a confession and took the man into custody. In April 1914 Sheriff Wheeler and Deputy Charley Cross drove in pursuit of two thieves who were heading east by horseback. At the ranch of Lee Hudspeth the lawmen abandoned their automobile for saddle horses, then continued the chase cross-country. Following the trail into New Mexico, Wheeler and Cross intercepted their prey near Cloverdale. The fugitives were arrested and taken to Tombstone.[23] Throughout his tenure as sheriff, Harry Wheeler readily left the routine of paperwork, subpoenaing jurors, and transporting prisoners to go into the field in pursuit of lawbreakers.

On Monday night, April 8, 1914, Sheriff Wheeler was in Pirtleville, a few miles northwest of Douglas. The sheriff was standing in the doorway of the justice of the peace, on the main street of the little town, when a fight erupted nearby. When Jesus Mimbres pulled a knife, Sheriff Wheeler darted forward. Mimbres whirled and extended the blade toward the lawman, but Wheeler whipped out a revolver and struck the threatening arm (instead of shooting Mimbres). An instant later Constable Clarence Reese struck Mimbres in the head with a rock, "knocking him insensible."[24]

A month later Sheriff Wheeler investigated a crime of the twentieth century: auto theft. There were more than 5,000 automobiles in Arizona by 1914, and one of them, a new seven-passenger Studebaker, was stolen from in front of a Douglas hotel on May 11. Sheriff Wheeler launched his usual relentless pursuit, traveling to El Paso before finding the thieves and the missing car in Albuquerque, a week after the theft.[25]

Allyn Wheeler continued to be a popular member of Tombstone's youthful society. A happy participant in local parties, Allyn frequently entertained friends in the Wheeler home on Toughnut Hill. In April 1914 his pals surprised him in his own house. "About twenty-five young people were present, and together with dancing, games, music and dainty refreshments, the evening passed in a most enjoyable manner." Two months later, again at his home, Allyn "was the recipient of a pleasant party given by several of his young friends in his honor." There was a similar occasion in September. "The Wheeler home, on the hill, was the scene of one of the most enjoyable parties of the season . . . when about twenty-five young folks congregated. . . . [T]here was not a dull moment

Gun Safety

On Friday morning, May 16, 1913, Sheriff Wheeler was on the streets of Tombstone without a gun belt and holster. He slipped his revolver into a coat pocket, a common practice, but somehow the heavy weapon dropped out of his pocket onto the boardwalk. There was no safety on the old single-action revolvers, and the gun discharged. Fortunately the accidental round did no damage, but Wheeler was disgusted with his carelessness. "Sheriff Harry Wheeler had a warrant sworn out against himself," reported the *Prospector* the next day, "charging the careless discharge of firearms within the city limits." The embarrassed sheriff paid a $10 fine, although the justice of the peace, who seemed amused, reminded Wheeler "that the maximum penalty was $300 and six months in jail."

during the entire evening and it was after midnight when the young people departed. ...."[26] Whatever tensions existed in their marriage, Harry and Mamie regularly opened their home on behalf of their sociable son.

Both father and son were regular participants with the local baseball teams, the Stars and the Regulars, during the summer of 1914. Allyn played second base for the youthful Stars, while Harry pitched and played shortstop for the Regulars. The two teams usually played each other on Sunday afternoons, and there was out-of-town competition as well. During a July doubleheader, for example, "the boys' team was too much for the Regulars and they went down to defeat in both games, despite the good work of Sheriff Wheeler in the box." By August the Regulars had lost six games in a row to the Stars, but prior to the next contest Sheriff Wheeler good-naturedly suggested "that the vanquished nine should appear on the grounds the following Sunday and play in dresses." The older Regulars finally beat the Stars in extra innings, 10–7, but the younger players came back for revenge in the second game of the doubleheader, trouncing the Regulars, 14–3. Later in the month the Regulars swept a doubleheader from the Stars. Allyn banged out a double in the first game, while the second contest featured "the excellent work of Sheriff Wheeler at shortstop."[27]

By this time Sheriff Wheeler was running for a second term in office. As sheriff of Cochise County, Wheeler had maintained the high public profile he had become accustomed to, at least in southeastern Arizona. Wheeler was comfortable financially, and as chief law enforcement officer of one of Arizona's largest and most prosperous counties, his daily work was busy and challenging. Porter McDonald, a Ranger private who had been fired from the company in 1907 by Captain Wheeler, offered a challenge for the Democratic nomination for sheriff. McDonald spent almost as much as Wheeler ($170 to $174) during the primary campaign, but he could have saved the money. The popular sheriff trounced McDonald, 4,076 votes to 1,275. The Tombstone *Prospector* predicted similar success in the general election in November: "Sheriff Wheeler has made one of the best officials Cochise County ever had and judging from indications he will receive a

Political A

Democratic

For State Senator

I hereby solicit the support of the voters of Cochise county in the general election November 3rd, 1914, for state senator from Cochise county. I offer as my qualifications my record of efficiency and business administration since the beginning of Cochise county.
WILLIAM M. RIGGS
Regular Democratic Nominee.

For Sheriff

I hereby announce myself as a candidate for re-election to the office of sheriff, at the General election November 3rd, 1914, and solicit the support of the voters of Cochise county.
HARRY C. WHEELER,
Regular Democratic Nominee.

Sheriff Wheeler's reelection announcement, Tombstone Prospector, *October 2, 1914.*

Stop That Turkey!

Early on Tuesday morning, December 30, 1913, Harry Wheeler stepped into his backyard, intending to execute "a big, round fat turkey" with an axe. The gobbler would be the centerpiece of the New Year feast for the Wheeler family. But the uncooperative turkey fled Harry and his axe. Armed as usual, Wheeler snapped off a pistol shot, but the agitated turkey took flight, "over the fence and across the prairie at a mile-a-minute gait—with the sheriff in pursuit." The chase continued, according to the Tombstone *Prospector,* "over the hills and through the brush," until Wheeler's marksmanship prevailed. The deceased turkey was brought back to the house, and the menu for New Year's proceeded as planned.

handsome majority at the polls." As predicted, Wheeler easily outpolled a Prohibitionist and a Socialist candidate, 5,742 to 1,683 to 534. The *Prospector* pointed out that the victorious incumbent had "been one of the most fearless officers the state has ever known, . . .while towards the conduct of his office Mr. Wheeler has devoted his entire attention." Sheriff Wheeler announced that his deputy force would remain intact, and the *Prospector* had special praise for Chief Deputy Guy Welch: "New ideas have been introduced in the office affairs by Mr. Welch which have been adopted throughout the state, and according to the report of the State Examiner, the Cochise sheriff's office was the best conducted in Arizona."[28]

During the general election, Arizona voters approved a statewide prohibition amendment, although the issue failed by a narrow margin in Cochise County. Sheriff Wheeler habitually shunned alcohol, and publicly supported the growing movement for national prohibition. But Cochise County had a predominantly male population—twice as many men as women—with a tradition of frontier drinking habits. Soon after his "overwhelming" reelection, the sheriff wrote a public letter expressing "my gratitude and appreciation to each and every one" and pledging renewed service. "There are several trials ahead of me," he hastily added. "Prohibition will be to this country a new and untried idea. I mention prohibition, specifically, because I anticipate prohibition enforcement as one of my most severe trials to be . . . . I will enforce this law with whatever power, intelligence and ability I may possess and I call upon every good citizen to aid me in all ways possible, regardless of how any of us felt before election."[29] But immediately it became apparent that prohibition would be unpopular in Cochise County, prompting Sheriff Wheeler to publish a lengthy letter of instructions that he had issued to his deputies. After detailing violations and arrest procedures under the new law, Wheeler issued another appeal to the citizenry: "I also expect all good citizens to assist me in enforcing this law, by swearing to a complaint before a justice of the peace who will issue warrant (which I or my deputies will be very glad to serve) for any person or persons violating any of the provisions of this law."[33] Despite his appeals, Sheriff Wheeler would find that the people of Cochise County would ignore and disobey prohibition with the same obstinence as many other Americans.

Immediately after his reelection, Sheriff Wheeler traded in his little Ford Roadster on a 1914 Overland touring car, purchased at a Douglas agency. "Sheriff Wheeler is still well efficient in the handling of an auto and in the performing of the duties of his office an auto is a valuable asset," the newspaper reported. At the same time, the county sold the "old Cole car," which had "traveled approximately 210,000 miles," to the highest bidder. A new Vehe "Six-60" was considered "the height of perfection, and will fill the needs of the sheriff's office."[31]

The Cochise County Board of Supervisors provided more than a new car. A major renovation of the 1882 courthouse included new steel jail cells, and the sheriff's office was moved from the front of the building to be nearer to the lockup in the rear. The steel and other material for the new cells arrived in June, and Sheriff Wheeler had to transfer several prisoners to Tucson. Throughout the remainder of 1914, the thirty-two-year-old building was repaired and re-painted, the walls were "calcimined," and structural alterations were made. These renovations were launched even though a proposal had been placed before the voters to move the county seat to Bisbee. This proposal regularly had appeared on the ballot for years, since Bisbee had outgrown Tombstone in size. Although the removal issue would pass within Cochise County (by more than two-to-one in 1914), it always failed statewide. Optimistically the people of Tombstone approved the paving of four blocks along Allen Street, to give the growing numbers of automobiles ready access to the business district.[32]

A continuing problem of 1914 occurred just across the international border of Cochise County. The Mexican Revolution erupted in 1910, generating war-ring factions and border raids for years. In April about 2,600 rebel troops be-sieged a garrison of a few hundred federal soldiers defending Mexican Naco. Sheriff Wheeler soon went to the point of danger, where his wife and Sunshine had just gone on a social visit. Wheeler sent Mamie and Sunshine back to Tombstone, as bullets fired from the Mexican side of Naco slammed into virtu-ally every structure on the American side. Sheriff Wheeler "had several narrow escapes, one bullet wounding his horse while riding on his warning mission." A force of United States troops, commanded by Maj. George Reed, was sta-tioned at American Naco to provide protection for U.S. citizens. Before dawn on Monday, April 13, the rebel force attacked Mexican Naco. The battle raged for hours before the border town was captured. Many of the defenders fled into American Naco, breaking their rifles before crossing the international line. The Tombstone *Prospector* reported: "During the fierce fighting many wounded stag-gered across the border seeking aid and Sheriff Wheeler, at imminent risk, took 16 of them to the hospital." More than 100 soldiers were reported slain, while over seventy wounded were taken to nearby American hospitals.[33]

Opposing Mexican troops again converged on Naco in October. United States cavalrymen again rode down from Fort Huachuca, and Sheriff Wheeler also returned, along with numerous spectators. The expected battle failed to materialize, but long-range sniping plagued the vicinity for days. On Tuesday morning, October 6, Sheriff Wheeler and "a negro trooper" from the Ninth Cavalry were riding along the international line when they suddenly came under fire. It was believed "that the attempt was made to kill Captain Wheeler, but failed in its purpose." Shrugging off this close call, Wheeler continued to work "day and night" in American Naco. "He is daily on the streets," observed one reporter, "where the bullets are thickest, watching to see that none are ex-posed." Although concerned about being absent from his office, Wheeler was confident that his deputies in Tombstone "are taking care of the business as fast as it comes in. . . ." Eventually Deputy Guy Welch traveled to Naco to give his boss a day of rest, but numerous citizens insisted "that Sheriff Wheeler should remain with them throughout the controversy across the line." Political candidates for the election of 1914 arranged a campaign trip around Cochise County for October 19–25, but Sheriff Wheeler remained on duty in Naco. Since military officers could not enter Mexico, Sheriff Wheeler courageously slipped into Mexican Naco from time to time as an emissary "attending to . . . critical matters across the line. . . ."[34]

Wheeler remained on duty in Naco for three weeks before finally feeling free to return to Tombstone. The sheriff resumed his usual duties, investigating cattle theft and an occasional murder, collecting jurors, and transporting prisoners. But in January 1915 Sheriff Wheeler assumed a constant and controversial responsibility. Prohibition went into effect in Arizona, but numerous citizens—including a great many in Cochise County—had no intention of observing the new laws.

Sheriff Wheeler now began a determined battle against bootleggers. Saloons

COCHISE COUNTY

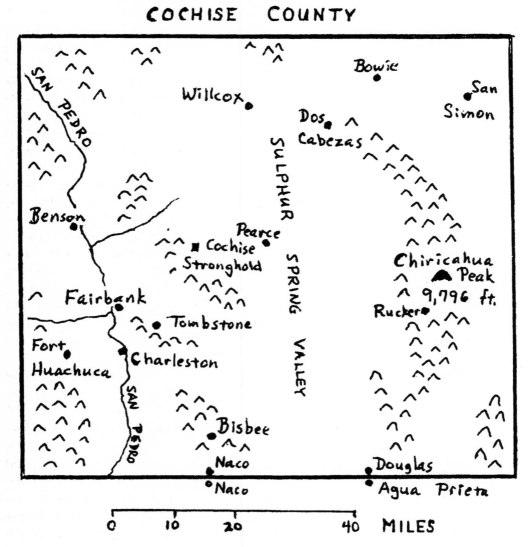

shut down (one barkeep in Pearce converted his building into a movie house),[35] but the demand for whiskey, wine, beer, mescal, and other spirits remained high in Cochise County. The sheriff and his deputies regularly apprehended bootleggers and their cargo. For example, on Sunday night, March 14, 1915, Sheriff Wheeler intercepted a bootlegger with "three large barrels of whiskey" headed for White City, the collection of dives near Fort Huachuca. There was praise for "the many captures made since the first of the year by Sheriff Wheeler, who is ever on the watch for these violators of the law."[36]

In May and June Wheeler concentrated on bootleggers operating around Douglas, seizing "80 quarts of whiskey, said to be of fair quality," and earning accolades from at least one pulpit. "SHERIFF HARRY WHEELER ARRESTS MORE BOOTLEGGERS AT DOUGLAS," proclaimed one headline, while a few weeks later another announced, "SHERIFF WHEELER SEIZES MORE BOOZE." In September the Tombstone *Prospector* proudly published "a tribute to Sheriff Harry C. Wheeler" from the Tucson *Citizen,* which lamented the open flaunting of the law in Tucson and Pima County: "Would that Pima county had a sheriff with the courage of Sheriff Harry Wheeler of Cochise county, who is doing his duty and enforcing the prohibition law in that border county against terrible odds. He is being sued for a large sum for false arrest and harassed by those whom he is prosecuting. . . . He says they will have to put him in jail if they want to get him off the trail of the lawbreakers." The *Citizen* emphasized: "If Tucson had a sheriff and other officers like Wheeler, this city would not be a paradise for bootleggers."[37]

The harassment and suits for false arrest came principally from Starr Williams and "women living in the Bisbee tenderloin district." Sheriff Wheeler defied Williams and other bootleggers with a public letter. "Every time I capture a consignment of liquor I expect to be harassed," announced Wheeler. "Starr Williams is involved in every suit against me in liquor cases. He attempts to intimidate me through my bondsmen. My answer is that last evening Deputy Prewitt and I captured another Bisbee outfit in the Dos Cabezas mountains with eighteen cases of intoxicating liquor and arrested two men, and I am now awaiting another suit or attempt to make me cease my activity in my endeavors to enforce the law. Mr. Williams can now get busy again, as I had no search warrant."[38]

Harry Wheeler had reason to harbor bitterness against Starr Williams and anyone else who illegally dispensed liquor in Brewery Gulch, Bisbee's notorious street of illegal saloons and houses of prostitution. On Tuesday, March 22, 1915, sixteen-year-old Allyn Wheeler and four other youthful adventurers drove from Tombstone to Bisbee for a night on the town. It is not known how parents of the boys were persuaded to approve this expedition, if they were told anything at all. The five boys piled into a Ford that belonged to Joe Norcross, manager of the Crystal Theater, and which apparently was borrowed by his young employee, Cole Noll. Allen Larison, Albert Fitzgerald, and Leo Hill were other members of the party. The drive to Bisbee was twenty-five miles along a

Allyn Wheeler as a teenager was confident and popular, and he bore a strong resemblance to his father. (Courtesy Pam Hamlett)

The street angling to the left of the Orpheum Theatre was Bisbee's notorious Brewery Gulch. (Courtesy Arizona Historical Society)

steep mountain road. Since the boys stayed all night, it is a likely assumption that they drank illegal liquor and sampled other recreational possibilities of Brewery Gulch.

The party started home about dawn, with Allen Larison at the wheel and the cloth top down. At 6:30 the Ford began rocketing down a steep grade along the Divide Road. Cole Noll "yelled to Larison to cut it out, that he was making too much speed." Larison shouted "that he had lost control of the car." The brakes probably had burned out on the long grade. A rancher, whose spread was nearby, saw the Ford hurtle off the road at the bottom of the hill. The car overturned completely, before landing on its wheels and "throwing all the occupants out" onto level but rocky ground. The windshield of the Ford was shattered, three wheels were broken, and the steering gear was bent.[39]

An ambulance was summoned. Allen Larison was unconscious, Allyn Wheeler, "received bad abrasions and cuts about the face," Cole Noll had a bad cut on his leg, and Albert Fitzgerald was bruised and badly shaken. Leo Hill was uninjured, but the other four were taken to the well-equipped C&A Hospital near Bisbee. Sheriff Wheeler was notified by telephone and immediately left for Bisbee, accompanied by Joe Norcross, owner of the wrecked Ford. At the hospital they found the boys "resting easily, not much the worse for their terrible experience." Wheeler and Norcross intended to return in the afternoon with those who were well enough to travel. "The parents of the boys were thunderstruck at the news of the accident," concluded the front page account in the *Prospector,* "but have been quieted by word that results will not prove serious."[40]

Hill, Noll, and Fitzgerald returned home by the next day. Larison was "resting easily" on the day after the accident, and it was thought that Allyn Wheeler would return "probably tomorrow." But by Saturday, five days after the wreck, both boys remained hospitalized. Mamie Wheeler had come to Bisbee to be "constantly with her son." Harry also was at Allyn's bedside as much as possible. When the sheriff returned to Tombstone on April 3, eleven days after his son was injured, he reported that Allyn "has been quite ill" but expressed hopes that he soon would be able to leave the hospital. It would be another week, however, before Allyn was released to return home Saturday, April 10. The *Prospector* again expressed optimism: "He is well on the road to recovery and will soon be out again."[41]

Unfortunately, the hoped-for recovery did not occur. Allyn remained bedridden in the house on Toughnut Hill. Details of his illness were never discussed in print. Although Allyn may have sustained internal injuries, the facial cuts and abrasions he suffered in the wreck suggest brain damage. On the last day of July, the *Prospector* reported "that the patient is still very low and weak, but doing as well as could be expected under the circumstances." Later that day, Allyn took a turn for the worse. On Monday, he was reported to be slightly improved. "The patient was left very weak from the attack of Saturday, but is holding out bravely. The many close friends of the Wheelers' sincerely hope that the danger mark is passed." Allyn's seventeenth birthday was on August 11, but there was little to celebrate. Later in the month, Harry and Mamie decided to take their stricken son to a Los Angeles hospital. The family traveled together to California, where Mamie had relatives, and Harry returned to Tombstone alone. The *Prospector* announced, "Captain Wheeler reports his son doing as well as could be expected."[42]

Sheriff Wheeler went about his duties, staying in touch with his wife and periodically visiting California. After a visit early in October, Wheeler related "that the physicians have only a slight hope of a change for the better." The newspaper reported, "Everything known to medical science has been sought to save his life," but the understanding grew "that it was only a matter of time." On October 14, Wheeler heard from his wife that Allyn "is very ill and has been for several days past and that the patient is slowly growing weaker from the continued strain." Sheriff Wheeler returned to the bedside vigil at the California hospital on October 22. Three days later, he telegraphed his chief deputy, Guy Welch: "Allyn beautiful and peaceful in death. Will wire you later."[43]

Harry and Mamie arrived at the Tombstone depot with the body of their son on the afternoon of October 28, 1915. "Many sorrowing friends met the heart-broken parents at the depot and the coffin bearing the body, accompanied by six boys, was taken to the residence where it will remain until interment to-morrow. . . . Floral offerings were numerous today, which expressed in their own humble way, sympathies which cannot be told in words." The following morning a funeral mass was conducted at the Catholic church by a priest from Bisbee. Deputies came from all over the county, and the courthouse was closed so the officials could join the afternoon funeral procession from the Wheeler home. Boys and girls who had been Allyn's friends formed a special choir to sing hymns at the residence and at the graveside. "Many automobiles from Bisbee and Douglas, containing friends of the family, arrived during the day and joined the procession to the last resting place of the deceased. Allyn was interred at the City Cemetery, on a hill half a mile west of Tombstone. The monument erected by the grieving parents proclaimed: "God's will not ours be done." Harry and Mamie were praised for having "borne their sad misfortune, through these many months of the illness, nobly."[44]

Harry and Mamie had suffered the most agonizing tragedy that can befall parents. Their only child, the reason for their marriage, had died slowly, seven months after a debilitating accident. Allyn was handsome and popular, with all of the promise of youth. Now he was dead. "Oh! the aching hearts of a sorrowing mother and father," empathized an obituary, "who . . . must bear still the thought and realization that he lives no more in this world, and has gone beyond before even he had a chance to enter into manhood."[45] That excruciating "thought and realization" would prove to be the final blow to a troubled marriage.

Harry dealt with his devastating loss by immersing himself into the busy schedule of a demanding job. The bereaved mother could only grope for solace by resuming visits to out-of-town friends. A few days after the funeral, Harry

CARD OF THANKS

We desire to extend our sincere gratitude to our friends and acquaintances, in Tombstone and throughout the county, for the many kind deeds extended in the period of sickness and death of our dear son, Allyn. For the unmerous beautiful floral offerings, and for kind deeds and words of sympathy throughout our misfortune, do we extend sincere thanks in the hour of our bereavement.

MR AND MRS. H. C. WHEELER

Left: Allyn Wheeler's gravesite at Tombstone's City Cemetery. (Photo by Karon O'Neal) Above: Published in the Tombstone Prospector, *October 30, 1915.*

accompanied his wife and Mrs. Owen E. Murphy to Douglas. He intended to return immediately, while the ladies would "remain for several days on a visit with friends." But hostilities were developing between the bandit army of Pancho Villa and Mexican troops around Agua Prieta, just across the border from Douglas. So Sheriff Wheeler stayed in Douglas while the two factions skirmished. Pancho Villa finally led his men toward Naco, and Harry and Mamie returned to Tombstone on Thursday evening, November 4. Mamie, however, restlessly took the Golden State Limited the next night, intending to visit relatives in San Francisco. Within a few months, Harry moved the Wheeler home from the house on Toughnut Hill, with its sad memories, to "the King residence next to the Fix It Garage on Allen Street."[46]

Sheriff Wheeler took up his customary activities. At the end of 1915 Chief Deputy Guy Welch left his desk in the sheriff's office for a ten-day California vacation with his wife. The previous October Sheriff Wheeler had filled a deputy's post in Warren by appointing Arthur Hopkins, who had spent more than three years as a headquarters sergeant of the Arizona Rangers. When Deputy Welch departed for California, therefore, Sheriff Wheeler brought the experienced Hopkins to the main office in Tombstone, where the two old Rangers briefly resumed their former working relationship.[47]

Illegal liquor may have played a crucial part in the death of his son, and Sheriff Wheeler apparently took a grim pleasure in hounding bootleggers. The Tombstone *Prospector* chronicled Wheeler's relentless pursuit of bootleggers, featuring the sheriff in one headline after another:

SHERIFF WHEELER AND CONSTABLE PREWITT MAKE BIG HAUL
   (November 23, 1915)
MUCH BOOZE WAS DESTROYED BY SHERIFF (December 28, 1915)
SHERIFF WHEELER DESTROYS BOOZE (January 3, 1916)
SHERIFF CAPTURES CASES BOOZE AT DOUGLAS (January 29, 1916)
SHERIFF MAKES ANOTHER BIG HAUL OF BOOZE (January 31, 1916)
SHERIFF AND CITY OFFICERS CLEAN UP BISBEE AND DOUGLAS BLIND PIGS
   (April 29, 1916)
SHERIFF WHEELER CAPTURES CONSIDERABLE BOOZE (June 20, 1916)

A report on the effects of prohibition in Arizona, compiled by "statistical expert" George H. Smalley, recorded detailed praise for the sheriff of Cochise County:

There were from 120 to 127 saloons in Cochise County. The record for murder was the greatest of any county in the Southwest. The first six months of 1914 the sheriff wore out an automobile chasing murderers, now several county jails are unoccupied and have not been used since prohibition came. Sheriff Harry Wheeler is enforcing the law vigorously throughout the county. He has the most difficult place of any sheriff in the state, owing the great size of [the] county and its long border line. Although his expense is heavy for ferreting out violations of the amendment, his account for deputies shows $8,567 for 1914 and $6,040 for 1915. . . . The number of violations are decreasing, owing to his vigilance and fearlessness in enforcing the law, and the end of the year should show a constant monthly decrease in sheriff's costs.

In Tombstone, where there are over 300 more men working in the mines than were employed the first six months of 1914, the arrests were only seven all told, against 35 for 1914. . . . The August record shows no arrests in Tombstone. . . .

Bisbee had more saloons than any city of its size in the state, and its percentage of crime since the saloons have been closed will be reflected materially in the ensuing year's budget. . . . There is a remarkable change in the tone of the city and there is bound to follow a decrease in cost of city government.

There were 229 less arrests in Douglas the first six months of 1915 than for the same period of 1914. As in Bisbee all of the places previously occupied by saloons are occupied by other businesses and the city is flourishing, with no empty buildings and the construction of new building going on. [47]

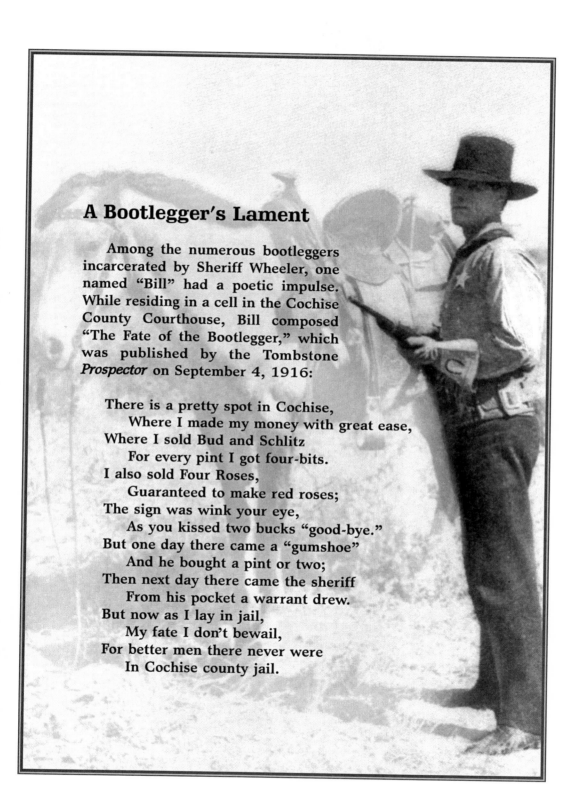

A Bootlegger's Lament

Among the numerous bootleggers incarcerated by Sheriff Wheeler, one named "Bill" had a poetic impulse. While residing in a cell in the Cochise County Courthouse, Bill composed "The Fate of the Bootlegger," which was published by the Tombstone *Prospector* on September 4, 1916:

There is a pretty spot in Cochise,
 Where I made my money with great ease,
Where I sold Bud and Schlitz
 For every pint I got four-bits.
I also sold Four Roses,
 Guaranteed to make red roses;
The sign was wink your eye,
 As you kissed two bucks "good-bye."
But one day there came a "gumshoe"
 And he bought a pint or two;
Then next day there came the sheriff
 From his pocket a warrant drew.
But now as I lay in jail,
 My fate I don't bewail,
For better men there never were
 In Cochise county jail.

Harry Wheeler's repeated notoriety in thwarting bootleggers reasserted his status as Arizona's preeminent lawman. "Sheriff Wheeler has been the most active officer in the state in the enforcement of the prohibition law," stated the Tombstone *Prospector,* "and under adverse circumstances has succeeded in upholding the law in a greater degree possibly than any sheriff in Arizona."

With such praise and publicity, Wheeler readily decided to run for a third term, announcing his candidacy late in June 1916. "Mr. Wheeler is perhaps the best known man in Cochise County," proclaimed the *Prospector,* adding that "the county will support him to a man in the county election."[48]

In July Wheeler announced to the public "the personal platform in which I believe." He reaffirmed his support for prohibition, pointing out that "murder and other serious crimes" had declined by almost half. Furthermore, "the banks have more depositors, the merchants have fewer unpaid bills, the mine fewer accidents." He urged voters to support him because of his experience, and because of his personal friendship with Mexican officials. Wheeler pointed out that he had reduced his office expenses by $7,000 during the past year, and that the state examiner had said of his office: "It is probably the best kept in the state." He also solicited support because this would be his last race: "I will not be a candidate for next election for this office."[49] No explanation was given for this curious decision. Wheeler was only in his early forties, and as sheriff of Cochise County he enjoyed prestige and financial security. Perhaps the antagonism of anti-prohibition citizens had begun to weigh on him, but it still seems confusing what Wheeler thought he might do in the future that offered better prospects than his sheriff's position.

In August he traveled around the county posting election notices, which offered the chance to campaign while on official business. No deputies were sent to perform this chore. And when a train was robbed shortly before the primary, Wheeler galloped into the Chiricahua Mountains on a grueling and well-publicized pursuit. Constable Sam Hayhurst, a six-year Arizona Ranger, ran against him in the Democratic primary, and so did J.F. McDonald. Hayhurst poled just 915 votes to 1,251 for McDonald and 2,556 for Wheeler. When Democratic candidates scheduled an October campaign tour, Wheeler found that he was needed to "investigate the report of speeding that caused several accidents on Sunday." Actually, Wheeler felt strongly about dangerous driving, because of Allyn's mortal accident. The sheriff called for a 25 MPH speed limit on county roads and enlisted several motorcycle deputies to patrol the county. In November he prevailed over Republican candidate, Lorenzo White, 5,434 to 4,232. He expressed his gratitude to Cochise County voters, "particularly those of Tombstone and the forty-two precincts who so loyally stood by me."[50]

During 1916, Sheriff Wheeler continued to be faced with border troubles. At one point he became so concerned about possible military action around Douglas that he wired President Woodrow Wilson, requesting that martial law be proclaimed along the border. In June, Sheriff Wheeler and Deputy Percy Bowden drove out of Tombstone to investigate "reports that a large force of

Mexicans had camped south of the line, and intended to raid the district and capture all horses." When Wheeler was not heard from for a couple of days, rumors erupted "that he undoubtedly had met his fate at the hands of the Mexicans." There was not much concern in Tombstone: "at the sheriff's office no alarm had been felt for them, nor by Mrs. Wheeler, owing to the fact that in pursuit of his duties the sheriff many times does not communicate with them." Wheeler and Bowden soon turned up, safe and hale.[51]

Also during 1916, Wheeler became involved in a welcome diversion, an activity which would engage him for the rest of his life. The Tombstone Rifle Club was organized, in affiliation with the National Rifle Association. By July, fifty-six members had paid an initiation fee of $10, and more members were being enrolled. With a treasury exceeding $500, the club ordered steel targets, purchased competitive rifles from the army (some members bought their own rifles from the government), and cleared a regulation range at a site below town. The club's first shoot was held on Thanksgiving morning, and practice shoots were scheduled for every Sunday. The public was invited as spectators. At a December practice shoot, at a range of 300 yards, Wheeler recorded by far the highest score among seventeen shooters. In order to remain in good standing, members were required to shoot for an official record under NRA conditions by the end of each year. Fifty rounds would be fired at distances from 200 to 600 yards. Wheeler scored 48 of 50 from 200 yards, 45 of 50 from 500 yards, and 37 of 50 from 600 yards. His total score was 215 out of a possible 250, which qualified him as an "expert marksman." The next closest score was 159, recorded by Charles Allen. Shortly before the end of the year, Wheeler shot a round that included twelve straight bull's-eyes at 600 yards and 246 points out of 250. During the state competition in Tucson in May 1917, "Capt. H. C. Wheeler won the state championship and will receive a gold medal for high individual gun."[52] Wheeler became an avid participant in state and national NRA competitions.

The rifle competition was deadly when Sheriff Wheeler and Constable Lafe Gibson engaged in a pitched battle with bootleggers on the night of March 6, 1917. One month earlier, Wheeler and Gibson had been fired upon by bootleggers near the New Mexico line. On Sunday night, February 4, the lawmen in Wheeler's car headed off a bootlegger driving into Cochise County from Lordsburg. The bootlegger bailed out of his big Mitchell Six, emptied a sixgun in the direction of the officers, and escaped on foot. Wheeler and Gibson refrained from shooting back, settling for taking possession of the Mitchell and more than 1,800 bottles of whiskey. Constable Gibson had never driven a car, but Wheeler provided a few basic instructions, and Gibson followed the sheriff all the way to Tombstone, where the whiskey was destroyed publicly. Two weeks later, Wheeler and Gibson intercepted another bootlegger, who fled before his Buick came to a halt. Once again, "Constable Gibson, who is fast becoming an expert chauffeur, drove the loaded car."[53]

On Tuesday night, March 6, Wheeler and Gibson were "out scouting for bootleggers in the vicinity of the Chiricahuas near the state line." They pulled off the road near tiny Kelton, then rolled up in their blankets beside the car. A short time later the silence of the night was broken by the crack of a rifle. A bullet crashed into the windshield, and Wheeler and Gibson scrambled to arm themselves. Wheeler grabbed a rifle and ammunition, while Gibson found his revolver. The lawmen moved to a nearby railroad grade, saw a movement ahead of them, and opened fire. Return fire came from four men spread out in front of them, positioned fifty to seventy-five yards away. Silhouetted in the moonlight, Wheeler and Gibson dropped to prone positions. During the ensuing firefight at least one hundred shots were exchanged, reducing Wheeler to about thirty rounds for his rifle and Gibson to only a few revolver cartridges. The bootlegger turned out to be four Mexicans, who shouted taunts and "a storm of vile oaths."[54]

One bootlegger crept close enough to trigger a round that kicked sand into the faces of the lawmen. Wheeler poured six rounds of rapid-fire at the gun flash. Groans were heard from this position, and examination after the sun came up "disclosed a large pool of blood and knee and elbow prints in the sand." Apparently the bootleggers skulked away with their wounded comrade. When the moon went down an hour later, the lawmen advanced on the bootleggers' camp. The camp was deserted and four burros, loaded with ten cases of whiskey, had been abandoned. Two of the animals had been wounded and later were killed.[55]

At daylight the lawmen spotted a horse trail leading into the mountains, but they drove to Courtland and telephoned Guy Welch in Tombstone. Welch and another deputy soon arrived with guns and ammunition, and the officers followed the trail into the mountains. The bootleggers temporarily had made their escape, so Wheeler returned to Tombstone with the whiskey. The next day the sheriff picked up Constable Gibson in Gleeson and again penetrated the Chiricahuas. In Apache Pass two of the Mexicans appeared "driving burros laden with booze." When ordered to halt, one bootlegger drew a gun, but wisely dropped it and submitted to arrest.[56]

This 1917 battle with bootleggers was Harry Wheeler's last gunfight. In 1904 he had killed Joe Bostwick in Tucson; in 1907, J.A. Tracy in Benson. Wheeler and a deputy killed outlaw George Arnett in 1908, and in 1917 he drilled a bootlegger. He displayed deadly skills each time he was compelled to use firearms. Clearly, Wheeler was one of the most lethal gunmen in the history of the West, but he wore his badges during the final years of frontier conditions. If Wheeler had been a lawman in an earlier, wilder West, it seems probable that he would have become embroiled in personal combat with dangerous regularity. Imagine, for example, how often he would have clashed with lawless elements if his service as sheriff of Cochise County had occurred during the late 1870s and 1880s. Certainly he would not have suffered the controversies and frustration he was about to experience in the era of the First World War.

CHAPTER SEVEN

The Bisbee Deportation

"Damn a man that is not patriotic!"

—Sheriff Harry Wheeler

The Great War erupted in Europe in August 1914. Horrified at the unprecedented slaughter, Americans intended to stay neutral. But the sinking of the *Lusitania* in May 1915 by a German submarine killed 1,198 passengers, including 128 Americans. Traditional ties with the British and French created considerable sympathy in the United States from the Allied side, while continued submarine warfare generated growing American hostility against Germany. Early in 1917 the continued sinking of American merchant ships and the revelation that Germany was attempting to persuade Mexico to invade the United States put many Americans in a fighting mood. Most Arizonans, hardened to frontier violence, harbored little fear of war.

President Woodrow Wilson, addressing a joint session of Congress on the evening of April 2, 1917, asked for recognition that a state of war existed between the United States and the German Empire. Following heated debates, the Senate on April 4 approved a resolution, 82–6. After the House concurred, 373–50, President Wilson signed a declaration of war on April 6.

On April 3 the Tombstone *Prospector* reported that "Old Glory is flying from every flagpole in town," while new flagpoles were hastily being erected and automobiles also were showing the colors. "The school children are making a flag survey of Tombstone," related the *Prospector* four days later, "taking account of business houses and residences that are—and are not—displaying the Stars and Stripes." On Sunday, April 8, there was "one mass of flags" at a community rally, and after patriotic speeches the audience stood to sing "My Country,

'Tis of Thee." Soon Sheriff Wheeler asked all men in the county who owned a horse, saddle, and rifle to send him a note, and he made the same request of automobile owners. Wheeler intended to be able to mobilize the manpower of his county if needed.[1]

Harry Wheeler, a former cavalryman and the son of a career soldier, immediately felt a personal call to arms. Aware that Governor Thomas E. Campbell intended to raise a volunteer regiment of cavalry, Wheeler eagerly wired on April 3, 1917: "I am capable of leading or being led. I offer myself in any capacity the country can best use me." More than one hundred men contacted the noted peace officer with hopes of serving under his command.[2] Wheeler also offered his services to President Wilson, and in May he received notification to report to the Officers Reserve Training Quarters at the Presidio in San Francisco. He obtained a sixty days' leave of absence from his duties as sheriff, intending to resign if he received a commission. Mrs. Wheeler and "little daughter Sunshine" also journeyed to California, to stay with relatives. The forty-one-year-old cavalry veteran passed his initial examinations with high marks, and during the first month of training the familiar military routines came back readily.

On June 7, however, a doctor rejected him because of the old injury with the cavalry horse at Fort Grant. Disappointed, Wheeler promptly submitted a new application, and returned to his duties as sheriff.[3]

Chief Deputy Guy Wilson had been running the office in Wheeler's absence. After Wheeler spent a few weeks with America's expanding military, returning to the sheriff's office must have been a severe letdown. Wheeler briefly had been in the mainstream of the nation's activities, but now he was on the sidelines while other men donned uniforms. Wheeler's frustrations were suffered alone; Mamie had stayed in California with a sister. But the Arizona sheriff was about to find himself thrust suddenly into an explosive situation that would place him into a far-reaching spotlight and create a controversy that would blot his distinguished career as a law officer.

By 1914, when war broke out in Europe, Arizona's economy had been dominated by mining. Demand soared for copper, an essential element of shell jackets, as well as for communication wire and cable. Arizona led the world in copper production by 1909. Arizona mining companies produced $40 million worth of copper in 1910, but wartime demands escalated production to $200 million in 1917. The Bisbee Mining District produced more than 190 million pounds of copper in 1916.[4]

Bisbee's Copper Queen, owned by the Phelps, Dodge & Co., Inc., was the richest mine in Arizona. The other two firms which dominated the Bisbee mining district were the Calumet & Arizona Mining Company and the Shattuck-Denn Company. Phelps Dodge began developing the Copper Queen during the 1880s, and the mining camp of Bisbee grew into a city, with Lowell and Warren substantial suburbs of the mining district. Bisbee became a company town, with handsome Victorian structures crowded into narrow canyons 5,400 feet

Wealthy, bustling Bisbee. Much of the town still would seem familiar to Harry Wheeler. (Author's collection)

above sea level. Houses were perched precariously above the city. Bisbee's Brewery Gulch became one of the West's liveliest and most infamous tenderloin districts. Wages were high, and by 1917 more than 4,700 miners were employed in the area's copper mines.

The big mining companies were the dominant political force in Arizona, exerting influence and power at local, county, and state levels. These companies united to restrict the increasing activities of labor unions. Union membership expanded to more than three million in 1917, but there was a severe labor shortage during the war (while demand for workers grew, four million men left the workforce for military service, and immigration temporarily ended). Aware of their increasing strength and of escalating wartime profits enjoyed by production companies, unions called more than 4,200 strikes during 1917. Although more than 400 of these strikes hit the mining industry, only twenty occurred in Arizona. Primarily because of the efforts of Phelps Dodge and other mining companies, Arizona was not congenial to wartime labor activities. Mining companies had no intention of permitting strikes to interfere with the immense profits of the era, and in Arizona a concerted effort against unions was led by Walter Douglas, president of Phelps Dodge and of the American Mining Congress.[5]

Intending to shatter the power of unions in their mines, Douglas and other industry leaders formulated a plan to expel or "deport" union agitators. The International Workers of the World unknowingly would play a key role in this stratagem. A small group of socialists and labor radicals had formed the IWW in 1905. Although the IWW never gained mass membership (only 14,000 in 1917), Bill Haywood and other controversial leaders turned up wherever violent strikes occurred, which made the small union appear to threaten public tranquility. The IWW called for the overthrow of industrial capitalism and for worker control of mines and factories. As the most openly revolutionary voice of labor, the IWW advocated sabotage and violence as necessary tactics. Union members were contemptuously called "Wobblies," and the IWW was said to stand for "I Won't Work." The IWW was infiltrated with spies, while company-controlled newspapers, such as the Bisbee *Daily Review,* described the Wobblies in unflattering and unpatriotic terms. With more than two million members, the American Federation of Labor dwarfed the IWW, but the impression was given that most union workers were Wobblies.[6]

Extralegal "deportations," executed in earlier labor disputes outside Arizona, became a traditional method of ridding towns of various undesirables. By July 1917 a coordinated plan apparently was launched to deport Wobblies and other militant labor leaders from Arizona mining towns. On July 7 in Kingman, the sheriff of Mohave County obtained warrants for the arrest of fifteen Wobblies who had called a strike that previously had been rejected decisively by the overall group of miners. On July 10 three other Mohave County mining towns, Chloride, Golconda and Mineral, notified Wobblies to get out within twelve hours. On the same day, Tuesday, July 10, action was taken in Jerome, about one hundred miles north of Phoenix, against a larger body of Wobblies. Out of 2,500 miners at Jerome, only about 125 were members of the IWW, but these Wobblies were so militant that they clashed with many other miners. On Monday, July 9, a large band of vigilantes had formed, agreeing to identify themselves by tying white handkerchiefs around their arms—the same signal that would be used in Bisbee a couple of days later. Before dawn on Tuesday, a force of more than 200 men seized 104 suspected Wobblies and hustled them to the vastly overcrowded city jail. A three-man committee permitted each suspect to try to prove that he was not a member of the IWW, a review that also would occur in Bisbee. Sixty-seven men finally were escorted to a waiting train: the United Verde Copper Company provided two boxcars for the deportees, along with a flatcar in front and a flatcar behind for fifty armed guards. Water barrels were placed in the cars, and the train pulled out for California.[7]

A similar scenario was about to be played out in Bisbee on a far larger scale. More than 4,700 miners were employed in the district, and about 400 were members of the IWW. "The Wobblies weren't really miners," reflected mine guard Harold Nichols. "They were troublemakers, loafers, sent in to stir up trouble."[8] Such was the general impression of Wobblies around Bisbee, a bustling company town where well-paid miners enjoyed vaudeville theaters, dancehalls, sporting houses, and a baseball league. Following a strike in the Clifton-Morenci mining district in the fall of 1916, "a Citizen's Protective League" with almost 1,000 members was organized in Bisbee, probably under the guiding hand of Walter Douglas and the Phelps Dodge Corporation. "The league was formed partly for the reason that it had been learned that industrial agitators of the type which had been doing its best to wreck the mining industry at Morenci and plunge the camp into disorder, were aiming at Bisbee also," reported the *Prospector*.[9]

Several months later, the IWW called a strike at the Bisbee mines for June 27, 1917. Officials of Bisbee's mining companies approached Sheriff Wheeler "with the request that they be allowed to appoint men, who would be deputized by him for the purpose of keeping the strikers from trespassing on company property. He flatly refused all such requests," reported William S. Beeman, who was present at the meeting. Beeman afterward was told by John C. Greenway, general manager of the Calumet and Arizona Mining Company, that "he was disappointed that Sheriff Wheeler would not permit the deputizing of men for the purpose of protecting property and keeping down disorder."[10]

Fifteen years earlier, Wheeler had worked briefly as a miner in Tombstone, and he had never demonstrated hostility toward workingmen. But now America was at war, and Bisbee's immense copper production was vital to the war effort. A great many Americans—including Harry Wheeler, who still hoped to join the army—regarded wartime strikes as unpatriotic. John Greenway and George Willcox, head of security for the C&A, had both served in the Rough Riders and understood the appeal of patriotism upon Wheeler. "Wheeler may have been slightly out of balance where patriotism is concerned," observed William S. Beeman. Greenway asked Willcox, a longtime friend of Wheeler's, to try to persuade the sheriff to cooperate with their plan. Later there were "many stories about the huge sum of money that was paid to Harry Wheeler . . . for allowing the mining companies to deport the men from Bisbee." William S. Beeman vehemently denied all such accusations: "I only wish that I was as sure of entering the Pearly Gates as I am that Harry Wheeler did not get one cent, either directly or indirectly, for any part he had in the Bisbee Deportation."[11]

Instead of bribery, Willcox revealed to Wheeler that Greenway had gathered evidence "that the strike was for the sole purpose of tying up the copper industry and preventing the government from entering the war at an early date." Beeman stressed that not until Wheeler was "convinced by Captain Greenway and Geo. B. Willcox that the strike was not being conducted in the interest of labor, but was for the purpose of embarrassing the government in her preparation to enter the World War, that he consented." Wheeler, though, "raised the question of the great expense that would follow such a move, and he told Willcox that he did not think the County Board of Supervisors would stand for the enormous expense." Willcox assured Wheeler "that the expense would be taken care of by the companies." Wheeler then expressed concern, on behalf of his bondsmen, about "any covert acts that might be committed by deputies selected by the mining companies and deputized by him." Willcox insisted that Greenway would not allow the sheriff or his bondsmen to suffer financially. "You know Jack Greenway well enough to know that he would never leave a friend in the hole." Willcox told Wheeler to meet with Greenway, who offered earnest assurances on every point. Finally, Wheeler told Greenway "to name the number of deputies" that would be needed. "As a result," recalled Beeman, "about three thousand men were deputized in the Warren District. ..."[12]

Sheriff Wheeler immediately "deputized more than 200 men ... and his assertion that more will be called into service is assurance that he expects to do his duty. His need for the extra deputies was made necessary by his determination to drive all IWW pickets from property owned by the mining companies and keep them away." The Wobblies were taunting miners on their way to or from work, "reviling them for not joining in the strike." The Douglas *Dispatch,* another company newspaper, strongly approved of the sheriff's actions: "Wheeler says these pickets will not be permitted to stand on company ground and insult honest workers—men with families—going to and from their places of toil, and his actions show that he means what he says. More power to him!"[13]

On July 3, 1917, Sheriff Wheeler was back in Tombstone for a trial appearance. "He reports so far absolutely no trouble of any nature and does not expect any serious trouble," related the Tombstone *Prospector,* "although if any should occur he and his deputies are prepared for any emergency." Wheeler immediately returned to Bisbee for the Fourth of July and "one of the biggest parades that has ever been staged in the district." Sponsored by the Loyalty League, the procession marched along Tombstone Canyon, Bisbee's main thoroughfare. "As the parade moved down the street," remembered William Beeman, "there could be heard hisses and jeers from the sidelines, and several fist fights resulted from remarks that were made by IWWs or sympathizers of the IWW."[14]

Following the parade, Sheriff Wheeler asked ten or twelve men, including Beeman, to bring "loyal and trustworthy" friends to a meeting that afternoon. About seventy or eighty men gathered to hear Wheeler state that he had become "convinced that the strike was being financed by German capital." Wheeler said that the ringleaders all were outsiders, brought to Bisbee "for the sole purpose of tying up the copper mines." He asserted that "the time had come for him to call upon all of the loyal citizens of the district," and he asked everyone who was willing to help to rise to his feet. "Every man rose to his feet," related Beeman proudly, "and the thing most noticeable was, every man rose at once; there was no waiting to see what the other fellow was going to do."[15]

Wheeler then asked five men to join him in a closed meeting. Beeman was one of the five, and he stated that Wheeler asked those present to list five more men who would help form a ten-man leadership group. The area would be divided into ten districts, with each of the leaders assigned to a district. Each leader would select four captains, who would organize at least seventy-five men apiece. (One of Beeman's companies was captained by a C&A mounted watchman, who recruited fellow watchmen and thus provided a mounted company.) The ten leaders would meet daily with Sheriff Wheeler. On Monday, July 9, "all leaders reported to Sheriff Wheeler that the organization was complete, and that three thousand men could be mobilized on short notice." Every unit was assigned a place to assemble.[16]

The IWW staged nightly meetings in Bisbee's city park. It was rumored that the Wobblies were collecting "rifles and firearms of different kinds," while citizens continued to be taunted and "jostled" by aggressive IWW members. On Wednesday, July 11, Bisbee mayor Jacob Erickson ordered the city park closed to further public meetings, whereupon Wobblies "publicly leveled threats at the mayor." That same day Mayor Erickson protested Wobblies blocking traffic in front of the post office in the center of town. An IWW leader reported that he could no longer control his men. Dismayed, Mayor Erickson related this exchange to Sheriff Wheeler. "My reply was that," said Wheeler pointedly, "if he could not control his men, I could."[17]

By this time "city authorities had expressed their entire willingness that Sheriff Wheeler should command the situation both in Bisbee and the Warren district." On Wednesday afternoon Wheeler assembled his ten leaders and asked them to attend a meeting at 8:00 that would include about thirty "of the representative citizens of the district." That night William Beeman noted that these citizens included "mine managers, doctors, bankers, merchants, machinists, miners and muckers." Following a general discussion, a motion was made to deport agitators, which "carried without a dissenting vote."[18]

A general discussion of plans followed. A suggestion to build a detention stockade was discarded. It was agreed that each deputy would tie a white handkerchief to his right arm as a mark of identification. Sheriff Wheeler stated his concern "that there would undoubtedly be considerable bloodshed," and several men present "made hasty wills" later that night. John Greenway outlined his ideas about sending the deportees by train to Columbus, New Mexico, where they would be "detained as enemies of the government" at Camp Furlong, the military encampment at Columbus. (Columbus was the site of the violent Pancho Villa raid of 1916.) "That seemed the most logical solution of the problem," said Beeman, "and it was adopted." Sheriff Wheeler asked Greenway and D. H. Dowell, manager of the Copper Queen mines, "to arrange for a train to take the men out the next day." The final item of business was the appointment of a committee to provide food and water for the train.[19]

Sheriff Wheeler prepared an announcement to the public which appeared at 6:00 Thursday morning, July 12, in the Bisbee *Review,* as well as in other county newspapers. (See page 121 for Wheeler's public proclamation.) According to Wheeler's statement, his "Sheriff's Posse" consisted of 1,200 men in Bisbee and 1,000 men from Douglas, while the Bisbee *Review* reported that the deputies numbered "1,800 strong." Hundreds of phone calls were made after midnight to alert the deputies. Sheriff Wheeler mounted a machine gun on a Ford, a vehicle appropriated for the day from a Catholic priest, and eight other machine guns were distributed among his men. One machine gun was set up facing the door of Union Hall, headquarters of the IWW. Wheeler moved before dawn to neutralize the IWW pickets around town. At 5:30, 1,200 men con-

Sheriff's Office

STATE OF ARIZONA. } ss.
County of Cochise

Know all men by these Presents:

That I, Harry C. Wheeler, Sheriff of Cochise County, State of Arizona, do hereby constitute and appoint

O. P. Mc Rae

my lawful deputy in all matters to act as if myself were present.

This commission expires automatically with the cessation of the present trouble in the Warren District, or upon any act of disloyalty on the part of the appointee herein named to the County, State or United States Government.

H C Wheeler
_____
Sheriff.

STATE OF ARIZONA, } ss.
County of Cochise

I, _O. P. Mc Rae_ , do solemnly swear that I will support the Constitution of the United States and the Constitution and laws of the State of Arizona; that I will true faith and allegiance bear to the same, and defend them against all enemies whatsoever, and that I will faithfully and impartially discharge the duties of the office of Deputy Sheriff according to the best of my ability, so help me God.

O. P. Mc Rae
_____

Subscribed and sworn to before me this 29 day of June, 1917.

John F. Bankerd

My Commission expires
April 3rd, 1920
Feby 17–1920

Notary Public.

Commission form signed by hundreds of Sheriff Wheeler's "special deputies" during the deportation crisis. This was the form of O.P. McRae, the only deputy who was killed.

verged on the pickets, taking them into custody within fifteen minutes. Backed by a force of his special deputies, Wheeler entered the Union Hall, then emerged with a number of IWW leaders. These initial captives were taken to the detention center in Warren, a fenced-in baseball park. Four miles from downtown Bisbee, the ballpark stood near the Calumet and Arizona office building, where a machine gun was placed overlooking the stadium.[20]

"After the pickets and leaders had been taken in charge," reported the Bisbee *Review*, "a house to house canvas was made by the citizens, and the trouble makers were marched to Warren."[21] Despite Wheeler's prediction of bloodshed, there was only one shooting incident. Orson McRae led several other deputies into a rooming house and tried to force the door of James Brew, a slumbering miner who was an IWW cardholder. Brew opened fire with a pistol, killing McRae, who was unarmed. The other deputies had guns, however, and Brew was shot to death. "Brew's mind is believed to have become unbalanced through brooding over the situation in the district," suggested one account. "He was an IWW but he had not been among the strikers."[22] Of course, if he was not on strike, he may have felt justified in going to his gun when a gang of men tried to burst into his bedroom.

A number of other deportees testified to being roughed up in various ways. James Byrkit compiled several of these incidents in *Forging the Copper Collar*, reporting beatings and the theft of money.[23] Brought first to the open area in

Bisbee's Main Street. The Bank of Bisbee is at right, while the three-story post office and library looms at left. On July 12, 1917, deportees by the hundreds were rounded up and brought into this plaza, before being marched four miles to the ballpark in Lowell. (Courtesy Arizona Historical Society)

front of Bisbee's post office, those who were rounded up were then marched by the hundreds to the ballpark in Warren. A great many spectators watched the proceedings at every point. "The sheriff was in command and remained so throughout the day," observed one reporter. James Byrkit described the sheriff's busy supervision from the Ford touring car with the "new 7.62 mm. Marlin machine gun with a loaded feed belt in position. As the car raced back and forth along the streets of Bisbee, Lowell, Bakerville and Warren, Wheeler shouted instructions, exhortations and praise."[24]

A large force of armed guards supervised the ballpark. Citizens were admitted to the stadium who could find "men who could be responsibly vouched for as innocent of IWW participation or sympathy, and who desired to be released to go to work." Furthermore, the men corralled inside the ballpark could call "for any person who could clear his name." Most men who announced that they wished to return to work were released. About 2,000 men—and three women—were herded into the ballpark, and several hundred were released.[25]

Around 11:00 a special train rolled into a siding near the ballpark. There were twenty-seven boxcars and cattle cars, rolling stock of the El Paso and Southwestern Railroad, which was owned by Phelps, Dodge & Co., Inc. Within half an hour the ballpark gates were opened and 1,186 men were marched to the train. Water and bread were supplied on the cars, but the water would rapidly be consumed in the July heat. The cattle cars were littered with manure. By half past noon the cars were loaded with deportees and guards, and the train pulled out for New Mexico. William Beeman overheard an army colonel (probably Lt. Col. J. J. Hornbrook, sent to Bisbee as an observer by the War Department) comment upon the roundup that had taken place throughout the morning: "It was the greatest piece of civilian work I have ever seen. I could not have done with any regiment what Sheriff Wheeler did with his deputies today."[26]

Wheeler enjoyed a flood of praise. "You are to be congratulated on your excellent work at Bisbee," read a telegram from Col. Fred S. Breen, head of the Selective Draft in Arizona, "and I want to as an American citizen say you are the 'real thing.' I agree with your actions. America for Americans sounds good to me." Resolutions were adopted by the executive committee of the Citizens' Protective League of Douglas tendering the "full and undivided support of our membership" for Sheriff Wheeler. The Cochise County Board of Supervisors upheld Wheeler's actions, claiming that all "commissions issued to nearly 2,000 special deputy sheriffs were scrutinized by the board before being issued and given its official sanction." The Tombstone *Prospector* offered an editorial of praise the day after the deportation. Entitled "WELL DONE, BISBEE, WELL DONE!" the editorial concluded: "It will go down in history as a great day for the Warren District, and credit is due to Sheriff Harry Wheeler and the patriotic citizens for assuming the responsibility they did, and executing their work in so masterly a manner."[27]

A few days later the Bisbee *Review* added its acclaim:

Wheeler's Announcement to the Public
(In the Bisbee *Daily Review,* July 12, 1917)

I have formed a Sheriff's Posse of 1,200 men in Bisbee and 1,000 men in Douglas, all loyal Americans, for the purpose of arresting, on charges of vagrancy, treason, and being disturbers of the peace of Cochise county, all those strange men who have congregated here from other parts and sections for the purpose of harassing and intimidating all men who desire to pursue their daily toil. I am continually told of threats and insults heaped upon the working men of this district by so-called strikers, who are strange to these parts, yet who presume to dictate the manner of life of the people of this district.

Appeals to patriotism do not move them, nor do appeals to reason. At a time when our country needs her every resource, these strangers persist in keeping from her the precious metal production of the entire district.

Today, I heard threats to the effect that homes would be destroyed because the heads of families insisted upon their rights as Americans to work for themselves and their families.

Other threats have and are daily made. Men have been assaulted and brutally beaten, and only today I heard the Mayor of Bisbee threatened and his requests ignored.

We cannot longer stand or tolerate such conditions! This is no labor trouble—we are sure of that—but a direct attempt to embarrass and injure the government of the United States.

I therefore call upon all loyal Americans to aid me in peaceably arresting these disturbers of our national and local peace. Let no shot be fired throughout this day unless in necessary self defense, and I hereby give warning that each and every leader of the so-called strikers will be held personally responsible for any injury inflicted upon any of my deputies of my posse, for those acts I, in turn, assume full responsibility as Sheriff of this County.

All arrested persons will be treated humanely and their cases examined with justice and care. I hope no resistance will be made, for I desire no bloodshed. However, I am determined if resistance is made, it shall be quickly and effectively overcome.

Harry C. Wheeler
Sheriff Cochise County, Arizona

A large crowd of onlookers watched the roundup and deportation on July 12, 1917. (Courtesy Bisbee Mining and Historical Museum)

The four-mile march from Bisbee to the ballpark in Warren. (Author's collection)

More than 1,100 deportees were forced into boxcars and cattle cars (center car). Note the deputies perched atop each car. (Courtesy Bisbee Mining and Historical Museum)

About forty or fifty deportees were loaded into each car. The special deputy in the foreground is brandishing a rifle and wearing a white handkerchief around his right arm. (Courtesy Bisbee Mining and Historical Museum)

Sheriff Harry Wheeler is becoming famous the country over as a result of the part he played in leading the famous drive on the IWW industry wreckers July 12. And the fine part of it is, the brave but modest little sheriff is worthy of all the praise and all the nice things that are being said about him. He just positively won't swell up over this "hero" business. Every day since the big drive has found him busily engaged in cleaning up the little sharks that escaped the net. . . . Many men win the name of heroes but few of them bear their blushing honors so modestly and so worthily as our sheriff.[28]

The Tombstone *Prospector* soon published another editorial which began: "Captain Harry Wheeler just a week ago today gave the Warren District a dose of medicine that cleansed it from top to bottom, when he rid the Warren District of that bunch of anarchists, the I.W.W.'s." At the end of this laudatory piece the editorialist added a little humor which seemed appropriate: "There is a rumor to the effect that Harry Wheeler, sheriff of Cochise county, is to be arrested for violating the medical laws of the state of Arizona. The charge against the doughty little captain is that he practiced surgery without being admitted to practice under state laws. On July 12, 1917, he removed a cancerous growth from the city of Bisbee."[29]

Meanwhile, another point of view was developing about the Bisbee Deportation. Nearly 1,200 deportees suffered through a long and difficult train ride to Columbus, New Mexico, only to be turned back by local officials, on the orders of New Mexico governor W. E. Lindsey. The train headed back, stopping on a siding at Hermanas, New Mexico, about twenty miles west of Columbus. A couple of hours after midnight on July 13, 1,200 men climbed out of the cars and built fires. During the following day, these "men were reported wandering about the little New Mexico town," as temperatures grew hotter and hotter. Many of the deportees sent telegrams to family and friends and IWW leaders. While concerns about the stranded deportees began to spread, the guards boarded a westbound train for Douglas and Bisbee. When rumors "said that it was the intention to bring the agitators back to Arizona as far as Douglas," officials and citizens prepared to defend their city. A report circulated that "Sheriff Wheeler also telephoned that he would come here to deal with the situation."[30]

But the deportees were still in Hermanas. Governor Lindsey, now better aware of their plight, made arrangements to transport them back to Columbus, where they could be fed. The governor wired President Wilson, who sent orders that Camp Furlong would provide rations. The deportees settled in at Camp Furlong, where they were divided into "eight companies" and maintained for a considerable period. IWW leader Bill Haywood learned of the deportation on July 13 and immediately began issuing outraged complaints. That same day, Governor Campbell of Arizona, who had received a stern telegram of inquiry from President Wilson, wired Sheriff Wheeler "requesting a statement of the reasons why the men were deported."[31]

Wheeler soon began to feel a need to defend his extraordinary actions.

Within a few days he tried to arouse widespread sympathy in an interview with an Associated Press correspondent. "We believe we were justified in doing what we did for the safety of the women and children of this district." Wheeler told the reporter that the night before the deportation "a reliable report" revealed Wobbly plans to dynamite the Bisbee water supply at Naco. "The day preceding the deportation American women were told their homes would be blown up, dinner pails were stolen from the miners and Finnish women sympathizers with the strikers attacked the miners going to work."[32]

Having explained the need to protect American women, Wheeler next expressed solicitude for the great number of deportees—more than half—who were not members of the IWW. "We are anxious to have those of the deported men who were caught in the roundup by mistake to return. We tried to segregate them at the ball park but the IWW leaders prevented this. We will welcome those who have homes and families here and are not agitators but we will not let the agitators and 'wobblies' come back." Indeed, deputies were manning checkpoints around Bisbee to deny entry to anyone suspected of being a labor agitator. Sheriff Wheeler asserted that "we intend to make this an American camp where American working men may enjoy life, liberty and the pursuit of happiness unmolested by any alien enemies of whatever breed."[33]

The Associated Press correspondent asked about the fate of the detainees at Camp Furlong. "What the solution is of the problem presented by their deportation and detention I cannot say," replied Wheeler. When the deportation train left Cochise County, the deportees no longer were the problem of the sheriff. "But I cannot think the United States will force these men upon us after we took the action we did through pure Americanism and did what we did because we honestly felt those men were injuring the best interests of the United States." Wheeler pressed home a point he saw as crucial to his defense. "It was not an ordinary labor dispute and I cannot and will not believe the government will censure us for what we did for the government."[34]

In a statement to a reporter from Douglas, Wheeler explained why persons coming to Bisbee were being monitored by deputies. "I am determined to keep out men who are continually making trouble in the camp and am not fearful of having overstepped any authority of my office." For the next several weeks the sheriff remained on duty in Bisbee, returning to the county seat only sporadically. On July 19, for example, the sheriff "drove up from his Bisbee headquarters to Tombstone this afternoon," and on August 2 he was "in town today for several hours."[35]

In the midst of his post-deportation duties in Bisbee, Sheriff Wheeler was suddenly called away to California. He received "news of the serious illness of his wife in San Francisco, where she is on a visit with relatives." Perhaps ready for a break from the tense situation in Bisbee, Wheeler caught a train on Monday morning, July 23, "and left for the bedside." It was more than a week before Mamie "recovered sufficiently from her recent serious illness to be able to travel." Harry and Mamie returned to Tombstone on Wednesday morning,

August 1. Perhaps accompanied by friends, Mamie proceeded on to a hospital in Bisbee, while Harry stayed in Tombstone for a short time to catch up at his office. Mamie Wheeler's hospital stay lasted for several weeks. On a visit to Tombstone "from his temporary headquarters in Bisbee" on September 9, Sheriff Wheeler reported that his wife finally had "recovered sufficiently to be moved" from the hospital. Two days later Harry brought Mamie to Tombstone, and after spending the night he left her to continue her recovery alone while he returned to Bisbee.[36]

While Mamie Wheeler still was in the hospital, a movement to recall Sheriff Wheeler was fostered in the little town of McNeal, "presumably by Socialists and IWW's and their sympathizers," according to the Tombstone *Prospector*. About forty voters signed the petition, but soon this movement was repudiated by "the leading citizens of McNeal." Further support of Sheriff Wheeler was provided by ladies of the Bisbee area, who met on August 23 at the gymnasium of Bisbee's YMCA and organized a chapter of the Women's Loyalty League of America. These women elected officers, adopted a constitution, and voted a resolution "that we most heartily commend the action of our fearless sheriff for his loyal and patriotic stand in the deportation of the undesirable element from the Warren District on July 12, 1917." The new organization offered Sheriff Wheeler "our heartfelt thanks" and assured him of their support. An editorial in the *Prospector* slurred the IWW as "Imperial Warriors of Wilhelm" and speculated (correctly, as it developed) that the recall petition "originating with the Socialists and Wobbly sympathizers will not secure the required signatures to call an election."[37]

In mid-August Sheriff Wheeler swore out almost 1,200 warrants "charging vagrancy and inciting a riot ... against any man who was deported from the Warren district during the round up of July 12." Wheeler announced that if any of the men returned to Bisbee, they would "be placed under arrest on one of the two charges." Wheeler used a number of these warrants a month later, after the deportees finally departed Camp Furlong. Some of the deportees tried to return to Bisbee, but Sheriff Wheeler and his deputies "continued arresting the deportees yesterday as fast as they arrived in the district from the detention camp at Columbus, N. M." The sheriff "conducted a personal examination of each man, and then classed him in one of three groups." A few were married men and/or property holders; others were deemed suitable to appear before the area draft board, which was headed by Sheriff Wheeler; and the rest, contending "that they had come back merely to gather their personal effects," had neither family nor property in the district.[38]

About one hundred men were taken into custody and delivered to Tombstone "as rapidly as they were arrested by deputy sheriffs ... and formal charges of vagrancy are made in the public court." The usual sentence was ninety days in jail. One detainee angrily "arose and damned the American government," which triggered an immediate response from Sheriff Wheeler. "I deported you men myself in the name of Cochise county and for the good of the

Hymn to Deportation

International Workers of the World agitators were gifted at annoying established society. In addition to strikes and rabble-rousing speeches, Wobblies composed satirical songs that were guaranteed to irritate sedate listeners. One "hymn," aimed at the forces which opposed the IWW began:

Onward Christian soldiers, rip and tear and smite,
Let the gentle Jesus bless your dynamite,
Smash the doors of every home, pretty maidens seize,
Use your might and sacred right to treat her
    as you please.

county," he snapped, "and it is me you want to talk to and about, and not this government. If you say another word I will arrest you on a treason charge instead of for vagrancy. This is not a time when any man can speak of the United States government except in terms of respect or loyalty."[39]

In August 1917 the attorney general of Arizona, Wiley E. Jones, placed a 200-page report about the Bisbee Deportation in the hands of Governor Campbell. The report primarily contained "statements of residents of the Warren District, including Sheriff Wheeler of Cochise county." Wheeler declared to Attorney General Jones: "I would repeat the operation any time I find my own people endangered by a mob composed of eighty percent aliens and enemies of my government." Shortly before the deportation, Wheeler had telegraphed both Governor Campbell and President Wilson for help, to no avail. He defended his actions: "I intend when deserted by all other departments who should aid and protect, yet who do not, to protect my own people by the best possible method and in the most effective way. . . . There were no jails in the county capable of holding so many prisoners, the state could not and the government would not aid us and I did what was left to me. I pursued the only course that promised freedom from bloodshed and anarchy." Asked about statements from IWW leaders that a labor revolution was at hand, the sheriff issued a challenge: "If the men shriek of revolution, I only hope they come here to begin their revolution. We will end it for them."[40]

Another investigation was taking place, by a federal "Mediation Commission" dispatched by President Wilson. The commission's findings and recommendations were released in November 1918. A letter was sent to Sheriff Wheeler, tactfully offering two recommendations while avoiding any criticism. The federal government probably was reluctant to criticize Wheeler because during the war about 1,500 anti-war agitators had been arrested by the government on charges of sedition, and the postal system had barred anti-war propaganda from the mails, among other actions. Furthermore, according to James Byrkit, wealthy Cleveland Douglas, Princeton classmate of Wilson and a partner and director of Phelps Dodge, was the president's closest friend and a key financial supporter. An obvious supposition is that the president's Mediation Commission would be unlikely, in the end, to come down very hard on the instigators of the Bisbee Deportation. But the commission did insist that "unimpeded admittance into the Warren district" should be restored. "Therefore, all deputy sheriffs now serving as patrol or pickets on the outskirts of the district for the purpose of passing judgment on the right of any one to enter the district should be at once withdrawn from such service, nor should deputies hereafter be stationed for such purpose." The commission's other recommendation insisted that all citizens should be allowed to move about freely and to continue to reside in the district. "This, of course, is in no wise intended to limit authority of the sheriff, under the usual restrictions of the law," the commission hastily added.[41]

Sheriff Wheeler promptly composed a response to the Mediation

Commission for public consumption. First he insisted that any criticism of his deputies should be directed at him. Then, incredibly, he seemed to suggest that restrictions might continue against certain persons trying to enter the district. "Trying to reach the spirit of your letter, I conclude all you desire is that all peaceably disposed persons not accused of any violation of law be permitted to enter the district without molestation." On this point, however, the letter seems so emphatic and clear-cut as to have no other "spirit." Wheeler's conclusion hinted that by this time he was beginning to suspect his action might have been excessive. "Please believe me personally willing to make any sacrifice for the best interests of the United States. If the Supreme Power would endow me with complete wisdom I should never be at fault. My findings through many trials have been, 'Tis easy to do right, but at times terribly difficult to distinguish the wrong from the right of things.' "[42]

Wheeler took a break in October, heading into the mountains for a hunting trip. In Arizona it was the season for deer, quail, and wild turkey, and the beleagured sheriff certainly needed a vacation. But while he was gone, Wobbly sympathizers began "circulating the report that he had been beaten up and his eyes blackened by some IWW, and that he was keeping from the public as a consequence." When he finally emerged from the mountains, his friends were relieved that he did "not carry the black eyes nor the marks of having been beaten up."[43]

But Wheeler continued to be "beaten up" by IWW spokesmen and sympathizers in articles and speeches. Legal action would be taken against him which would trouble his life for years. In a career punctuated by such spectacular occurrences as deadly shootouts, the Bisbee Deportation was the most spectacular and controversial event. Sheriff Wheeler longed to leave Arizona for military service, and he continued to try to enlist.

The Bisbee *Ore,* however, pointed out that Wheeler "gained more fame . . . than if he had been given his shoulder straps. There is slight chance that any of his companions now at Presidio will, during the World War now raging have the opportunity that Captain Wheeler had during the recent disturbance in this city. He was given an opportunity to show his qualities of manhood, of leadership and good, strong Americanism and he was there. He never faltered but did his duty as an official and as a consequence has added to his reputation as fearless officer and a brave and efficient official."[44]

On Thursday night, December 5, 1917, Bisbee's Commercial Club feted Sheriff Wheeler with a banquet at the country club. "The attendance at the banquet overwhelmed the committee on arrangements and there were not enough places for the guests at the long tables," reported the Bisbee *Review.* Three hundred leading citizens "gathered there to try to show the man who had led them . . . just how they felt about it." Speeches and musical entertainment accompanied the fine dinner. "One of the most modest men that ever lived, he faced the praise and the cheers with a downcast glance," described the *Review.* But responding to a clamor for him to speak, Wheeler stood up "and looked the throng in the face and spoke from his heart."

Wheeler spoke about the report of the President's Mediation Commission and about the IWW leaders. Wobblies "ought to be deported further than New Mexico," said Wheeler to a cheering audience. "They ought to be sent to an island in the sea where they could set up a kingdom of their own. The hyenas would howl over that kingdom in six months."

Remarking that his "mother"—the U.S.A.—had "spanked" him by refusing him an army commission, Wheeler nevertheless emphasized that "I love her with all my heart and strength and soul." More cheers followed. "I have been feeling bad about the failure to realize my life ambition and fight for my country," he admitted. "I was depressed and discouraged, but when I came here tonight and received your grand welcome and heard your kind words, I was thrilled with the feeling that I have done some small bit for my country after all. Your reception makes me believe that my mother loves me still.

"But, my friends, you pay me too much honor in this matter. There were scores of men in that drive the morning of July 12, who are entitled to more honor than I; who did more than I that day for the district and our home fires. I merely did my duty. I couldn't shirk. You could. But you didn't!" Duty was indeed the driving force of his life, and once he had become convinced of his patriotic duty, Sheriff Wheeler had used the authority of his office and the power of his leadership skills to coordinate the largest extra-legal action in the history of the West.

"And now, my friends, I want you all to stand up and pay tribute for a moment to the first American soldier killed in France." The crowd stood silently until Captain Wheeler, "with deep earnestness," said, "I thank you, gentlemen." As Wheeler took his seat, "the handclapping and cheers that followed then made the country club ring."

Reflecting upon Wheeler's talk, the *Review* pointed out that Wheeler's "intense patriotism blazed out time and again" throughout his remarks. Once he declared emphatically, "Damn a man that is not patriotic!"[45]

CHAPTER EIGHT

Captain in the Great War

"The one ambition of Sheriff Wheeler since this war began has been to have his service accepted in some capacity in the army."

—Douglas *International*

Early in October 1917, Harry Wheeler received a letter from his younger brother, Lt. William Wheeler of the 165th Infantry. When the war broke out William, a bachelor, was living in Brooklyn. He had served a hitch in the infantry during the Spanish-American War, and after the United States entered the Great War he obtained a commission. William graduated from the inaugural training camp in Plattsburg, New York, as a first lieutenant, and was posted to the Rainbow Division, 165th Infantry, which formerly was the famous "Fighting 69th." "They are a splendid bunch—and mostly Irish. We are the Rainbow Division (42nd) and expect to sail to France," he wrote. The division was encamped at Mineola, Long Island. Lieutenant Wheeler described a vast number of men in uniform, along with high enthusiasm and hard work, and he expressed the hope that he would serve his country well. He closed with a request for letters.[1]

Sheriff Wheeler proudly showed off his brother's letter, eliciting a story in the Tombstone *Prospector*. The Rainbow Division soon was shipped to France, and in December Harry told the country club banquet crowd that William was overseas. "The crowd cheered, and cheered again," described the Bisbee *Review*. Despite Harry's obvious pride in his brother, he quietly envied William's trip "over there" with a combat division. Harry, of course, had volunteered early, and he had reported eagerly to the Reserve Officers' Training Camp at the Presidio of San Francisco on May 13, 1917. Disappointment followed in less than a month, when he was "found physically disqualified."[2]

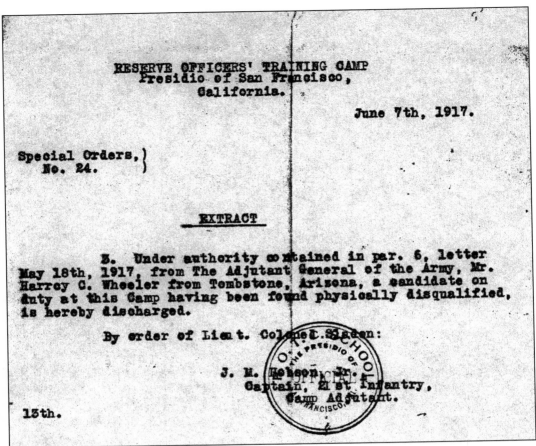

RESERVE OFFICERS' TRAINING CAMP
Presidio of San Francisco,
California.

June 7th, 1917.

Special Orders,
    No. 24.

EXTRACT

3. Under authority contained in par. 6, letter
May 18th, 1917, from The Adjutant General of the Army, Mr.
Harrey C. Wheeler from Tombstone, Arizona, a candidate on
duty at this Camp having been found physically disqualified,
is hereby discharged.

By order of Lieut. Colonel Sladen:

J. M. Hobson, Jr.
Captain, 21st Infantry,
Camp Adjutant.

13th.

Wheeler's medical discharge from the Reserve Officers' Training Camp at the Presidio early in the war. (Courtesy National Archives)

Harry had made repeated efforts to obtain a commission, having joined the Arizona National Guard in April 1908, while he was captain of the Rangers. Assigned to Company A of the First Infantry, Harry enlisted for three years. Apparently he did not re-enlist, but while trying to join the army at the age of forty-two, he could list National Guard service, as well as five years in the U.S. Cavalry. After he was discharged from the first Reserve Officers' Training Camp at the Presidio, Wheeler immediately applied for the second Training Camp, but he was not accepted. Then he tried "to join the First Arizona Infantry at Naco," applying for a captain's commission. "LET WHEELER FIGHT," headlined the Tombstone *Prospector* in a typical editorial. Another editorial, in the Douglas *International,* made a similar plea: "The one ambition of Sheriff Wheeler since the war began had been to have his service accepted in some capacity in the army."[3]

Still Wheeler was not accepted. He tried unsuccessfully to enter the Reserve Officers' Training Camp at Leon Springs, Texas. Meanwhile, former Arizona Ranger sergeant Arthur Hopkins was commissioned a captain in the regular army, which must have caused Wheeler more silent envy. In desperation,

Wheeler tried to enlist in his brother's regiment as a private, but at forty-two he was two years past the age limit for an enlisted man. Next Wheeler applied to the Canadian government for military service. The Tombstone *Prospector* pointed out that if Wheeler was successful in entering the Canadian Army, "he will be joined by a number of other prominent citizens of the Warren district who are also above the age limit and who are desirous of getting into the trenches in France." However, the trenches in France were spared the presence of the middle-aged men of Bisbee, because once more Wheeler was denied.[4]

Wheeler's efforts to enlist were opposed by labor leaders. Spokesmen for the International Workers of the World railed against him, and in October 1917 the Warren District Trades Assembly voted a set of resolutions "that protest his appointment in the U.S. army." Wheeler responded with a lengthy newspaper statement, complaining that

> labor seems to have taken up the IWW cause against me and, as a means of hurting me most, is opposing my entrance into the army of the United States. I have no wish to permanently enter the army, being in the old age of my youth; I realize I could yield but a short period of usefulness to the army, but such as I am I have offered freely—still offer freely and if accepted even the supreme sacrifice of a soldier would be met gladly and with the willingness and the pride under such circumstances a soldier would know and feel in the knowledge of duty well performed in the service of the country he loves above all else.
>
> To you men who would take from me the privilege of serving the flag; to you men who would deprive the country in time of war of the service of an experienced man and soldier, I would say: I have four times tried to enter the service of the United States; how often have you done likewise? If through your actions prompted by pique or spite, I am denied the high privilege of becoming a member of the army and the army in turn through your actions loses the services of one willing man, which one of you gentlemen, married and beyond the draft age, contemplates a voluntary service to make up the loss?[5]

There were four other long paragraphs as Wheeler vented his frustration at not being accepted by the military and his bitterness against the men who worked to thwart his enlistment. Now he could continue his efforts to enlist while going about his duties as sheriff. Whenever there was an opportunity, Sheriff Wheeler eagerly drilled hopeful recruits. On October 29, for example, he met seven "colored men" who had been drafted and who were about to depart to join their regiment. Wheeler "put them through drill yesterday afternoon and again gave them some additional instructions today, before they left." Two weeks later Wheeler received a letter from these men, expressing gratitude "for the drill he gave them" as well as for the "fine banquet and the big send off" they were provided by the ladies of the Loyalty League.[6]

At dawn on February 10, 1918, a four-man posse, led by Graham County

Sheriff Wheeler showing draftees basic drills at Bisbee's City Park in September 1917. (Courtesy Bisbee Mining and Historical Museum)

Sheriff Robert McBride, closed in on a remote log cabin in Kilburg Canyon, seventy miles northeast of Tucson. Inside the cabin were fifty-four-year-old Thomas J. Powers, Sr., his two grown sons, Tom and John, and hired hand Tom Sisson. These men were working four nearby mining claims, and the Powers brothers had not responded to draft notices. The posse intended to arrest the brothers on charges of draft evasion, but a vicious gun battle erupted when the elder Powers came to the doorway brandishing a rifle. Powers was fatally wounded, and Sheriff McBride and two deputies were shot to death. The Powers brothers nursed their dying father, while the surviving posse member rode for help. Finally the Powers brothers headed into the wilderness, guided by Sisson, an army scout during the Apache wars of the 1880s.[7]

A massive manhunt soon developed, with perhaps a thousand men searching for the fugitives. On the day of the killings, Graham County officials "sent word to Sheriff Wheeler that the three men were supposed to be headed for the San Pedro valley country where they would undoubtedly attempt to cross into Mexico. . . ." Wheeler immediately led a posse of deputies into the Dragoon Mountains, where they soon encountered other posses. Within another day there were sheriff's posses from eight counties along with military patrols. "Sheriff Wheeler and deputies are hot on the trail in the mountains," reported the Tombstone *Prospector,* but Sisson skillfully eluded capture. Sheriff Wheeler used bloodhounds and four Indian scouts, but the hunted men disappeared into the rugged Cochise Stronghold. While the outlaws struggled on foot, fresh horses were brought to the lawmen, and Sheriff Wheeler was termed "in supreme charge of the searchers. . . ." But a deep snowfall wiped out the trail.[8]

At one point in the Chiricahua Mountains, "Sheriff Harry Wheeler was within 40 feet from where the three outlaws were in hiding, but did not know it. They had their guns trained on him," related the fugitives after their capture, "and were ready to kill him if he came up to where they were." But Wheeler turned onto another trail and disappeared without spotting them. "They then turned in another direction and never saw him again."[9]

Sheriff Wheeler and two trackers returned to Tombstone on Tuesday afternoon, February 26, "having gone without food, water and sleep." Wheeler and his trackers were "the last part of the posse of several hundred men" which returned the previous week, while the soldiers had been withdrawn the day before. The sheriff sported "a ten-day's growth of beard, with clothes torn to shreds." Despite abandoning the search for the time being, Sheriff Wheeler stated "that he believes the outlaws will be captured within a short time."[10]

Wheeler's prediction proved correct. On March 8 the fugitives were taken prisoner by a cavalry patrol. Although they were eight miles below the international border, a "hot pursuit" agreement permitted their capture in Mexico and their return to the United States. Taken to Safford, the seat of Graham County, the prisoners were displayed in jail "for a ravenous populace." Because the citizens of Graham County were regarded as "too aroused for a fair trial," a change of venue placed the trial in Clifton in Greenlee County. After a sensational seven-day trial, all three men were convicted of murder and sentenced to life in prison. (On December 8, 1916, capital punishment in Arizona had been repealed, but immediately after the Powers brothers and Sisson thus escaped execution, the death penalty was restored on July 3, 1918.) Sisson died in prison, but the Powers brothers were paroled in 1960. After forty-two years behind bars, John was seventy and Tom was sixty-eight.[11]

Harry Wheeler was not in Arizona when the Powers brothers and Tom Sisson were apprehended and tried. In January 1918, Sheriff Wheeler appeared before the Cochise County Board of Supervisors, requesting "a leave not to exceed 60 days." The board granted Wheeler's request, but the Powers-Sisson manhunt unexpectedly delayed his departure. After the bedraggled sheriff returned from the mountains, how-

Capt. Harry Wheeler, United States Army. Note the crossbelt through his shoulder strap to his Sam Browne belt, which indicated that he was an officer. (Courtesy Pam Hamlett)

Watch Your Step, Sheriff

On Wednesday morning, January 9, 1918, fire broke out in a house near Harry Wheeler's residence. Hurrying across a vacant lot to help, Wheeler fell through the boards covering what he assumed "was an old cess pool." He managed to clutch the timbers, then clambered out and rushed to fight the fire. Later, Wheeler and several other firefighters walked back across the lot. They discovered that the "cess pool" was an abandoned mine shaft. That afternoon the *Prospector* accurately headlined, "SERIOUS ACCIDENT NARROWLY AVERTED," and Sheriff Wheeler had the shaft opening securely covered.

ever, he shaved and bathed, donned his traveling clothes, and boarded an eastbound train. He was vague about his destinations, and the Tombstone *Prospector* speculated that "it is believed he went to visit relatives in New York and will take a trip to Washington while away."[12]

Washington was the object of Wheeler's journey. He had determined to take his quest for an army commission to the nation's capitol, and he brought an impressive collection of letters of recommendation. Wheeler had obtained letters from Governor Campbell, former Governor Joseph E. Kibbey, both Arizona senators, Superior Court Judge A.C. Lockwood, and two army officers, Col. J.J. Hornbrook and Capt. John C. Walker. As the wartime army expanded to four million men, a new cavalry regiment, the 308th, was being organized in Arizona, and Wheeler intended to make an all-out effort to become an officer in this outfit.[13]

"HARRY WHEELER GETS CAPTAIN'S COMMISSION," trumpeted a Tombstone *Prospector* headline on March 9. Word arrived in Arizona by telegram and telephone that Wheeler "has been given a Captain's commission and has been assigned to the 308th Cavalry regiment now forming at Douglas, which will be an Arizona unit." The IWW campaigned unsuccessfully to have Captain Wheeler's commission rescinded, but the army put him to work immediately. He was a veteran cavalry non-com, and recently he had undergone reserve officer's training at the Presidio. With the army's explosive influx of new soldiers, Captain Wheeler could be put to immediate use. The new captain was sent to an encampment at Hoboken, New Jersey, "in charge of several hundred recruits." Undoubtedly he was proud of the captain's bars on the shoulder straps of his wool uniform, and of the brown leather belt with the cross strap over his right shoulder. This "Sam Browne" belt indicated to all enlisted men that the wearer was an officer.

Captain Wheeler's service revolver and scabbard, with "U.S." embossed on the leather. Note the lanyard ring on the bottom of the gun butt. (Courtesy Pam Hamlett, photo by Karon O'Neal)

As a captain, Wheeler earned $2,400 annually, considerably less than his $4,000 sheriff's salary plus fees. Yet, after finally obtaining a wartime commission, Captain Wheeler did not hesitate to submit his resignation as sheriff of Cochise County. The resignation was effective May 1, sixty days after he left Tombstone. Chief Deputy Guy Welch was placed in charge of the sheriff's office.[14]

Mamie Wheeler, who had become an inveterate traveler, did not miss the opportunity to visit the northeast. She journeyed cross-country by train to Hoboken, although Captain Wheeler soon was transferred to Camp Merrit in New Jersey. Wheeler was assigned to the Signal Reserve Corps, Aviation Section, "much against his wishes." Captain Wheeler wanted a combat command, and he pointed out that he was "not qualified for the Signal Corps." Wheeler, of course, was hardly the only soldier unhappy with his duties, and the army was notably impervious to such complaints.[15]

Captain Wheeler could not have complained about the dispatch with which he was sent to France. In what surely was one of the most rapid deployments of the war for a new soldier, Wheeler sailed for France late in March, only three weeks after receiving his commission. The American Expeditionary Force was increasing troop strength as rapidly as possible, and transport ships usually reached France within ten days of departure. Mamie Wheeler caught a westbound train, arriving in Tombstone on Monday, April 3. A week later she received word that her husband had arrived safely in France. "The Captain asks that all the Cochise county papers be sent to him," reported the *Prospector,* "beginning with the date when he left." Several days later Mamie received "the regulation army official postcard," which stated: "I have arrived safely overseas." Captain Wheeler added, in his bold handwriting, "Will write later."[16]

Within a few weeks Mamie received two letters, which she shared with the *Prospector.* Captain Wheeler stated that he "has several hundred reserve men under his command, preparing them for duty at the front. . . . He states that he is already tired of playing 'feather bed' soldier away from the front and expects orders for himself and command to get into active duty at the front soon."[17] In France, as well as in New Jersey, the overage captain was given training assignments. He chafed for front-line duty, but so did another officer who excelled at training new men, Capt. Dwight D. Eisenhower. Eisenhower remained in the United States throughout the war, training other men for the AEF and fearing that his career was permanently damaged. At least Captain Wheeler reached France.

Late in May 1918 Wheeler injured a hand badly enough to be hospitalized for a few days. Soon afterward he learned that he had recently been indicted by a federal grand jury in Tucson on kidnapping charges related to the Bisbee Deportation. Although two dozen other men also were indicted, the case was titled *United States v. Harry Wheeler, et al.* Captain Wheeler promptly cabled a public reply to the indictment.

Wish my friends to know that I am anxious to protect them by again assuming all responsibility of deportation. Would do the same thing over again under same circumstances. No traitors or I.W.W. sympathizers over here, all American soldiers. My country needs me here now. When I can be spared, if still alive, will find myself ready to go home and stand with my friends and fellow Americans, undergo any tribulation for the deportation of the politicians, I.W.W. sympathizers and other traitors can inflict. The Eagles in France feel only contempt for the vultures at home but do not fear them.

Capt. Harry C. Wheeler[18]

Captain Wheeler continued to train the 350 men under his command, while persistently applying for transfer to the infantry. He managed to contact his brother, who soon moved out with the Rainbow Division for the front lines of Château-Thierry. On June 30, Captain Wheeler was stunned to receive orders to return immediately to the United States to answer legal charges. There were delays, though, and a couple of weeks passed while he maintained his training duties. Then, when about to embark in mid-July, he received from his commanding officer the orders he had wanted so fervently:

You have been designated by the commander in chief for duty with the front corps. This was based on your application and on the recommendation of the chief of the air service due to your special qualifications for service with combat troops at the front. The chief of the air service hopes that you will soon be able to complete the duty for which you are ordered to Washington and that the War Department may see fit to expedite your return to France at the front.[19]

This sketch of Capt. Harry Wheeler was widely published in Arizona newspapers. (Author's collection)

It was the ultimate frustration. At last, like his brother, he was assigned to the front lines. But first he had to leave France and journey to Arizona to answer charges stemming from the detested Wobblies. Captain Wheeler departed France at the beginning of a massive Allied offensive which would continue until the end of hostilities in November. Of course, the return to the United States may have saved Wheeler's life, but he must have been exasperated almost beyond endurance at missing the decisive action.

Mamie Wheeler received a cablegram on July 1 that Harry was ordered back to the United States, but she waited with growing anxiety before finally hearing from him again. She received a telegram on July 26 that Harry had "just arrived in Washington under special orders." He had landed in New York, then had traveled to Washington, no doubt hoping that somehow he might be sent back to France. But there would be no sudden return to the front. Captain Wheeler was granted "a short furlough," and on Sunday, July 28, Mamie and Sunshine left Tombstone to meet Harry in Alamogordo, New Mexico.[20]

Within a few days Harry, Mamie, and Sunshine returned to Tombstone. The captain was asked to speak about the war at the local Crystal Palace, as well as at Bisbee and Douglas. To his audiences and to reporters, Captain Wheeler praised the Red Cross and the food and, of course, his fellow soldiers. He urged everyone to write to anyone they knew in France, "for what they crave and clamor for is letters and mail from their loved ones at home." Captain Wheeler offered anecdotes about France and about the trips across the ocean. He spoke of how determined United States forces were to seize victory. "We are all confident that we will win this war and believe it is only a matter of time until the Hun is beaten," he stated. Then Wheeler expressed his frustration over having been pulled away from a combat role. "Let me go back and do my best at the front, and then when I come back let them try me before a jury of my American peers, and if they decide that I shall go to the penitentiary, Harry Wheeler will go. But not until I have served my country. I want to go back and am going as soon as possible and do my best. After that I don't care what they do with me."[21]

Wheeler would not go back. Legal action, not surprisingly, underwent long delays. The captain could have remained in France until the final shots were fired and he would not yet have been needed in court.

On August 21 he learned that his brother had been wounded in France. His sister in Florida had received a cablegram from the War Department that Lt. William D. Wheeler was wounded and would be invalided back to the United States. Although Sallie was provided no further details, she telegraphed Harry what she knew.[22] Undoubtedly, he was concerned about his brother, but secretly, perhaps subconsciously, Harry must have coveted for himself William's wound on the field of battle.

The day after receiving word of his brother's injury, Captain Wheeler was scheduled to travel to Washington to report for duty to the War Department. With the indictments pending further action, Wheeler hoped to be shipped back to France. He boarded a train in Tombstone on August 22, but within a few miles he received a telegram at the depot in Fairbank. Wheeler was ordered to report to General Cabell at Douglas, where he was told "to report to Fort Huachuca pending further orders." At Fort Huachuca he was attached to the Tenth Cavalry and sent to Nogales to head a machine gun company on the border until his legal trouble "is definitely settled."[23] While the AEF gradually overwhelmed German forces on the Western Front, Capt. Harry Wheeler commanded a machine gun company in Nogales, Arizona.

Mamie and Sunshine periodically traveled from Tombstone to Nogales, staying at the Bowman Hotel. On the night of October 25, Harry was driving his automobile on the Tucson-Nogales road, when the auto "turned turtle on a bad spot in the road," pinning Mamie beneath the car. Harry was unhurt, but it was feared that Mamie had suffered internal injuries. Harry and Mamie must have flashed back to Allyn's tragic auto accident in 1915. Mamie was only bruised, however, and she returned with Sunshine to Tombstone on November 3.[24]

On Monday, November 11, 1918, an armistice ended the combat of the Great War. Captain Wheeler, bored and exasperated with his humdrum assignment, immediately applied for a discharge. On Sunday, December 1, he visited his wife in Tombstone. Returning to Nogales, Wheeler was notified of his discharge, then quickly went back to Tombstone. During the next few days he visited Douglas "on business," lining up a job on the police force of "Smelter City." At this time Wheeler received word that the indictments in *United States v. Harry Wheeler, et al.*, after a lengthy review, had been dropped from federal court. Defense attorneys contended that no federal laws had been violated, and on December 2 this appeal was upheld: if there was any offense, it was to be pursued in the state court. Wheeler's discharge became official on December 19, 1918.[25]

During the Great War, Harry Wheeler attracted national attention with the Bisbee Deportation, which brought him unwanted repercussions. Finally obtaining an army commission, he came tantalizingly close to seeing combat before being sent back to Arizona. Now, with the war ended and his patriotic ambitions largely unfulfilled, Wheeler faced an immediate future which included an unhappy marriage, the possibility of more legal action, and a low-level law enforcement job. Now forty-three, this man who had experienced adventure and fame, tragedy and notoriety, may have felt that his best years were behind him. Harry Wheeler needed a rejuvenating new lease on life.

CHAPTER NINE

A New Family

"Let every man hoist his own colors and be true to them, be what they may. I am true to mine, and shall so remain."

—Harry Wheeler

The year 1919 began inauspiciously for Harry Wheeler. The former captain of the Arizona Rangers and three-term sheriff of Cochise County now was a "Special Officer" on the Douglas police force. Recently Wheeler had commanded 350 men as an army captain, but now he took orders from a municipal chief of police. While Mamie and Sunshine stayed at the Wheeler residence on Allen Street in Tombstone, Harry bunked on a cot at the Douglas City Hall. Every couple of weeks he traveled to Tombstone to visit his family.[1]

Wheeler was reunited on the Douglas police force with a former deputy. "Harry Wheeler and Percy Bowden have been employed by Douglas to help eradicate bootlegging there," explained the Tombstone *Prospector*. Wheeler was an old hand at thwarting bootleggers, and occasionally there was other action, such as apprehending an escapee from New Mexico's penitentiary in February.[2] But such activities provided little excitement or challenge or fame, and Special Officer Wheeler soon grew restless.

During this depressing period of his life, Harry Wheeler fell in love. The object of his affections was Jessie Leona Wills, a waitress at the Modern Café in Douglas. Jessie was a native of Georgia, born in Cornelia on February 24, 1901.[3] In 1919 she turned eighteen, while Harry was forty-three. Jessie was youthful and adventurous—she rode both horses and motorcycles—and already she had experienced a brief and unsuccessful marriage. (Jessie may have learned to ride a motorcycle during the two weeks that Harry worked traffic in

Douglas as a motorcycle cop.) Jessie found in Harry a handsome, mature man who was prominent and widely known for heroic deeds. Wheeler could provide an eighteen-year-old waitress with security and immediate advancement in social status. According to her descendants, Jessie developed a love for Harry that did not diminish during a widowhood that lasted more than half a century. As this young woman fell for Harry, he experienced a romantic ardor that he must have never expected to feel again. Excited and rejuvenated over this unlikely bonus to his life, Wheeler was reluctant to leave Jessie, and during his brief visits to Tombstone his heart stayed in Douglas.

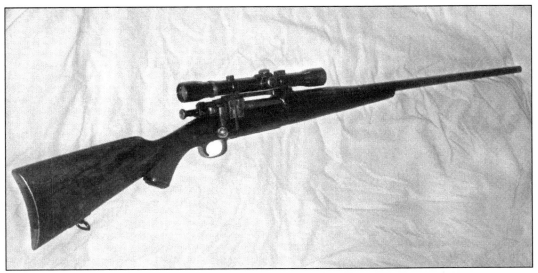

Harry Wheeler's target rifle. He was a highly successful, competitive marksman. (Courtesy Pam Hamlett, photo by Karon O'Neal)

Another activity which restored zest to Wheeler's life was his return to rifle competition. In 1917, with the United States at war, the Tombstone Rifle Club had enjoyed an increase in active members and in marksmanship scores. The qualifying scores, under National Rifle Association rules, produced seven "marksmen" (scores ranging from 160 to 189), three "sharpshooters" (190 to 209), and three "experts" (201 or higher). Wheeler, of course, was an expert at 222, but he was edged out as high gun by H.C. Almy.[4] During 1918 Captain Wheeler did most of his shooting on army ranges, but in 1919 he eagerly rejoined the Tombstone Rifle Club, now presided over by H.C. Almy, who soon would be elected president of the state association. In March a general call went out to all civilian and military teams to participate in the Arizona State Rifle Association matches, to be held on the Tucson rifle range on Saturday and Sunday, April 26 and 27. "Matches will be on the program for the big meet at from 200 to 1200 yard ranges, with eight big matches for trophies, medals and cash prizes. Revolver and pistol matches will also be held," the newspaper announced.[5]

The National Rifle Association

In 1871 a small group of National
Guard officers in New York organized the
National Rifle Association of America. "An association should be organized . . . to promote and
encourage rifle shooting on a scientific basis . . . ,"
wrote Col. William Church, one of the NRA's
founders.

For years the NRA promoted marksmanship and
helped train National Guardsmen. When the Great
War broke out, the NRA elevated military pre-
paredness and, with substantial aid from the national government, aggressively fostered marksmanship with the 1903 Springfield army rifle. The
government helped support the NRA national
shooting matches at Camp Perry, Ohio, twenty-five
miles east of Toledo. Camp Perry is located beside
Lake Erie, near the site of the naval victory led by
Commodore Oliver Hazard Perry during the War of
1812. When Harry Wheeler participated in shooting events at Camp Perry, the ranges were situated
so that spent bullets dropped harmlessly into the
water.

Approximately 300 participants from 120 Arizona rifle clubs gathered in Tucson for the state cup match. Tucson hosted the event with entertainments that included a boxing exhibition at the Armory and a banquet at the Santa Rita Hotel. Not surprisingly, Harry Wheeler "carried off the cup" and proved himself "the champion shot of the state." He was awarded a gold medal for high individual gun. Wheeler was modest by nature, but surely he took deep pleasure in claiming the state championship at a time in his life when he was dissatisfied with his work and his marriage. In a match on the Tombstone range on Sunday, June 1, Wheeler led a three-man team to victory over a Douglas team. And inevitably he was selected as one of seventeen members of the Arizona Civilian Rifle Team to compete in the National Rifle Shoot, to be held at the Navy Rifle Range at Caldwell, New Jersey, from August 4 through August 30, 1919.[6]

More than one thousand participants, civilian and military, were expected to compete in Caldwell. The federal government sponsored this event, providing "transportation, equipment, meals, and lodging." J.P. Sexton of Douglas acted as captain of Arizona's team; "Col. George J. Roskruge of Tucson, dean of rifle shots in Arizona, will go as quartermaster." Team members assembled in El Paso at the end of July, then traveled together to Chicago and on to New York, twenty miles from Caldwell. Some participants brought their wives, but by this time Wheeler's personal life was in turmoil, and he traveled alone.[7]

National matches had been held for years for military shooters, but not until 1916 were civilians permitted to compete. Working in conjunction with the National Rifle Association, which had been organized in 1871, the government during the war made "every effort to get the men in civil life to learn the use of the military arm." A Department of Civilian Marksmanship was established, distributing free ammunition, guns, and supplies to civilian rifle clubs, while selling these items to civilian members at the same prices the army was charged. (In November 1919, for example, "the Director of Civilian Marksmanship was good enough to slip something over 7,500 rounds of free ammunition" to the Tombstone Rifle Club.) Participants at Caldwell in 1919 were welcomed by the personable assistant secretary of the navy, Franklin D. Roosevelt: "All competitions must be open to civilians and they must receive the same consideration as the service men because in time of war our army and navy are made up not of service men, but of civilians."[8]

A reporter from the New York *Globe* found the Arizonans exotic and "most unique." The *Globe* reporter was especially impressed by Sheriff Wheeler of deportation notoriety, who "has retained his office for years by virtue of a quick draw, and by his ability with the gun." One member of the Arizona team attended a silent movie in New York, and in the crowded lobby he noticed "an especially attractive young woman [who] seemed to be in difficulty. I stepped up to her and asked if I could be of assistance." She thanked him, but said no and left. Moments later the Arizonan realized that his pocket had been picked.

Assistant Secretary of the Navy Franklin D. Roosevelt, shown here in his Washington office during World War I. FDR offered the official greeting to Harry Wheeler and more than 1,000 other participants at the 1919 National Rifle Shoot held at the Navy Rifle Range in Caldwell, New Jersey.

The Tombstone *Prospector* regarded this incident philosophically: "It is never safe to do the Sir Walter Rawleigh act outside of Good Old Arizona."[9]

The Arizona team arrived too late to sight their rifles, but they competed impressively, even though the match was plagued by rain and fog. There was a great variety of different matches. Harry Wheeler's performance was noteworthy, for example, in a "match consisting of 20 shots at 200 yards rapid fire and kneeling: 10 shots prone, 5 shots kneeling, 5 shots sitting at 500 yards." At the end of the matches, the *Prospector* proudly reported that "the Tombstone team emerged from the contest holding sixteenth place among the 72 rifle teams competing, only eight of which were civilian teams, the balance being made up of crack teams selected from the various branches of the army, navy and marines."[10]

For Harry Wheeler, the travel to state and national meets, the pleasures of socializing with fellow marksmen from across the land, the satisfaction of competing successfully at the highest level, provided high points in an otherwise disappointing and unhappy period of his life. Dissatisfied as a common police-man, he indicated in April 1919 that he expected "to complete his work in Douglas within the next couple of weeks, when he will return to Tombstone." But Wheeler lingered in Douglas for several weeks, and on June 1 he accepted a change of assignment, from special officer to motorcycle patrolman. But even getting to ride a motorcycle soon lost its appeal, and Wheeler resigned from the Douglas police force, effective June 15. He said that he was "tired" of law en-forcement, and he wanted to "make a living in some other way than by being a peace officer." Wheeler told the Tombstone *Prospector* that "he intended to take a month's vacation before entering business of any kind. He plans to go to the mountains and take life easy, hunting, fishing, and resting." Asked about his plans following this vacation, Wheeler said that he had not "definitely de-cided . . . , but will probably engage in the cattle business in this county."[11]

Unfortunately, Wheeler's return to Tombstone, according to his wife, proved tumultuous. Mamie claimed that for the past six years Harry had charged her "with being untrue and unfaithful to him," and during quarrels he "called her vile and vulgar names." During Harry's frequent absences from home, Mamie said that he would "leave her without money." On Friday, June 20, 1919, Mamie related that Harry accused her of "infidelity," then began packing his belongings, "threatening to leave [her] destitute." When she begged him not to leave, she stated that "he deliberately spit in her face, pushing her away and called her a whore [and] a bitch." According to her own account, Mamie became hysterical and dropped unconscious across the bed. Perhaps be-cause of some threat she had made, Harry thought that Mamie may have taken poison. He left the house and soon returned with a physician, who induced vomiting. Not detecting any poison, the doctor "pronounced her trouble Nervous Histeria [*sic*]" and recommended that Mamie be sent "where it was quiet and to a lower altitude."[12]

This prescription soon was adopted by the Wheelers. On Wednesday morn-ing, July 2, Mamie and Sunshine boarded a train for San Francisco, "where they will spend several months as guests of Mrs. Wheeler's sister, who lives there." Almost three weeks later, Harry journeyed to California. Mamie testified that "about July 20" Harry visited her, and during a quarrel he "violently struck her, and threw her across the room." He told her "that he had $8,000 on his per-son, and that he was going to leave her." Mamie "asked him to at least divide the money with her, which he refused, and said he never expected to see her again." The Tombstone *Prospector* reported that Wheeler returned to town on Sunday, July 27, then left to spend "several days in Douglas." From Douglas he proceeded on to El Paso, where the Arizona Rifle Team assembled to go to Caldwell, New Jersey.[13]

While he was away from Douglas, Harry stayed in touch with Jessie. For ex-ample, when he returned to Arizona from his unhappy visit to California, he wired Jessie in Douglas from the Tucson depot at 7:10 on the morning of July, 26, 1919: "Will arrive Tombstone noon. Please wire me there if convenient to

Jessie Wills Wheeler, Harry's spirited young wife and mother of three of his children. (Courtesy Pam Hamlett)

see you this evening. Otherwise I will go to Douglas tomorrow. Have much to tell you and would like to see you." Harry and Jessie were together in Douglas for only a few days before he had to leave again, this time with the State Rifle Team. But soon after arriving in New Jersey, Harry sent a postcard to Mrs. Jessie Wills, 913 16th St., Douglas, Arizona. "Hello, Jessie!" began his brief message.[14] When Wheeler returned from New Jersey, he stayed in Douglas. The cot at the Douglas city hall no longer was available to him, and it is not known where he found lodging, but surely he took his meals at the Modern Café.

According to Mamie, on October 2, 1919, Harry sent her a telegram refusing to send her any more money, or to in any way support her, and announced that if she came back home "he would leave the county." Mamie returned to Tombstone, obtained the services of an attorney, and filed for divorce in the Superior Court of Cochise County on October 14, 1919. Papers were served to Harry a week later. Mamie accused him of being "cruel and inhumane," and she recounted details of the June 20 and July 20 quarrels. But Mamie did not accuse Harry of infidelity, and in turn he did not contest her version of events. (Perhaps, then, he was not as "cruel and inhumane" as Mamie claimed). Even if Mamie's accusations were exaggerated, Harry may not have defended himself, on advice of attorney, as the quickest path to divorce.[15]

Their common property was listed as an automobile, furniture, and "goods," with a total value of $3,000, "and a large sum of money—about $12,000—that he kept in a New York City bank." Mamie was awarded $100 per month alimony, all furniture and half of all other property, and Harry also had to pay attorney and court costs. The divorce was finalized on October 30, 1919.[16]

How had Wheeler accumulated such a large sum of money, and why was it in New York? Mamie claimed that he had $8,000 in cash when he visited California. Perhaps he deposited most of his money in the New York bank. Possibly he had been saving for years, attempting to build up a substantial sum in a faraway place in anticipation of a divorce. Obviously, Mamie somehow knew about the New York account. But how could Harry accumulate $12,000 on a $4,000 annual salary, plus fees? The estate of his parents was negligible, but he had never purchased a house or other real estate, so it is possible he had managed to save a large portion of his income through the years. It is also possible that the copper mining companies, as rumor suggested, had placed a sum of money on deposit for Wheeler in New York. However he accumulated the $12,000, he had to split it with Mamie, according to the divorce decree. Wheeler retained $6,000 or so to begin a new life with Jessie.

In Arizona a divorced person could not remarry for one year, but Harry and Jessie had no intention of waiting that long. In December the couple traveled to El Paso, obtained a marriage license at the courthouse, and married on Wednesday, December 10, 1919. A telegram to Douglas informed friends, and the Tombstone *Prospector* was alerted. Out of deference to the highly respected former sheriff, there had been no newspaper stories about Wheeler's messy divorce, but a small item about the wedding mentioned: "HARRY WHEELER AGAIN MARRIES." Harry and Jessie moved into a house he rented in Douglas at 1224 10th Street.[17]

While Harry was juggling a love affair, a divorce, and a new marriage, he

Marriage license for Harry and Jessie, issued at El Paso on December 10, 1919.

also had to deal with recurring legal action about the Bisbee Deportation. For two years Cochise County Attorney John F. Ross and his successor, Robert N. French, had been compiling evidence to resurrect the deportation case. In July 1919 one of the deportees, Fred W. Brown, swore a blanket warrant charging more than 200 citizens with kidnapping. County Attorney French arranged to have the "biggest preliminary hearing ever held in the southwest" conducted in Douglas before Justice of the Peace William C. Jack. "One of the biggest theaters in Douglas will be used as a courtroom during the big joint hearings," explained the Tombstone *Prospector,* "Justice Jack's court being far too small to accommodate the hundreds who will attend." Since the law required every defendant to attend every session, and since most of these men were "business and professional men and miners in Bisbee, Warren and Lowell," it was decided to hold sessions in the theater-courtroom only in the afternoons so that business could be conducted in the mornings throughout the district. A train called the "Deportation Special No. 2" would leave Bisbee every afternoon at 12:10 and arrive at Douglas at 1:25, then commence the return journey each evening at 6:10 and pull into Bisbee at 7:25.[18]

Harry Wheeler, who was in New Jersey, and a few other defendants were absent. These men would be subject to individual hearings during the next month. The blanket hearings began in the Douglas theater on Monday afternoon, August 25. The mining companies provided a crack team of defense lawyers, headed by W.H. Burgess of El Paso. By September 9, Burgess had agreed to have his clients bound over to the Superior Court in Tombstone. Harry Wheeler, now back from New Jersey, was scheduled to appear before Justice Jack the following Monday, September 15, at 2:00. At that time Wheeler, through his attorney, waived preliminary formalities and was bound over. County Attorney French then revealed that he had intended to dismiss the kidnapping charges against Wheeler, since evidence had shown that "he was in no way connected with the planning of the deportation and that he only acted in his capacity as sheriff of Cochise County." The front-page headline in the Tombstone *Prospector* proclaimed: "WHEELER ASKS TO BE BOUND OVER; COUNTY ATTORNEY HAD INTENDED TO DISMISS HIS CASE."[19]

Wheeler responded a day later to French's surprising announcement. Once again Wheeler tried to assume complete responsibility: "I insisted upon being bound over for trial yesterday on the charge of kidnapping because I am the man responsible for the deportations." He cited the proclamation he had issued on July 12, 1917, as proof of his responsibility. "I have never denied my part in the deportations and I am willing and wish right now that all of the citizens arrested and bound over so far would be released and I alone be held to trial for any wrong that may be charged. The majority of the citizens who took part in the deportations were my deputies and whatever they did was in discharge of their duties as deputy sheriffs in my posse."[20]

Despite Wheeler's protestations, French eventually decided to drop the charge against the popular ex-sheriff. When a list of 211 defendants was published on January 21, 1920, Wheeler's name was not included. On that date the defendants gathered at Tombstone's ornate old courthouse to enter their pleas. "The defendants alone filled the courtroom to capacity," reported the *Prospector,* "while spectators either remained standing or out in the lobby." For the first time in many years, the streets of the declining town teemed with activity. "Tombstone presents an appearance similar to the days when she held first place among the cities of the southwest, as the greatest mining camp," the newspaper described.[21]

By early February 1920, County Attorney French had decided to try one defendant at a time. The highly respected Harry Wheeler would have been an obvious target of the first trial, which may be why French dropped the charges against him, but now the former sheriff would be a key witness. A defendant of decidedly lower profile, Bisbee hardware merchant H. E. Wootten, would be tried for kidnapping deportee Fred W. Brown. Hundreds of potential jurors were examined before a jury finally was seated, on March 10. A day later, in his opening argument, W. H. Burgess contended that "self-defense" and "necessity" were the principles under which the defendants had acted. "The right of a community to defend itself against aggressors whether armed or unarmed, who may imperil the lives and property of that community, is a principle established by law and rooted in the very nature of human existence." Burgess then explained that necessity is "the maxim that the safety of the public is the supreme law."[22]

Judge S. L. Pattee took the opening arguments under considerations for a number of days. On Wednesday, March 24, 1920, Judge Pattee read his decision in court (thirty-five double-spaced typewritten pages). He denied the right of defendants to show self-defense for the deportation, but the defense would be allowed to prove necessity. On this basis the trial of H. E. Wootten would be conducted. Former sheriff Wheeler took the stand on Monday, March 29, and he would testify in this familiar courtroom for three days. Wheeler began by describing in detail the conditions and events which led to the deportation. At one point he refrained from reciting "an epithet" he had heard "on account of the presence of ladies," so the women were ushered out of the courtroom.[23]

Wheeler stressed that "he asked for aid from state and Federal governments," but he was left to his own resources. IWW leaders issued threats, and Wheeler's deputies reported "that among the Mexicans were many ex-Villa soldiers and they had arms and ammunition cached away." Wheeler decided that as sheriff "he would have to strike first or the law abiding citizens would be stricken." But Wheeler "considered it an impossibility to arrest and hold 1,000 men in jail . . . [and] he wanted to get the men out of Bisbee to stop killing or bloodshed and had no other means in his power to cope with the situation." The questioning of the former sheriff continued until shortly before 5:00, when he was turned over to the state for cross-examination. After a brief conference, the court recessed until 10:00 the following morning.[24]

Wheeler spent all of Tuesday on the witness stand, undergoing a "grilling cross-examination . . . by County Attorney R. N. French." French questioned the

Capt. Harry Wheeler Again Takes Responsibility For the Deportation

An old photo illustrated another attempt by Wheeler to assume all responsibility for the Bisbee Deportation. (Tombstone Prospector, May 1, 1920)

former sheriff about details regarding numerous individuals, at one point making accusations which Wheeler rejected as "false statements." While French tried to establish conspiracy by attributing various acts to different defendants, Wheeler continued to assume all responsibility. Finally, French sarcastically stated, "'I am not trying to deprive you of any laurels, Mr. Wheeler,' to which the witness heatedly replied: 'Mr. French, I want no laurels.'" Judge Pattee interceded "with a strong admonishment of both." Following recess for lunch, the duel between Wheeler and French continued all afternoon. In reply to one query, Wheeler replied with satisfaction: "My government comes first and everything afterward. I would sink the whole Warren district for my government."[25]

On Wednesday French examined "numerous details connected with almost every phase of the situation." French was attempting "to show that conditions in the district from the time of the arrival of Mr. Wheeler . . . grew better instead of worse, but this was denied by the witness, who stated he believed conditions grew worse." After lunch, French continued to grill Wheeler into the afternoon of the third day.[26]

Following the long struggle between Wheeler and French, a parade of witnesses testified about numerous happenings before and during the deportations. Governor Thomas E. Campbell was summoned by the state on April 26, and during his testimony he brought telegrams from his files, including messages from Harry Wheeler. The appearance of Governor Campbell, of course, was a "big drawing card." During closing arguments on April 30, French pointedly said, "Wheeler is only the goat for the companies and the other defendants. He said he would take care of Wheeler and has told Wheeler so."[27]

The case went to the jury early that evening. After enduring weeks of testimony, the jury deliberated only seventeen minutes before arriving at a verdict on the first ballot. "About 7 o'clock the word spread about the city that the jury had arrived at a verdict and in a few moments the courtroom was crowded to overflowing," reported the Tombstone *Prospector*. Wootten was declared not guilty, but French immediately launched plans for a "blanket trial."[28]

The next day, Saturday, May 1, Wheeler issued a lengthy public statement. "CAPT. HARRY WHEELER AGAIN TAKES RESPONSIBILITY FOR THE DEPORTATION," proclaimed a *Prospector* headline above a large photo of the lawman astride a horse. "Do I ever regret my actions? Do I still believe the deportations to have been necessary?" Wheeler answered his own questions. "I can truthfully say I regretted then, and I regret now, that necessity made the deportation the only possible solution of a danger, national and local, too great to be faced without state or federal aid." After expanding his statement, Wheeler emphasized his main point: "I regret the necessity—I do not regret the action taken. Was it the only course? No. There was one other course: To have awaited the inevitable conflict of thousands of armed men in those narrow, winding streets of Bisbee." After reiterating what had become standard statements of his regarding the deportation, Wheeler staunchly declared his personal philosophy: "A man can but determine the right or wrong of a thing according to the influence of his own conscience. This I have done. I stand by what I did. Let every man hoist his own colors and be true to them, be what they may. I am true to mine, and shall so remain."[29]

A few days after the trial, the Tombstone *Prospector* announced that the jurors "are unanimous in their opinion that the deportation was justified." For example, Fred Brown of Willcox said that after hearing the evidence, "I, for one, feel that Harry Wheeler and the citizens of the Warren District did what they thought was right and necessary." Eldorado cattleman B. K. Riggs spoke for his fellow jurors: "I think that we all wished that our one verdict could have spiked the prosecution of all the cases." Such opinions boded ill for the "blanket trial." Scheduled for June, W. H. Burgess obtained a postponement until November. The Cochise County Board of Supervisors did not want to spend more money on pointless trials, and legal action in the Bisbee Deportation finally was discontinued.[30]

Harry Wheeler spent so much time in Tombstone that he once more began participating in the local rifle club. In May he was part of a five-man team that competed in the state meet at the Tucson Rifle Club range. The meet opened with a dinner at the Tucson Country Club, and Governor Campbell was present throughout the meet. "The Tombstone team was composed of the three Harry C's, Wheeler, Kendall and Almy, James F. McDonald and Norman Abel." Wheeler, who certainly had experienced numerous recent distractions, was unable to repeat as state champion. But for the second year in a row the Tombstone Rifle Club produced Arizona's state champ. Harry Almy won "the gold medal and the individual state championship," while the Tombstone team "made a splendid showing, winning six trophies out of a total of twenty." Wheeler was selected to the state team that traveled to Camp Perry, Ohio, in August for the National Rifle Association matches. Wheeler did not distinguish himself, but the Arizona team performed competitively.[31]

By June 1920 a number of Wheeler's Cochise County friends were urging him to run for sheriff in the Democratic primary. Knowing that some potential candidates would not enter the primary if he did, Wheeler publicly invited them to run, announcing "my determination against seeking office this year." Wheeler expressed gratitude to those who had supported him, then left the door slightly ajar by saying that he wanted "to allow politics this year, at least, to go its own way."

In July, Harry and Jessie traveled to possible ranch sites as he contemplated becoming a cattleman. It was a buyer's market, because much of Arizona's rangeland suffered from drought. By September Harry had bought a ranch in the Chiricahua Mountains near tiny Rucker. When the primary elections were held on Tuesday, September 7, 1920, Wheeler could not resist the excitement, and spent several days in Tombstone. Although Wheeler had shrugged off any suggestion of again running for sheriff, clearly he remained interested in politics.[32]

Within two more weeks, range conditions were so dry that Cochise County ranchers began shipping their cattle to Texas ranges. Wheeler, who had no experience as a cattleman, stayed busy at his ranch. He came out of the mountains briefly on Monday, December 20. "Harry Wheeler, former sheriff and now operating a cattle ranch in the Chiricahua Mountains," reported the *Prospector*, "was in Tombstone yesterday for a short while, returning to his home in the afternoon." Three weeks later Wheeler, "accompanied by Mrs. Wheeler," came into Tombstone for Saturday shopping. Although four inches of snow fell near Rucker in February, the grasslands were still dry. With little winter moisture, the range was in bad shape in April. But early in April Wheeler sold his cattle interests, although he had found a certain charm in living in the Chiricahuas which he would not forget.[33]

Apparently Wheeler had taken time from his ranching chores to hone his shooting eye. At the 1921 state meet, held at Fort Huachuca on Friday and Saturday, May 6 and 7, Wheeler won the "50-yard slow and rapid pistol event," and he recorded the third highest individual grand aggregate score. Now apparently living in Tombstone, Wheeler was selected to the fourteen-man civilian team for the national meet in Camp Perry, Ohio (Arizona also sent a fourteen-man National Guard team in 1921). But the civilian team did not fare as well as usual at Camp Perry. "The Arizona team composed of 12 men, has eight Douglas men on it," remarked the Tombstone *Prospector*. "Two of Arizona's best shots were unable to attend and seriously handicapped the team." Wheeler is not mentioned in the numerous *Prospector* stories about the Camp Perry events, so evidently he was one of "Arizona's best shots" who was "unable to attend."[34]

Harry and Jessie had their first child in 1921, William J. "Jack" Wheeler. In the spring of 1922 Harry announced his candidacy for the Democratic nomination for sheriff of Cochise County. A major factor in his decision to run for another term doubtless was the $4,000 salary, now that he had a new family to support. He also may have missed the authority that he had exercised in one capacity or another—cavalry sergeant, Ranger captain, sheriff, and army cap-

A Life of Service

U.S. Cavalry, private, sergeant (1897-1902)
Arizona Rangers, private, sergeant, lieutenant,
    captain (1903-1909)
Cochise County, deputy sheriff (1909)
U.S. Customs, mounted inspector (1909-1911)
Cochise County, sheriff (1911-1918)
U. S. Army, captain (1918)
Douglas Police Department (1919)

tain—throughout much of his life. James F. McDonald, chief deputy of Cochise County, and Henry C. Bohmfalk, constable of Lowell, also challenged for the nomination. In the September primary, Bohmfalk collected 1,052 votes, Wheeler 2,093, and McDonald 2,697. Wheeler, whose popularity clearly had been damaged by the deportation controversy, lost the Democratic nomination by more than 600 votes. In November McDonald defeated the Republican candidate by just 400 votes.[35]

Wheeler moved his family to a rented house in Douglas at 1367 13th Street, where they would live for the next couple of years. Wheeler tried to develop a mining lease, although there had been severe layoffs and the industry was in decline in the district. Harry and Jessie welcomed a daughter, Jessie Jacqueline Wheeler, in 1923. In October 1923 Wheeler "purchased the famous peach orchard of H. S. Buckley in Cochise Stronghold, consisting of 70 acres . . . , the consideration being placed at $12,000." The Tombstone *Prospector* explained that the "Buckley orchard is famous for its delicious fruits, which is grown entirely by sub-irrigation, and thousands of tons of fruit are marketed yearly." Wheeler intended to "take charge of the place immediately."[36] A cabin was located there, nestled against a cliff in the Cochise Stronghold of the Chiricahuas.

Wheeler continued to try to develop mining properties, operating for a time in 1924 from an office in Bisbee with a partner. In February 1924 Wheeler "sustained a broken leg while working on his lease in Bisbee yesterday," noted the *Prospector*. "He was taken to the C. & A. Hospital, where he will be confined for some time."[37]

Soon Jessie was pregnant again, and another son, Robert W. "Bobby" Wheeler, was born in December 1924. Sadly, the baby died three months later and was buried at Lowell's Evergreen Cemetery. Wheeler had lost another son, although a little boy and girl remained healthy at home. Soon after his son's death, Wheeler moved his family to a rented house at 600 Hoveland in Warren, not far from Evergreen Cemetery. He belonged to the Bisbee Elks Lodge and the Bisbee Masonic Lodge, and he maintained a membership in the Douglas American Legion. "Wheeler was especially active in the Bisbee rifle club, and seldom a Sunday passed that did not find him on the range, participating in the weekly shooting matches," related the Bisbee *Review*. "The famous ranger never lost his marksmanship ability and was considered the best shooting eye on the local team."[38]

Wheeler turned fifty on July 23, 1925. The last few years had been prosaic for a man who was accustomed to prominence and responsibility. There had been a divorce, controversial trial proceedings, the loss of a baby boy, an election defeat, and uncertain economic developments. Although he had entered his fifties and seemed to be going nowhere, at least he had a loving young wife, a son and daughter, and a legion of friends.

In December 1925, however, Wheeler fell ill. Within a few days he developed pneumonia and was taken to the nearby Calumet and Arizona Hospital.

Harry and Jessie, along with Jack and baby Jessie, lived in this house at 1367 13th Street in Douglas in 1922 and 1923. (Photo by Karon O'Neal)

The front door of Harry and Jessie's home at 600 Hoveland in Lowell. (Photo by Bill O'Neal)

Jack and little Jessie were ages four and two when their father died. (Courtesy Pam Hamlett)

The 50-bed Calumet and Arizona Hospital, where Harry died in 1925 and where Allyn was hospitalized in 1915. From the front of the C&A Hospital the Wheeler home at Hoveland can be seen (in the direction of the viewer). (Photo by Bill O'Neal)

From the hilltop hospital, Jessie Wheeler could look down at her house. She had lost a baby in March, and now the "attending physicians held little hope for [Harry's] recovery." The high altitude contributed to his respiratory difficulties, and he died on Thursday, December 17. The following Saturday at 4:30 a military funeral was held from his home, conducted by members of the Spanish-American War Veterans and American Legion posts of both Douglas and Bisbee.[39]

"A FRIEND TO EVERYONE," proclaimed a eulogy in the Bisbee *Review* on the day of his funeral. "No man in the public life of the county or state was loved and admired more than the former ranger and sheriff of Cochise, for even his few enemies honored him for his bravery and fairness. . . . Wherever he went, the late Captain Wheeler made friends. Of a quiet disposition, he possessed a personality that made one feel his presence the moment he arrived. None of the numerous tales of his physical prowess and success in capturing fearless fugitives of justice . . . were told by Captain Wheeler, for he was modest almost to a fault, and the stories of his exciting adventures were spread by admiring friends." The *Review* commented upon how "well-deserved" were the military honors about to be bestowed over his grave: "all that is mortal of him will be lowered from the sight of man forever, but memory of the quiet, unassuming, brave, friend-to-every-one will live long, long after the echoes of the plaintive bugle notes and the reverberation of the final salute are silenced by distance."

The young widow moved with her two children to the cabin in the Cochise Stronghold. One day in 1927, upon returning from a three-mile walk with her children to the post office, they found the house on fire. The only possession

In December 1925 Harry Wheeler was buried (center) beside his baby boy, Bobby (right). More than half a century later Jessie Wheeler Adams (left) joined Harry and Bobby in Evergreen Cemetery. (Photo by Karon O'Neal)

Jessie could reach was a Navajo rug. Everything else was lost in the flames, and there was no insurance. Neighbors took her to a nearby home, but she soon moved to Douglas. There she was courted by a border patrolman named Happy Adams. Jessie and Happy married in 1929, and he was a kind and loving stepfather to Jack and little Jessie. Never losing her love for Harry Wheeler, after half a dozen years she divorced, never to remarry. A self-reliant woman, Jessie treasured Harry's guns and documents (stored elsewhere and thus saved from fire), and these family treasures were handed down to her daughter.[40]

Jessie died of a heart attack in 1977 at the age of seventy-six. She was buried in Evergreen Cemetery, beside Harry and little Bobby. Harry's legacy was carried on by his descendants. His son Jack was wounded in the Pacific during World War II, who then served with the Border Patrol, the Arizona Highway Patrol, and the Arizona Game and Fish Commission before his death in 1982. Jack shot competitively, and so did his daughter, Debbie Wheeler. Another of Harry's granddaughters, Pam Hamlett, works as an adult probation officer and is a firearms instructor. Harry Wheeler would be proud.

Jack and Jessie Wheeler, not long after the untimely death of their father. (Courtesy Pam Hamlett)

Jack Wheeler, with his wife Fern and their three daughters, visiting Harry's grave. (Courtesy Pam Hamlett)

There are substantial remains of the nineteenth-century military posts where Harry was reared. The 1882 courthouse at Tombstone is a major tourist attraction, and many other structures remain from Wheeler's years there. Bisbee appears much the same as it was during the first years of the twentieth century. The stone foundation and chimney of the cabin in the Cochise Stronghold are still there, and so is the orchard (of quinces, not peaches). Harry and Jessie's final home still is inhabited, and so are other houses of theirs in Douglas. The C&A Hospital, where Harry died, has been converted into apartments. A handsome gravestone in the Evergreen Cemetery reads:

CAPT. HARRY C. WHEELER
JULY 23, 1875
DECEMBER 17, 1925
BORN JACKSONVILLE, FLA.

Contemporary Arizona Rangers have proudly added a bottom line:

ARIZONA RANGERS 1903-1909.

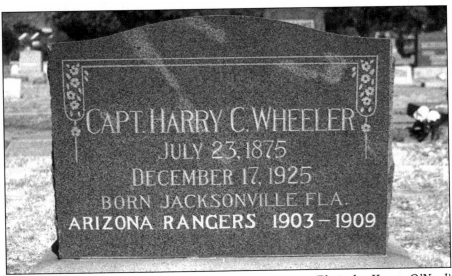

(Photo by Karon O'Neal)

Endnotes

Introduction to a Lawman

1. The shooting in the Palace Saloon is described in the Tucson *Daily Citizen,* October 31 and November 5, 1904.

Chapter One: Early Life on the Frontier

1. This biographical information was repeatedly given by Wheeler on documentary inquiries throughout his life, except for his second marriage license, when he wed a woman a quarter century his junior. Correspondence with authorities in Jacksonville—letter from Priscilla R. Smith, supervisor, Certification Unit, Officer of Vital Statistics, State of Florida, February 18, 1985, and letter from S. Morgan Slaughter, clerk of the Circuit Court, Duval County, Florida, February 11, 1985—uncovered no birth records for Harry Wheeler. Until further research reveals a different date and place, these birth statistics must suffice.

2. For a detailed record of Wheeler's military career, see William B. Wheeler, Military Personnel Record, National Personnel Records Center (NPRC), St. Louis, Missouri. Colonel Wheeler's descendants hold his degree from the U.S. Military Academy, his commission, and his promotions. An obituary for Harry Wheeler (Bisbee *Daily Review,* December 16, 1925), stated that his father "saw service in both the Civil War and Spanish-American wars." Entering West Point in 1867, Colonel Wheeler might have enlisted late in the Civil War, but his service record does not indicate service prior to 1867.

3. Utley, *Frontier Regulars,* 16-24.

4. Hart, *Old Forts of the Northwest,* 177-178.

5. *Ibid.,* 140-142.

6. Robinson, *Frontier Forts of Texas,* 47-48.

7. *Ibid.,* 26-28; Simmons, *Fort Ringgold: A Brief Tour.*

8. Arizona historian Joseph Miller wrote, in a biographical sketch in Miller, *The Arizona Ranger,* 141-143, that Wheeler "attended a military school" and that "he was rejected by the United States Military Academy because of his not being quite tall enough, much to his distress."

9. Robinson, *Frontier Forts of Texas,* 72-78; Hart, *Old Forts of the Southwest,* 25-29.

10. Wheeler enlistment document, April 1, 1897. A letter from United States Military Academy Assistant Archivist Kenneth W. Rapp (February 11, 1985) provided the qualifications for USMA candidates during the 1890s.

Chapter Two: Family Man and Cavalryman

1. Wheeler enlistment document, April 1, 1897.
2. Hart, *Old Forts of the Southwest,* 116-119.
3. Cavalry uniforms, equipment, and weapons are described and illustrated in meticulous detail by Randy Steffen in *The Horse Soldier,* Vol. III (1881-1916).
4. Records from Comanche County, Oklahoma, go back only to 1901 (letter from Jamie Mitchell, district court clerk, Lawton, Oklahoma, June 3, 1951), but the Wheeler wedding date is recorded in their 1919 divorce case. Allyn Wheeler's birthdate is found on his gravestone in the City Cemetery in Tombstone, Arizona.
5. Bisbee *Review,* December 16, 1925; Tombstone *Prospector,* October 6, 1917; El Paso *Herald* quoted in the Tombstone *Prospector,* July 5, 1917. Heitman, *Historical Register,* Vol. II, 449, cites Companies A, B, C, D, E, G, I and K in action during June and July in Cuba.
6. Pvt. William Wheeler kept a daily journal for time following his enlistment. The journal is in the possession of family members.
7. *Ibid.*
8. Wheeler Enlistment Papers, National Archives.
9. *Ibid.* For information on the Fourteenth Cavalry and Col. Lebo, see Heitman, *Historical Register*, Vol. I.
10. Hart, *Old Forts of the Far West,* 154-156; Heitman, *Historical Register,* Vol. II, 503.
11. Harry Wheeler, Certificate of Disability for Discharge, September 4, 1902, and Discharge Papers, September 22, 1902, National Archives.

Chapter Three: Arizona Ranger

1. Harry Wheeler, biographical file, Arizona Historical Society.
2. Hunt, *Cap Mossman,* 143-145.
3. The best account of the creation of the Rangers was related by contemporary observer and Ranger historian Mulford Winsor, "The Arizona Rangers," *Our Sheriff and Police Journal,* 49-50.
4. The act creating the *Rangers is in Revised Statutes, Arizona Territory, 1901,* Chapter II, "Arizona Rangers," 833-836.
5. Mossman's acquaintance with the 1895 Winchester is described in Hunt, Cap Mossman, 121-122. Also see Ernenwein, "Lucky Star," *Ranch Romances,* 44. An excellent photographic description of this rifle may be studied in Rattenbury, "A Portfolio of Firearms," *American West,* 44.
6. Act No. 64 expanding the Ranger company is in *Acts, Resolutions and Memorials, Twenty-second Legislative Assembly 1903,* 104-106.
7. Wheeler's enlistment papers are in his personnel file in the State Archives in Phoenix. Rynning's praise is in Wheeler's personnel report, July 6, 1905. Wheeler was informed of his promotion to sergeant in a letter from Governor Brodie, October 15, 1903.
8. The shooting in the Palace Saloon is described in the Tucson *Citizen,* October 21 and November 5, 1904.
9. For Wheeler's aborted pursuit, read the Tucson *Citizen,* November 1, 1904.
10. Tucson *Citizen,* October 21, 1904.
11. Willcox is described in Schultz, *Southwestern Town.*
12. Tucson *Citizen,* April 20, 1905.
13. The Ranger arrest of Hobbs is detailed in the Tucson *Citizen,* April 10, 1905.
14. *Border Vidette,* June 3, 1905.
15. Tucson *Citizen,* July 14 and 28, 1905.
16. *Ibid.,* August 11, 1905.
17. Rynning's inspection trip is described in the Tucson *Citizen,* August 11 and September 20, 1905.

18. Tucson *Citizen,* October 16, 1905.

19. The murder of Plunkett and Kennedy was reported in the Tucson *Citizen,* July 22, 1905.

20. The organization of a Ranger pursuit posse is described in the Tucson *Citizen,* August 7, 1905. Also see the personnel files of Hickey and Shute.

21. Ranger personnel records.

22. The story of the rigorous search through Sonora was related by Wheeler in 1910 to a reporter for the Tucson *Star,* quoted in Miller, *Arizona Rangers,* 109-115.

23. For the story of Wheeler versus the Douglas criminals, see the Tucson *Citizen,* January 24, 1906.

24. For Wheeler's apprehension of Howard, see the Tucson *Citizen,* January 29, 1906.

25. For Wheeler's clash with Jiminez, and the resulting correspondence between Rynning and Torres, see the Douglas *Dispatch,* a 1906 issue quoted in Miller, *Arizona Rangers,* 126-127.

26. Eperson's hearing and exoneration are reported in the *Border Vidette,* August 18, 1906, and the Tucson *Citizen,* August 6 and 10, 1906.

27. Tucson *Citizen,* August 10, 1906.

28. Tucson *Citizen,* August 17, 1906.

29. The background of Silverton, Tracy, and their paramour was reported in the Bisbee *Review,* March 1, 1907, and the Tucson *Citizen,* March 2 and 4, 1907. Reddoch's comments may be found in the *Border Vidette,* 363, in Peck memoirs. These three sources provide the best description of the Tracy-Wheeler duel. In addition see: Rynning, *Gun Notches,* 278-282; Winsor, "The Arizona Rangers," *Our Sheriff and Police Journal,* 58-59; Tucson *Citizen,* February 28, 1907.

30. Bisbee *Review,* March 1, 1907.

31. *Ibid.*

32. Tucson *Citizen,* March 4, 1907.

33. Wheeler's recuperation and refusal of the reward was reported in the Tucson Citizen, June 25, 1907, and in Ligitt, *My Seventy-Five Years Along the Mexican Border,* 53.

Chapter Four: Ranger Captain

1. Millay's resignation was reported in the Tucson *Citizen,* February 19, 1907. Rynning's appointment and arrival in Yuma were reported in Rynning, *Gun Notches,* 320, and the *Border Vidette,* March 30, 1907.

2. Sheriff White to Governor Kibbey, January 23, 1907.

3. Predictions of Wheeler's promotion may be found in the Tucson *Citizen,* February 19 and 28, 1907. Wheeler's promotion is confirmed in his Ranger personnel file.

4. The improving moral climate of Douglas was remarked upon in the Tucson *Citizen,* December 2, 1905.

5. Interesting descriptions of Naco are in the Citizen, September 26, 1901; December 24, 1902; June 12, 1906; Liggitt, *My Seventy-Five Years along in Mexican Border,* 25; and Peterson, "Naco," *American West.* Wheeler's baseball challenge was reported in the *Citizen,* August 10, 1907.

6. General Orders, June 1, 1907, Ranger Records, Arizona State Archives, Phoenix. In a June 2 letter to the governor, Wheeler stated: "I have the honor to enclose, for your consideration, General Orders one to seven, of this year." But only six orders are pinned to this letter. "General Order # 6," however, was originally typed # 7, suggesting that Wheeler simply miscounted before the strikeover was made.

7. For Wheeler's scrupulous observance of border protocol, see his letter to Sims Ely, June 8, 1907.

8. Wheeler to Governor Kibbey, June 2, 1907.

9. *Ibid.*

10. *Ibid.*, August 15, 1907.

11. Enlistments and discharges under Wheeler are detailed in the personnel records.

12. The Emett controversy may be followed in: [Illegible] to B.F. Saunders December 1, 1907; [Illegible] to E.S. Clark (December 5, 1907); B.F. Saunders to Judge John J. Hawkins, December 9, 1907. These letters are in the Ranger correspondence in the Arizona State Archives.

13. Wheeler to Sims Ely, October 24, 1907.

14. *Ibid.*

15. The arrest records and personnel records prove Larn's disappointing performance. Larn dated his letter of resignation December 3, 1907, but this date was scratched out and someone, in a clearly different style of handwriting, wrote in "January 4, 1908." Larn's personnel file records his resignation as December 21, 1907. Larn's letter, addressed to "Cap C H Wheeler," reads:

"Pleas Except my resignation as territorial Ranger. I will make out my Report for Dec. 1907 as soon as Mr. W A Olds returns from Clear Creek

Yours very Truly
W A Larn"

On January 11 Wheeler forwarded Larn's resignation to the governor, commenting: " I never saw this man Larn, he was enlisted by Lieut. Old." Old apparently was deeply disappointed in Larn's performance; Wheeler gathered that the erstwhile undercover man was "not deserving of a good discharge." Wheeler to Governor Kibbey, January 11, 1908.

16. For the Olney-Wheeler confrontation, see Olney to Wheeler, November 18, 1907, and Wheeler to Governor Kibbey, November 26, 1907, in Olney's personnel file.

17. McDonald to Wheeler, November 23, 1907.

18. Wheeler to Governor Kibbey, November 26 and 27, 1907.

19. Wheeler's personnel file.

20. Wheeler to Sims Ely, May 19, 1907.

21. *Ibid.*

22. Ranger performance in the latter months of 1907 may be studied in the monthly reports for August, October, November, and December.

23. Wheeler's desire to station his men in pairs was related in his Monthly Report, July 1908. Beaty's corroborating remark is quoted in the *Border Bidette,* 365, in Peck memoirs.

24. Wheeler requested a machine gun in letters to Governor Kibbey, July 18 and 27, 1907.

25. The 1907 attempts to abolish or reduce the Rangers may be followed in the Tucson *Citizen,* February 26 and March 4, 1907. Kibbey is quoted in *Report of the Governor of Arizona,* 1907, "Arizona Rangers," 13-14.

26. The act preventing "Steer Tying Contests" was described in the Tucson *Citizen,* April 3, 1907.

27. Bisbee *Review,* April 14, 1907.

28. *Ibid.*

29. Criticism against gamblers ("men of the green table") quoted from the Tucson *Citizen,* November 23, 1904.

30. Descriptions of the Nogales resistance to the anti-gambling laws are described in letters from Kidder to Wheeler, May 16, 1907, and from the Arizona attorney general to Kidder, June 14, 1907.

31. Captain Wheeler discussed the situation in two letters to Governor Kibbey, August 27 and 29, 1907.

32. The problem in Yuma was described in: Frank Wheeler to Harry Wheeler, November 23, 1907; and Peter Robertson to Governor Kibbey, September 7, 1907. For resistance elsewhere in the territory to anti-gambling efforts, see: Harry Wheeler to Governor Kibbey,

November 25, 1907; Wheeler's monthly reports for October, November, and December 1907.

33. Detailed information on Mother Jones, see: Jones, *Autobiography of Mother Jones*; Atkinson, *Mother Jones, The Most Dangerous Woman in America; Fetherling, Mother Jones, The Miners' Angel.*

34. Mother Jones's arrival in Arizona was described in the Tucson *Citizen,* February 22, 1907.

35. For the story of the Sarabia kidnapping, see: Tucson Citizen July 3, 1907; Bisbee *Review,* 1907 issue quoted in Miller, *Arizona Rangers,* 147-154.

36. Jones, *Autobiography,* 139.

37. Sarabia's fate is described in Miller, *Arizona Rangers,* 155-156.

38. The ominous situation in El Cubo was described in the Tucson *Citizen,* September 16, 1907.

39. The formation and progress of the posse was reported by Captain Wheeler in a letter to Governor Kibbey, September 14, 1907. Also see Miller, *Arizona Rangers,* 163-170.

40. Wheeler described his attempt to halt the roulette game in Naco in two letters to Governor Kibbey, February 3 and 7, 1908. Wheeler's confrontation with the saloon owners was reported in the Tucson *Citizen,* February 13, 1908.

41. Wheeler's activities and Hayhurst's trip to Texas were reported in Wheeler to Governor Kibbey, January 9 and 22, 1908.

42. Wheeler's stopover in Yuma was reported in Wheeler to Governor Kibbey, January 31, 1908.

43. Wheeler to Governor Kibbey, January 14, 1908.

44. For Gunner's undercover activities, see: Gunner to Wheeler, February 29, 1908; Peter Robertson to Wheeler, February 21, 1908; Wheeler to Sims Ely, February 23, 1908.

45. Gunner to Wheeler, February 29, 1908; and Robertson to Wheeler, February 28, 1908.

46. Gunner to Wheeler, March 3, 1908.

47. *Ibid.*

48. *Ibid.,* March 5, 1908.

49. The dismayed complaints of Gunner and Robertson are in: Gunner to Wheeler, March 5, 1908, and Robertson to Wheeler, March 5, 1908.

50. Gunner to Wheeler, March 5, 1908.

51. Wheeler to Governor Kibbey, March 7, 1908.

52. *Ibid.,* March 16, 1908.

53. *Border Vidette,* December 8, 1906.

54. For Jeff Kidder's background and traits, see: Tucson *Citizen,* April 4, 1908; DeArment, "Arizona Ranger Jeff Kidder," Tombstone *Epitaph,* 9-11; Arcus Reddoch, in the *Border Vidette,* 345, 359, 360, in Peck memoirs.

55. The quotations about Kidder's marksmanship are in the Tucson *Citizen,* April 6, 1908. Kidder had his name engraved on the back strap of his fancy Colt. He sent this gun (serial number 246844) back to the factory late in 1907 and it was returned in mid-January 1908. During the interim, Kidder carried a single-action Colt .45 with a four-and-three-quarter-inch barrel. Late in her life Jeff's mother gave one of his Colts to a collector in San Jacinto, California. See Donoho, "Death of an Arizona Ranger."

56. The shooting is described in the Bisbee *Review,* December 31, 1906.

57. *Border Vidette,* February 15, 1908.

58. For Kidder's actions against the "undesirables," see the *Border Vidette,* March 28, 1908.

59. For the recent complaints against Kidder, see: Willson, "Sergeant Jeff Kidder," *Arizona Republic*; and Wheeler to Governor Kibbey April 8, 1908.

60. Willson, "Sergeant Jeff Kidder," *Arizona Republic.*

61. The account of the shooting and Kidder's final hours are taken from: Bisbee *Review,* April 4, 1908; Tucson *Citizen,* April 4 and 6, 1908; Wheeler to Governor Kibbey, April 8, 1908. Also see Donoho, "Death of an Arizona Ranger."

62. Bisbee *Review,* April 4, 1908.

63. For speculation and motivation about Kidder having been trapped, see the Tucson *Citizen,* April 6, 8, and 24 and May 1, 1908.

64. The disposal and condition of Kidder's body were related in Bisbee *Review,* April 5, 1908; Tucson *Citizen,* April 6, 1908; Wheeler to Governor Kibbey, April 8, 1908.

65. Citizen Wheeler to Governor Kibbey, April 8, 1908.

66. For the sad ride of Wheeler and his men into Bisbee, see: Wheeler to Governor Kibbey, April 8, 1908; and Bisbee *Review*, April 7, 1908.

67. Bisbee *Review,* April 8, 1908.

68. Kidder's funeral services were described in the Tucson *Citizen,* April 8, 1908. For the plight of Jip see the Bisbee Review, April 5, 1908, and the Tucson *Citizen,* April 30, 1908.

69. Bisbee *Review,* April 4, 1908.

70. For the recovery of Kidder's recovery and badge, see Wheeler to Governor Kibbey, April 10, 13, and 15, 1908.

71. Tucson *Citizen,* April 24, 1908.

72. *Ibid.*

73. Wheeler to Governor Kibbey, April 9, 1908.

74. *Ibid.,* April 12, 1908.

75. *Ibid.,* May 7, 1908.

76. This account of the Arnett shooting is taken from Wheeler's seven-page report of the incident—Wheeler to Governor Kibbey, May 7, 1908—and from the Tucson *Citizen,* May 6, 1908 and the Bisbee *Review,* May 7, 1908. Also see Egerton, "A Brazen Horse Thief," *Arizona Republic,* July 12, 1981.

77. Bisbee *Review,* May 7, 1908.

78. For Heflin as an informer, see Wheeler to Acting Governor John H. Page, May 11, 1908.

79. A copy of Heflin's agreement with Wheeler is in the Ranger correspondence.

80. Heflin's revelation that Ells aided Arnett is in Wheeler to J.F. Cleaveland, June 10, 1908. Heflin's disclosure about the high Mexican official is in Wheeler to J.F. Cleaveland, May 15, 1908. For the exodus of wary bad men, see Wheeler to Cleaveland, May 16 and 19, 1908.

81. Wheeler to J.F. Cleaveland, May 19 and 29, 1908, and Wheeler to Governor Kibbey, May 26, 1908.

82. Wheeler to J.F. Cleaveland, June 4 and 6, 1908.

83. For the organization of Wheeler's posse, the enlistment of Humm, the leaves of absence, and the trek into Mexico, see Wheeler to J.F. Cleaveland, June 4, 9, and 10, 1908, and Humm personnel file.

84. Wheeler to J.F. Cleaveland, June 19, 1908.

85. *Ibid.*

86. Downing's troubles with Speed are described in the Bisbee *Review,* May 7, 1908, and Tucson *Citizen,* August 5, 1908.

87. Wheeler to Sims Ely, February 5, 1908, and Wheeler to Governor Kibbey, February 2, 1908. Speed's reenlistment and demotion are verified in his personnel file.

88. General Order # 5, June 1, 1907.

89. Wheeler quoted his instructions to Speed in a letter to Governor Kibbey, August 7, 1908.

90. For details of the shooting, see: Bisbee *Review,* August 5, 1908; Tucson *Citizen,* August 5, 1908; and Proceedings of the Coroner's Jury, August 5, 1908.

91. Wheeler's telegram was wired to Governor Kibbey on August 5. The quote from Wheeler about Downing is from a detailed report, Wheeler to Governor Kibbey, August 7, 1908.

92. Wheeler's discussion of the likely move of various Rangers to other offices was in Wheeler to Sims Ely, February 23, 1908.

93. Wheeler to Sims Ely, February 23, 1908.

94. Wheeler to Governor Kibbey, June 30, 1908.

95. Wheeler to J.F. Cleaveland, August 25, 1908.

96. For the outbreak of criminal activities in Naco in the absence of Rangers, see Wheeler to Governor Kibbey, October 16, 1908.

97. For Wheeler's soul-searching in regard to Chase, see, in order: Wheeler to J.F. Cleaveland, November 2, 1908; Wheeler to Governor Kibbey, November 4, 1908.

98. Wheeler's disillusionment with Gunner was recorded in: Wheeler to Governor Kibbey, November 30, 1908; and Gunner's personnel file. In Gunner's fitness report, Wheeler stated that he was "a good man when not drinking."

99. For Wheeler's reaction to Black's arrest of his brother-in-law, see Wheeler to Governor Kibbey, August 19, 1908. For Wheeler's decision to discharge Black, see Wheeler to Governor Kibbey, August 19, 1908. For Wheeler's decision to discharge Black, see Wheeler to Governor Kibbey, November 30, 1908.

100. See A.E. Ehle's personnel file. For Anderson's resignation, see Wheeler to Governor Kibbey, May 7, 1908.

101. The termination of Fraser is reported in Wheeler to Governor Kibbey, July 10, 1908. For Wheeler's conflict with Bates, see: J.F. Cleaveland to Wheeler, August 5, 1908, and Bates personnel file.

102. Wheeler's anti-Texan feelings are described in letters to Sims Ely, January 11, 1908; Governor Kibbey, February 2, 1908; and Sims Ely, February 5, 1908.

103. The peculiar circumstances of Horne's termination may be studied in: Wheeler to Governor Kibbey, April 27, 1908; Horne's discharge papers; and Wheeler to J.F. Cleaveland, April 29, 1908.

104. Wheeler's request for Springfields is outlined in a letter to Governor Kibbey, October 1, 1908. His request for bloodhounds is in the Monthly Report, October 1908, 2-3.

105. Wheeler's pleas to be allowed to make extensive inspection trips were made in two letters to Governor Kibbey, August 19 and October 1, 1908.

106. Wheeler's October sweep was described in his report to Governor Kibbey, October 25, 1908. Other forays are frequently mentioned in correspondence and newspapers.

107. Wheeler to J.F. Cleaveland, August 22, 1908.

108. The October capture of a horse thief was reported to Governor Kibbey, October 25, 1908.

109. Wheeler to Governor Kibbey, August 7, 1908.

110. Monthly Report, August 1908.

111. Wheeler to Governor Kibbey, August 4, 1908.

Chapter Five: The Last Ranger

1. For Wheeler's 1908 request to go to Florida, see: Telegram, Wheeler to Governor Kibbey, April 15, 1908; Wheeler to Governor Kibbey, April 15, 1908. For Wheeler's decision not to go, see Wheeler to J.F. Cleaveland, September 4, 1908.

2. Wheeler, William B., Service Record, National Archives. For the death of Colonel Wheeler, see the Tucson *Citizen*, December 3, 1908.

3. Wheeler to Governor Kibbey, January 1, 1909; Telegram, Governor Kibbey to Wheeler, January 2, 1909.

4. Wheeler to Governor Kibbey, January 3, 1909.

5. For Wheeler's activities prior to departure, see Wheeler to Governor Kibbey, January 3, 1909.

6. The family items that Harry Wheeler brought back to Arizona remain in the possession of his descendants.

7. For the dismissal of McGee and King, see: Wheeler to Governor Kibbey, January 25 and 26, 1909; personnel file, McGee; personnel file, King.

8. For Wheeler's inquiry about the letters of support, see Wheeler to J.F. Cleaveland, January 26, 1909.

9. Telegram, Acting Governor John J. Page to Wheeler, January 27, 1909.

10. For the situation in Globe, see: Telegram, Wheeler to J.F. Cleaveland, January 28, 1909; Telegram, Wheeler to J.F. Cleaveland, January 29, 1909; Telegram, J.F. Cleaveland to Wheeler, January 29, 1909; Telegram, Wheeler to J.F. Cleaveland, January 30, 1909.

11. Tom Gadberry's personnel file.

12. For the Rangers as a campaign issue, see: Tucson *Citizen,* January 14, 1909; Winsor, "Arizona Rangers," *Our Sheriff and Police Journal,* 61.

13. Tucson *Citizen,* November 13, 1908.

14. *Ibid.,* November 19, 1908.

15. *Ibid.,* January 13, 1909.

16. For the Democratic caucus, see: *Arizona Republican,* February 16, 1909; Winsor, "Arizona Rangers," *Our Sheriff and Police Journal,* 61. For first-day activities of the Assembly, see the Tucson *Citizen,* January 18, 1909.

17. The full text of the governor's Tuesday message is given in the Tucson *Citizen,* January 19, 1909.

18. For Weedin's introduction of the bills to abolish the Rangers and the office of public examiner, see the Tucson *Citizen,* January 23, 1909. For the Deputy Ranger bill, see the *Citizen,* January 16, 1909.

19. For an example of Democratic criticism of the Rangers, see the *Arizona Republican,* February 16, 1909.

20. Tucson *Citizen,* January 25, 1909.

21. Winsor, "Arizona Rangers," *Our Sheriff and Police Journal,* 61.

22. Tucson *Citizen,* January 29, 1909.

23. *Ibid.,* January 30, 1909.

24. Wheeler described the decline in Ranger morale and the perceived increase in crime in two letters to Governor Kibbey, February 6 and 10, 1909. For the letter from his headquarters clerk, see Emil Lenz to Acting Governor John H. Page, February 3, 1909.

25. Wheeler to Governor Kibbey, February 5, 1909.

26. For Wheeler's offer to resign, see: Wheeler to Governor Kibbey, February 5, 1909; Tucson *Citizen,* February 8, 1909. For Wheeler's invitation to Phoenix, see Telegram, J.F. Cleaveland to Wheeler, February 11, 1909.

27. The Tucson Chamber of Commerce plea was reported in the Tucson *Citizen,* February 12, 1909. For samples of other support for the company, see the Ranger correspondence for February 1909; "do all in your power . . . ," quoted from Marshall Young to Governor Kibbey, February 9, 1909.

28. Slaughter's statement of support was run in the Tucson *Citizen,* February 3, 1909. Mossman's plea was in the *Citizen,* February 8, 1909, and Wheeler's appeal was in the *Citizen,* February 11, 1908.

29. Finley's letter to the editor was published in the Tucson *Citizen,* February 12, 1909. The editorial reply came in the *Citizen,* February 13, 1909.

30. For hope that the caucus might relent, see the Tucson *Citizen,* February 15, 1909.

31. The return of the bills to each house, the text of the governor's veto message, and the subsequent legislative action is described in: *Arizona Republican,* February 15, 1909.

The official text of the governor's message is in *Legislative Journals, Territory of Arizona,* 1909, 94-21.

32. *Arizona Republic,* February 16, 1909.

33. Ranger expenses were declared in Report of the Governor of Arizona, 1908, "Arizona Rangers," 23.

34. *Arizona Republican,* February 16, 1909.

35. Section 3 of the abolishment bill is quoted from *Acts, Resolutions and Memorials, Twenty-fifth Legislative Assembly,* 1909, Chapter 4:3.

36. Ranger arrests on the last day were reported in Wheeler's Monthly Report (February 1909).

37. Bisbee *Review,* quoted in Miller, *Arizona Rangers,* 225.

38. Wheeler to Governor Kibbey (both letters are dated February 17, 1909).

39. The seventeen-page handwritten January report is in the Ranger correspondence. Wheeler mentions his Oliver typewriter in a letter to Governor Kibbey, February 19, 1909.

40. Wheeler's letter is quoted in Miller, *Arizona Rangers,* 223-225; G.L. Coffee, February 18, 1909, and J. Frank Wootton, February 19, 1909, were among those who wrote to Governor Kibbey.

41. Monthly report, February 1909.

42. For Wheeler's discharge and the accompanying letter, see Governor Kibbey to Wheeler, March 25, 1909.

Chapter Six: Sheriff of Cochise County

1. Wheeler's service as a mounted inspector is outlined on two handwritten cards deposited in the Customs Service Index to Letters Sent and Received, 1902-1912, Records of the Bureau of Customs, Record Group, 36, National Archives.

2. Wheeler discussed his political prospects in a letter to Sims Ely, February 23, 1908.

3. Tombstone *Prospector,* September 21 and October 7, 1911.

4. *Ibid.,* October 31, 1911.

5. *Ibid.,* December 2, 4, and 5, 1911.

6. *Ibid.,* December 13 and 27, 1911 and January 30, 1912: Wheeler Bond, February 7, 1912.

7. For a study of the sheriff's office in Arizona, see the master's thesis of Charles A. Hollister, "The Organization and Administration of the Sheriff's Office in Arizona," 32-60.

8. Tombstone *Prospector,* February 14, 1912.

9. *Ibid.,* February 15 and 16, 1912.

10. *Ibid.,* February 16, March, 1, 2 and 4, and December 6, 1912.

11. *Ibid.,* March 25 and November 11, 1912.

12. *Ibid.,* June 8 and July 15, 1912.

13. *Ibid.,* November 26, 1912.

14. *Ibid.,* December 20, 1912.

15. *Ibid.,* December 9, 1912, and January 17 and 18, 1913. The first mention of Sunshine as the Wheelers' "daughter" was in the *Prospector,* April 12, 1913.

16. *Ibid.,* April 22, 25, 26, 1913.

17. *Ibid.,* ,May 10 and July 28, 1913.

18. *Ibid.,* August 1 and September 2, 1913.

19. *Ibid.,* September 3 and 8, and October 23, 1913.

20. *Ibid.,* April 2, 7, November 8, 1913, and June 23 and 24, 1914.

21. *Ibid.,* March 18, September 24, December 1, 1914.

22. *Ibid.,* April 28 and 29, May 4 and 17, 1914.

23. *Ibid.,* October 6 and December 4, 1913, and April 8, 1914.

24. *Ibid.,* April 8, 1914.

25. *Ibid.,* May 12, 13, 16, and 18, 1914.

26. *Ibid.,* December 28, 1913, and June 20, and September 8, 1914.

27. *Ibid.,* July 28, August 8, 10, 20 and 31, 1914.

28. *Ibid.,* September 9, 10, 16 and 24, October 8 and 24, November 2, 5, 6 and 7, and December 31, 1914.

29. *Ibid.,* November 21, 1914.

30. *Ibid.,* December 30, 1914.

31. *Ibid.,* November 5 and 6, 1914.

32. *Ibid.,* June 4 and 8, October 23, November 6 and 26, and December 23, 1914.

33. *Ibid.,* April 9, 12, and 14, 1914.

33. *Ibid.,* October 3, 6, 8, 26, and 28, 1914.

35. *Ibid.,* March 6, 1915.

36. *Ibid.,* March 15, 1915.

37. *Ibid.,* May17, June 8, and September 7, 1915.

38. *Ibid.,* December 15, 1916.

39. The accident is described in the *Prospector,* March 23, 1915.

40. *Ibid.*

41. *Ibid.,* March 24 and 27, April, 3, 4 and 10, 1915.

42. *Ibid.,* July 31, August 2 and 24, 1915.

43. *Ibid.,* October 15, 22, and 25, 1915.

44. *Ibid.,* October 28 and 31, 1915.

45. *Ibid.,* October 31, 1915.

46. *Ibid.,* October 30, and November 3, 4 and 5, 1915, and April 14, 1916.

47. *Ibid.,* October 12 and December 28, 1915.

48. *Ibid.,* June 27, 1916.

49. *Ibid.,* July 29, 1916.

50. Tombstone *Prospector,* August 19, September 7, 8, 9, 11, 12, and 25, and October 10, 25, and 26, and November 18 and 27, 1916.

51. *Ibid.,* March 28 and June 26, 1916.

52. *Ibid.,* June 21, July 18, November 27 and 28, and December 1, 10, 18, and 23, 1916.

53. *Ibid.,* February 7 and 15, 1917.

54. *Ibid.,* March 7, 1917.

55. *Ibid.*

56. *Ibid.,* March 7 and 10, 1917.

Chapter Seven: The Bisbee Deportation

1. Tombstone *Prospector,* April 3, 7, 9, and 23, 1917.

2. *Ibid.,* April 3 and May 10, 1917.

3. Tombstone *Prospector,* May 10 and 11, and June 23, 1917. Harry Wheeler Service Record, National Archives. Wheeler was paid $73.99 for travel expenses at 3½ cents per mile.

4. James W. Byrkit created a monumental study which featured the Bisbee Deportation: *Forging the Copper Collar, Arizona's Labor-Management War of 1901-1921,* published by the University of Arizona Press in 1982. See p. 69 for details on Arizona's mining production.

5. Byrkit, *Forging the Copper Collar,* 146.

6. Byrkit provides a description of the IWW and intrigues against the Wobblies in *Forging the Copper Collar,* 126-143.

7. *Ibid.,* 168-177; Tombstone *Prospector,* July 11, 1917.

8. Tucson *Daily Citizen,* July 12, 1967.

9. Tombstone *Prospector*, September 20, 1916.

10. Beeman, "History of the Bisbee Deportation," 2-3.

11. *Ibid.*, 2, 4.

12. *Ibid.*, 2, 4-5.

13. Douglas *Dispatch* editorial, reprinted in the Tombstone *Prospector,* July 2, 1917.

14. Tombstone *Prospector,* July 3, 1917; Beeman, "History of the Bisbee Deportation," 5.

15. Beeman, "History of the Bisbee Deportation," 5-6.

16. *Ibid.*, 6.

17. "Deportations From Bisbee," pamphlet written soon after the deportation, on file at the Arizona Historical Society; Tombstone *Prospector,* July 18, 1917.

18. Beeman, "History of the Bisbee Deportation," 7-8.

19. *Ibid.*, 8-9.

20. "Deportations From Bisbee," 2; Bisbee *Review,* July 12, 1917.

21. Bisbee *Review,* July 12, 1917.

22. "Deportations From Bisbee," 3.

23. Byrkit, *Forging the Copper Collar,* 194-200.

24. "Deportations From Bisbee," 3; Byrkit, *Forging the Copper Collar,* 200.

25. "Deportations From Bisbee," 4.

26. Beeman, "History of the Bisbee Deportation," 10.

27. Tombstone *Prospector,* July 13 and 14, 1917.

28. Bisbee *Review,* reprinted in Tombstone *Prospector,* July 18, 1917.

29. Tombstone *Prospector,* July 20, 1917.

30. Byrkit, *Forging the Copper Collar,* 210-215; Tombstone *Prospector,* July 13 and 23, 1917.

31. Tombstone *Prospector,* July 12, 1917.

32. *Ibid.,* July 18, 1917.

33. *Ibid.*

34. *Ibid.*

35. *Ibid.,* July 14 and 19, and August 2, 1917.

36. *Ibid.,* July 23, August 1, September 10 and 13, 1917.

37. *Ibid.,* August 18, 20 and 25, 1917.

38. *Ibid.,* August 16 and September 14 and 15, 1917.

39. *Ibid.,* September 15, 1917.

40. *Ibid.,* August 20, 1917.

41. *Ibid.,* November 8, 1917. See also "The President's Commission at Bisbee," *New Republic,* December 8, 1917.

42. Tombstone *Prospector,* November 8, 1917.

43. *Ibid.,* October 19 and 22, 1917.

44. Bisbee *Ore,* reprinted in the Tombstone *Prospector,* August 4, 1917.

45. The banquet was described, including Wheeler's remarks, in the Bisbee *Review,* December 6, 1917. Also see Bruere, "Copper Camp Patriotism," *Nation,* 203.

Chapter Eight: Captain in the Great War

1. Tombstone *Prospector,* October 6, 1917.

2. Bisbee *Review,* December 6, 1917; Special Orders No. 24, Reserve Officers' Training Camp, Presidio of San Francisco, June 7, 1917.

3. Harry Wheeler, Service Record, National Archives; Harry Wheeler, Arizona National Guard enlistment form, April 18, 1908; Tombstone *Prospector,* September 10, 1917; Douglas *International,* reported in the Tombstone *Prospector,* November 16, 1917.

4. Tombstone *Prospector,* August 16 and November 22, 1917.

5. *Ibid.,* October 6, 1917.

6. *Ibid.,* October 30 and November 16, 1917.

7. The Powers-Sisson manhunt was a front-page story in Arizona newspapers for a month in 1918. The Tombstone *Prospector* describes Sheriff Wheeler's activities in detail in the following issues of 1918: February 11, 12, 13, 14, 16, 18, 19, 20, 21, 25, 26, 28, March 9. Also see, for aftermath and trial, March 12, 22, May 18, 23, June 11, August 12. There also is a useful file on the brothers and their life in prison.

8. Tombstone *Prospector*, February 11, 12, 15, 16, 18, 19, 20, and 21, 1918.

9. *Ibid.,* March 9, 1918.

10. *Ibid.,* February 26, 1918.

11. Tucson *Sun,* March 25, 1960.

12. Tombstone *Prospector,* February 23 and March 4, 1918.

13. *Ibid.,* March 11 and 13, and April 2, 1918.

14. *Ibid.,* March 9 and April 4, 1918. For uniform details see Gawne, *Over There! The American Soldier in World War I.*

15. Tombstone *Prospector,* April 4, 1918.

16. *Ibid.,* April 11 and 22, 1918.

17. *Ibid.,* May 23, 1918.

18. *Ibid.,* June 10 and 19, 1918.

19. *Ibid.,* August 1, 1918.

20. *Ibid.,* July 26 and 28, 1918.

21. *Ibid.,* August 1, 3, and 5, 1918.

22. *Ibid.,* August 21, 1918.

23. *Ibid.,* August 23, 1918.

24. *Ibid.,* October 10 and 25, November 4, 1918.

25. *Ibid.,* December 2 and 8, Byrkit, *Forging the Copper Collar,* 288-289.

Chapter Nine: A New Family

1. The Tombstone *Prospector* mentions Wheeler's visits on January 29, February 13, March 15 and 31, April 19, May 8, and June 9 and 24, 1919. The *Douglas City Directory, 1919,* 147, lists "Harry Wheeler, policeman" residing at city hall.

2. Tombstone *Prospector,* January 29 and February 21, 1919.

3. J essie's descendants know little about her early life, but birth information is on her marriage license in El Paso.

4. Tombstone *Prospector,* January 15, 1918.

5. *Ibid.,* March 31, April 21, and May 29, 1919.

6. *Ibid.,* April 21 and 28, May 29, June 2 and 6, and July 22, 1919.

7. *Ibid.,* July 28 and 30, and August 4, 1919.

8. *Ibid.,* November 13, 1919.

9. *Ibid.,* August 27 and September 10, 1919.

10. *Ibid.,* August 14, 21, 26, and September 3 and 18, 1919.

11. *Ibid.,* April 19, June 17 and 24, 1917.

12. *Mamie O. Wheeler v. Harry C. Wheeler,* Divorce Proceeding, Superior Court of Cochise County, October 14, 1919.

13. *Ibid.;* Tombstone *Prospector,* July 2 and 29, 1919.

14. Telegram, Wheeler to Jessie Wills, July 26, 1919; postcard, Wheeler to Mrs. Jessie Wills, August 6, 1919. Both items are in the possession of family.

15. *Mamie O. Wheeler v. Harry C. Wheeler,* Divorce Proceeding, Superior Court of Cochise County, October 14, 1919.

16. *Ibid.*

17. Harry C. Wheeler and Jessie Leona Wills, Marriage License, El Paso County, Texas,

December 10, 1919; Tombstone *Prospector,* December 11, 1919; *Douglas City Directory, 1920,* 149.

18. Tombstone *Prospector,* August 20 and 23, 1919.

19. *Ibid.,* September 9, 13, and 15, 1919.

20. *Ibid.,* September 17, 1919.

21. *Ibid.,* January 8 and 21, February 2, 1920.

22. *Ibid.,* February 2, 3, 12, and 16, and March 10 and 12, 1920.

23. *Ibid.,* March 29, 1920.

24. *Ibid.*

25. *Ibid.,* March 30, 1920.

26. *Ibid.,* March 31, 1920.

27. *Ibid.,* April 6, 7, 9, 15, 26, and 30, 1920.

28. *Ibid.,* May 1, 1920.

29. *Ibid.*

30. *Ibid.,* February 13, May 6 and 26, June 2, 1920.

31. *Ibid.,* May 8 and 10, July 19 and 24, August 7, 13, 16, 17, and 26, September 2 and 14, 1920.

32. *Ibid.,* July 15, September 6 and 9, 1920.

33. *Ibid.,* September 22 and December 21, 1920, and January 15, February 8, April 4 and 7, 1921.

34. *Ibid.,* February 19, May 7 and 9, August 2 and 13, September 22, 1921.

35. *Ibid.,* September 15 and November 10, 1922.

36. *Douglas City Directory, 1922,* 110; *Douglas City Directory, 1923,* 106; Tombstone *Prospector,* October 20, 1923.

37. *Bisbee Business District Directory, 1924-1925,* 151; Tombstone *Prospector,* February 21, 1924.

38. Bisbee *Review,* December 16, 1925.

39. *Ibid.,* December 17, 1925.

40. Family information was provided to the author by Harry Wheeler's granddaughter, Pam Hamlett.

Bibliography

Documents

The Arizona State Archives, Phoenix, houses the Arizona Ranger files and has collected the material in four boxes: *Box One*—Enlistment and discharge papers; *Box Two*—Miscellaneous correspondence; *Box Three*—Salary claims; *Box Four*—Expenses, receipts, and other financial data. *Note:* Ranger correspondence was stored in the basement of the old Capitol. On August 21, 1921, Cave Creek flooded west Phoenix, completely cutting off the Capitol and filling the basement with water. All documents were a soggy mass, and within a week reams of various papers had been spread out to dry on the Capitol grounds. High winds came up, and among the documents that blew away were the first six years of Ranger correspondence. Thirty-six letters survive from 1907; more than 160 from 1908; and about fifty from 1909. A majority of the letters are from Capt. Harry Wheeler to Governor Joseph Kibbey or his secretary. Many of the other letters are from the governor's office to Wheeler, while there is a scattering of miscellaneous correspondence. Also included are sixteen monthly reports from 1907 to 1909.

The Arizona Historical Society, Arizona Heritage Center, Tucson, maintains a mine of information about the Rangers. A large Ranger file has been collected, biographical information is available on many Rangers, and a great variety of related materials are on deposit. There also is a substantial file on Harry Wheeler.

Acts, Resolutions, and Memorials, Twenty-second Legislative Assembly, 1903. Act 57, p. 93.

Acts, Resolutions, and Memorials, Twenty-second Legislative Assembly, 1903. Act 64, secs. 1-10, pp. 104-106.

Acts, Resolutions, and Memorials, Twenty-second Legislative Assembly, 1903. Act 4, p. 3.

General Orders (6) for the Arizona Rangers from Captain Harry Wheeler. June 1, 1907. Arizona Ranger Correspondence File, State Archives.

Governor's Message, "The Arizona Rangers," to the Twenty-fifth Legislative Assembly, 1909, pp. 22-23.

Mamie O. Wheeler v. Harry C. Wheeler, October 14, 1919, Superior Court Records, Cochise County Courthouse, Bisbee, Arizona.

"Message of Governor Joseph H. Kibbey to the Council of the Twenty-fifth Legislative Assembly," *Journal of the Twenty-fifth Legislative Assembly, 1909,* pp. 94-111; reply of Councilman Thomas F. Weedin, pp. 111-122.

Report of Captain Burton Mossman of Arrests Made by Arizona Rangers from October 2, 1901 to June 30, 1902.

Revised Statutes of the Arizona Territory, 1901. Pars., 3213-30, pp. 833-836.

U.S. Dept. of the Interior, *Report of the Governor of Arizona to the Secretary of the Interior,* "Arizona Rangers," 1902, 1903, 1904, 1905, 1906, 1907, 1908, 1909.

Wheeler, Harry C., Mounted Inspector. Customs Service, Index to Letters Sent and Received, 1902-1912. Records of the Bureau of Customs, Record Group 36, National Archives.

Wheeler, Harry C. Military Personnel Record. National Personnel Records Center, St. Louis, Missouri.

Wheeler, Harry C. Official Bond, $10,000, February 20, 1912. United States Fidelity & Guaranty Company, San Francisco.

Wheeler, Harry C. Official Bond, $10,000, January 4, 1915. United States Fidelity & Guaranty Company, San Francisco.

Wheeler, Harry C., and Jessie L. Wills. Marriage License, December 10, 1919. Office of the County Clerk, El Paso County Courthouse, El Paso, Texas.

Wheeler, William C. Military Personnel Record, National Personnel Records Center, St. Louis, Missouri.

Manuscripts and Theses

Bassett, James H. "Reminiscences." Typescript in Arizona Heritage Center, Tucson.

Beeman, William S. "History of the Bisbee Deportations." Typescript available at the Arizona Historical Society, Tucson.

Cox, Annie M. "History of Bisbee, 1877 to 1937." Master's thesis, University of Arizona, Tucson, 1938.

"Deportations From Bisbee." Pamphlet on file at the Arizona Historical Society, Tucson.

Hollister, Charles A. "The Organization and Administration of the Sheriff's Office in Arizona." Master's thesis, University of Arizona, Tucson, 1946.

Pearce, Joe, and Richard Summers. "Line Rider." Lengthy transcript available at the Arizona Heritage Center, Tucson.

Peck, Arthur (Artisan) Leslie, Sr. Memoirs. Biographical Files, Arizona Heritage Center, Tucson. Lengthy transcript contains numerous excerpts from the Nogales *Border Vidette*.

"Reminiscences of Sam Hayhurst," as told to Mrs. George F. Kitt, September 27, 1937. Biographical Files, Arizona Heritage Center, Tucson.

Wheeler, William D. Diary, 1898. In possession of Pam Hamlett, Tucson.

Letters

Miscellaneous correspondence available at the Arizona Heritage Center, Tucson:

Bassett, J.H., to Mulford Winsor (February 14, 1936, and March 15, 1936).

"C P C" to Harry Wheeler (September 23, 1925).

Donoho, Ron, to Lori Davisson (December 3, 1982).

Hopkins, Arthur A., to Mulford Winsor (April 28, 1936).

Letter from Joe Pearce (1937).

Mitchell, Jamie, District Court Clerk, Comanche County, Lawton, Oklahoma, to the author (June 3, 1985).

Pearson, Pollard, to Mulford Winsor (December 1936).

Rapp, Kenneth W., United States Military Academy Assistant Archivist, to the author (February 11, 1985).

Rynning, Thomas, to Joe Pearce (October 1903).

Slaughter, S. Morgan, Clerk of the Circuit Court, Duval County, Florida, to the author (February 11, 1985).

Smith, Priscilla R., Supervisor, Certification Unit, Office of Vital Statistics, State of Florida, to the author (February 18, 1985).

Interviews

Barnes, Will C., interviewed by Mulford Winsor (May 12, 1936).

Hamlett, Pam, interviewed by the author in Tucson, Arizona (July 10, 2002).

Mossman, Burt, interviewed by Will C. Barnes at the Raleigh Hotel, Washington, D.C. (April 17, 1935).

Pace, Scott, interviewed by the author in Solomon, Arizona (March 12, 1983).

Payne, John, interviewed by the author in Naco, Arizona (March 12, 1983).

Zearing, Wally, interviewed by the author in Benson, Arizona (March 13, 1983).

Newspapers

Apache County Independent News
Arizona Blade and Florence Tribune
Arizona Daily Star
Arizona Journal Miner
Arizona Republic
Arizona Silver Belt
Bisbee *Ore*
Bisbee *Review*
Clifton *Copper Era*
Coolidge *News*
Courtland *Arizonian*
Douglas *American*
Douglas *Dispatch*
Douglas *International*
Graham County Advocate
Los Angeles *Times*
Navajo Apache Independent
Nogales *Border Vidette*
Phoenix *Democrat*
Phoenix *Gazette*
Phoenix *Tribune Sun*
Roswell *Daily Record*
Solomonville *Bulletin*
Tombstone *Epitaph*
Tombstone *Prospector*
Tucson *Citizen*
Tucson *Star*
Yuma *Sun*
Miscellaneous Obituary Files, Arizona Heritage Center, Tucson, Arizona

Books

Atkinson, Linda. *Mother Jones, The Most Dangerous Woman in America*. New York: Crown Publishers, Inc., 1978.

Bailey, Lynn R. *Bisbee: Queen of the Copper Camps*. Tucson: Westernlore Press, 1983.

Ball, Larry D. *The United States Marshals of New Mexico and Arizona Territories, 1846-1912*. Albuquerque: University of Oklahoma Press, 1978.

Bellah, James Warner. *Reveille*. Greenwich, CT: Fawcett Publications, Inc., 1962.

Bisbee Business City Directory, 1924-25.

Brent, William, and Milarde Brent. *The Hell Hole*. Yuma, AZ: Southwest Printers, 1962.

Burgess, Opie Rundle. *Bisbee Not So Long Ago*. San Antonio: Naylor Company, 1967.

Byrkit, James W. *Forging the Copper Collar, Arizona's Labor Management War of 1901-1921*. Tucson: University of Arizona Press, 1982.

Chisholm, Joe. *Brewery Gulch*. San Antonio: The Naylor Company, 1949.

Colquhoun, James. *The History of the Clifton-Morenci Mining District*. London: John Murray, 1924.

Coolidge, Dane. *Fighting Men of the West*. New York: E.P. Dutton & Co., Inc., 1932.

Cosulich, Bernice. *Tucson*. Tucson: Arizona Silhouettes, 1953.

Douglas City Directory, 1919, 1920, 1921, 1922, 1923, 1924, 1925.

Eisenhower, John S. D., Yanks, *The Epic Story of the American Army in World War I*. New York: The Free Press, 2001.

Erwin, Allen A. *The Southwest of John H. Slaughter, 1841-1922*. Glendale, CA: Arthur H. Clark Company, 1965.

Espito, Brigadier General Vincent J., chief editor. *The West Point Atlas of American Wars*, Vol. 1, 1689-1900. New York: Harry Holt and Company, 1995.

Fetherling, Dale. *Mother Jones, The Miners' Angel*. Carbondale and Edwardsville, IL: Southern Illinois University Press, 1974.

Fuchs, James R. *A History of Williams, Arizona, 1876-1951*. Tucson: University of Arizona Press, 1955.

Gawne, Jonathan. *Over There! The American Soldier in World War I*. London: Greenhill Books, 1997.

Haley, J. Evetts. *Jeff Milton: A Good Man with a Gun*. Norman: University of Oklahoma Press, 1948.

Hart, Herbert M. *Old Forts of the Far West*. Seattle: Superior Publishing Company, 1965.

———. *Old Forts of the Northwest*. Seattle: Superior Publishing Company, 1963.

———. *Old Forts of the Southwest*. Seattle: Superior Publishing Company, 1964.

Heatwole, Thelma. *Ghost Towns and Historical Haunts in Arizona*. Phoenix: Golden West Publishers, 1981.

Heitman, Francis B., comp. *Historical Register and Dictionary of the United States Army*. 2 vols. Washington, D.C.: Government Printing Office, 1903.

Hunt, Frazier. *Cap Mossman: Last of the Great Cowmen*. New York: Hastings House, 1951.

Jeffrey, John Mason. *Adobe and Iron*. La Jolla, CA: Prospect Avenue Press, 1969.

Jones, Mother [Ann]. *Autobiography of Mother Jones*. Edited by Mary Field Paron. Chicago: Charles H. Kerr, 1925.

Kelly, George H., comp. *Legislative History: Arizona, 1864-1912*. Phoenix: Manufacturing Stationers, 1926.

King, Frank M. *Wranglin' the Past*. N.p., 1935.

Liggit, Wm. (Bill), Sr. *My Seventy-Five Years Along the Mexican Border*. New York: Exposition Press, 1964.

Macmillan Compendium. *America at War*. New York: Macmillan Library Reference USA, 1994.

Manchester, William. *American Caesar, Douglas MacArthur, 1880-1964*. Boston: Little, Brown and Company, 1978.

Martin, Douglas D., ed. *Tombstone's Epitaph*. Albuquerque: University of New Mexico Press, 1958.

Miller, Joseph. *Arizona, the Grand Canyon State*. New York: Hastings House, 1966 ed.

————. *The Arizona Rangers*. New York: Hastings House, Publishers, Inc., 1972.

O'Neal, Bill. *The Arizona Rangers*. Austin: Eakin Press, 1987.

Patton, James M. *History of Clifton*. Clifton, AZ: Greenlee County Chamber of Commerce, 1977.

Pringle, Henry F. *Theodore Roosevelt*. New York: Harcourt, Brace and Company, 1931.

Raine, William MacLeod. *Famous Sheriffs and Western Outlaws*. Garden City, NY: Garden City Publishing Company, Inc., 1903.

Reps, John W. *Cities of the American West: A History of Frontier Planning*. Princeton, NJ: Princeton University Press, 1979.

Robinson, Charles M., III. *Frontier Forts of Texas*. Houston, Texas: Lone Star Books, 1986.

Roosevelt, Theodore H. *The Rough Riders*. New York: Signet Classic Edition, 1961 [1899].

Rynning, Thomas H. *Gun Notches, The Life Story of a Cowboy-Soldier*. New York: Frederick A. Stokes Co., 1931.

Schultz, Vernon B. *Southwestern Town, The Story of Willcox, Arizona*. N.p., 1964.

Sherman, James E., and Barbara H. Sherman. *Ghost Towns of Arizona*. Norman: University of Oklahoma Press, 1969.

Simmons, Thomas E. *Fort Ringgold: A Brief Tour*. Edinburg, Texas: University of Texas- Pan American Press, 1991.

Sonnichsen, C. L. *Billy King's Tombstone*. Tucson: University of Arizona Press, 1942.

————. *Tucson*. Norman: University of Oklahoma Press, 1982.

Sparks, William. *The Apache Kid, A Bear Fight, and Other True Stories of the Old West*. Los Angeles: Skeleton Publishing Company, 1926.

Steffen, Randy. *The Horse Soldier, 1776-1943*, Vol. III, 1881-1916. Norman: University of Oklahoma Press, 1978.

Turner, John Kenneth. *Barbarous Mexico*. Austin: University of Texas Press, 1969.

Utley, Robert M. *Frontier Regulars, The United States Army, and the Indian, 1866-1891*. New York: Macmillan Publishing Co., Inc., 1973.

Vanderwood, Paul J. *Disorder and Progress—Bandits, Police, and Mexican Development*. Lincoln: University of Nebraska Press, 1981.

Wachholtz, Florence, comp. *Arizona, the Grand Canyon State*. 2 vols. Westminster, CO: Western States Historical Publishers, Inc., 1975.

Wagoner, Jay J. *Arizona Territory, 1863-1912*. Tucson: University of Arizona Press, 1970.

Walker, Henry P., and Don Bufkin. *Historical Atlas of Arizona*. Norman: University of Oklahoma Press, 1979.

Walters, Lorenzo D. *Tombstone's Yesterday*. Tucson: Acme Printing Co., 1928.

Wentworth, Frank L. *Bisbee With the Big B*. Iowa City, IA: Mercer Printing Company, 1938.

Woody, Clara T., and Milton L. Schwartz. *Globe, Arizona*. Tucson: Arizona Historical Society, 1977.

Articles

"The Arizona Copper Strike." *Outlook* (July 18, 1917): 434 and *Outlook* (July 25, 1927): 466.

"The Arizona Rangers." *The Arizona Highway Patrolman* (Spring 1979): 11, 13.

Bruere, Robert W. "Copper Camp Patriotism." *Nation* (February 21, 1918) :202-203.

DeArment, Robert K. "Arizona Ranger Jeff Kidder." Tombstone *Epitaph* (National Edition, March 1982): 1, 9-11.

Donoho, Ron. "Death of an Arizona Ranger." *Nevada Peace Officers Association* (December 1971).

Egerton, Kearney. "The Arizona Rangers Hang Two Men." Clipping in the files of the Arizona Heritage Center, Tucson.

———. "The Arizona Rangers Settle a Labor Dispute." *Arizona Republic* (July 4, 1982).

———. "A Brazen Horse Thief's Comeuppance." *Arizona Republic* (July 12, 1981).

———. "The Case of the Cow Thief." *Arizona Republic* (March 28, 1982).

———. "Pursuit in Mexico." *Arizona Republic* (April 18, 1982).

———. "A Tale of Two Petitions." *Arizona Republic* (February 6, 1983).

Ernenwein, Leslie. "Lucky Star." *Ranch Romances* (July 8, 1949): 43-47.

Hewes, Charles. "Captain of the Arizona Rangers." *Saga* (June 1958): 53-60.

"Honor the Past . . . Mold the Future," *Gila Centennial Historical Celebration and Pageant* (1976).

Hornung, Chuck. "Fullerton's Rangers." Tombstone *Epitaph* (National Edition, January 1981): 7-9.

Jensen, Jody. "Birth of the Arizona Rangers." *Old West* (Spring 1983): 30-33.

Keen, Effie R. "Arizona's Governors." *Arizona Historical Review* (October 1930): 7-20.

Kelley, Edward J. "The Killing of Jack the Ripper." *Arizona Highways* 15 (November 1939): 20-21, 33.

Kildare, Maurice. "Arizona's Toughest Ranger." *Old West* (Summer 1967).

"'The Law of Necessity;' State of Arizona v. Harry E. Wootton." *Bisbee I.W.W. Case,* University of Arizona Library.

McCool, Grace. "With Grace McCool" (untitled articles on the Arizona Rangers), *Gateway Times* (September 14, 1961; September 16, 1961; April 16, 1964; April 19, 1964; April 23, 1964).

Myers, John Myers. "A Chivalrous Killer." *Arizona Days and Ways* (December 13, 1964).

Nichols, Roger L. "A Miniature Venice, Florence, Arizona, 1866-1910." *The Journal of Arizona History* (Winter 1975): 335-356.

Park, Joseph F. "The 1903 'Mexican Affair' at Clifton." *The Journal of Arizona History* (Summer 1977): 119-148.

Pearce, Joe, and Richard Summers. "Joe Pearce—Manhunter." *The Journal of Arizona History* (Autumn 1978): 249-260.

Peterson, C.O. "Naco, Arizona's Accidental Place in History." *American West* (January/ February 1983): 44-47, 70-71.

"The President's Commission at Bisbee." *New Republic* (December 8, 1917): 140-141.

Rathbun, Carl M. "Keeping the Peace Along the Mexican Border." *Harper's Weekly* 50, no. 2604 (1906).

Rattenbury, Richard. "A Portfolio of Firearms from the New Winchester Museum." *American West* (May/June 1980): 34-45.

Spangenberger, Phil. "Thomas H. Rynning." *Guns and Ammo Guide to Guns of the Gunfighters* (1975): 31-37.

Stocher, Joseph. "The Arizona Rangers . . ." *Arizona Highways* (August 1982): 35-39.

Virgines, George E. "The Arizona Rangers . . . Birth of a Commemorative." *Guns* (June 1975): 46-47, 56-58.

———. "The Arizona Rangers." *Arms Gazette* (December 1973): 26-31, 34-35.

———. "Return of the Rangers." *Gun World Magazine* (February 1970): 82-85.

Wahmann, Russell, comp. "Front Street, Flagstaff, From Trail to Thoroughfare." *The Journal of Arizona History* (Spring 1973): 31-46.

Waltrip, Lela, and Rufus Waltrip. "Top Man of the Fearless Thirteen." *True West* (December 1970): 22-25, 72, 74.

Willson, Roscoe G. "Arizona Days and Ways, Sergeant Jeff Kidder." *Arizona Republic* (February 22, 1948).

Winsor, Mulford. "The Arizona Rangers." *Our Sheriff and Police Journal* 31, no. 6 (1936): 49-61.

Index

Abel, Norman, 153
Adams, Happy, 159
Agua Prieta, 105
Aguinaldo, Emilio, 20
Al Peck's Livery, 63
Alamo, 12
Alamogordo, New Mexico, 140
Alexander, James, 40-41
Allen, Charles, 109
Almy, Harry C., 143, 153
Alvarez, Lariano, 58
Alvord, Burt, 40-41
Amador, Victoriano, 64-65
Amador, Tomas, 64
American Expeditionary Force, 138
American Federation of Labor, 114
American Mining Congress, 113
Anderson, Bob, 72, 73
Anderson, George, 30
Apache Pass, 110
Apache War, 23
Arizona Cattle Grower's Association, 31
Arizona Civilian Rifle Team, 145-146
Arizona Heritage Center, 2
Arizona National Guard, 132
Arizona Range News, 30
Arizona Rangers: abolishment of, 31-32, 55, 78-86; arrests by, 31, 54, 75, 80, 81, 84, 86; and bloodhounds, 74; bru-

tality in, 39; costs of, 31, 55, 74, 80, 81, 82-83, 84; created, 25-27; deaths in, 27, 67; and entry into Mexico, 50-51, 65, 67, 70; inspectors in, 52-53, 74, 82-83; pay in, 28, 74; purpose of, 26, 31, 80, 82-83, 84; reenlistment in, 67; required skills of, 52; rules regarding, 49-51; size of force, 28, 55, 74, 80; testimony by, 54; travel by, 38, 54, 80, 85, 86; turnover rate in, 51; warrants issued to, 48; weapons of, 54, 74
Arizona Rangers, The, 2
Arizona Rifle Team, 147
Arizona State Archives, 2
Arizona State Industrial School, 22
Arizona State Rifle Association, 143, 145
Arizona statehood, 87, 89
Arizona Territory, 25-26, 27, 32
Arnett, George, 67-70, 75, 110
Ascension, ———, 33-38
Atlanta, Georgia, 6
Austin, Texas, 12
Austin, Art, 2

Bailey, Neill, 81-82
Baker, John, 46
Bank of Bisbee, 36, 119
Bareras, Ramos, 57
baseball, 91, 96

Bates, W.F., 51, 59, 73
Battle of Bear Paw Mountain, 7
Beaty, Chapo, 54
Beede, M.D., 1, 29
Beeman, William S., 115, 116, 117, 120
Bellah, James Warner, 16
Benson, Arizona, 41-44, 72, 88
Bird Cage Theatre, 92
Bisbee, Arizona, 10, 27, 66, 88, 92, 99, 101, 106, 112-130, 140, 160
Bisbee Deportation, 111-130, 150-153
Bisbee Mining District, 112
Black, Samuel, 73
Bohmfalk, Henry C., 156
Bolan, Jack, 88, 89
Boot Hill, 92
Bootjack Ranch, 64
Boquillas Land and Cattle Company, 93
Bostwick, Joe, 1, 29, 30, 110
Bowden, Percy, 94, 108, 142
Bowman Hotel, 141
Brackettville, Texas, 11
Breen, Fred S., 120
Brew, James, 119
Brewery Gulch, 101, 102, 103, 113
Brocius, Curly Bill, 92
Brodie, Alexander, 27, 31, 32
Brooks, Johnny, 32
Brown, Fred W., 150, 151, 153
Browning, John M., 27
Bruce, Dave, 2
Buckley, H.S., 156
Buffalo War, 16
bulldogging, 55
Burgess, W.H., 150, 151, 153
Burnett, Rube, 36
Byrkit, James, 119, 120, 128
Byrne, Cy, 57

Cabell, General, 141
Caldwell, Kansas, 55
Caldwell, New Jersey, 145
Caldwell, New Jersey, 147
Calumet and Arizona Hospital, 103, 156, 158, 160
Calumet and Arizona Mining Company, 112, 115, 116, 119
Camp Del Rio, 12

Camp Furlong, 117, 124, 125, 126
Camp Merrit, New Jersey, 138
Camp Perry, Ohio, 144, 153, 154
Campbell, Thomas E., 112, 124, 128, 137, 152, 153
Canadian Army, 132
Cananea, Arizona, 46, 64, 72, 77
capital punishment, 135
Castaneda, Eduardo, 42
cattle industry, 90
Caw Ranch Saloon, 59
Chacon, Augustin, 27
Chase, A.F., 73
Chateau-Thierry, 139
Cheever, Mark, 34
Cheever, Mrs., 34
Chia, 64
Childs, Tom, 58
Chiricahua Mountains, 63, 85, 108, 134, 154
Chloride, Arizona, 114
Church, William, 144
Citiano, 59
Citizen's Protective League, 114-115, 120
Clark, E.S., 51-52
Clifton, Arizona, 135
Clifton-Morenci mining district, 114
Cloverdale, Arizona, 94
Cochise County, 1, 40, 59, 67, 72, 81, 82, 87, 88, 90, 91, 92, 93, 98, 99, 101, 106, 107, 121, 154
Cochise County Board of Supervisors, 98, 120, 135, 153
Cochise County Courthouse, 90, 98
Cochise County Stock Growers Association, 90
Cochise Stronghold, 156, 158, 160
Coleman, Charles, 68
Colon, 20
Columbia, South Carolina, 6
Columbus, New Mexico, 117, 124, 126
Comanches, 16-17
Commercial Club, 128
copper production, 112, 115, 116, 149
Copper Queen, 46, 112, 117
Cornwall, Harry, 5
Courtland, Arizona, 81, 88, 110
Cox, Frank, 26

Cross, Charley, 94
Crystal Palace, 92, 140
Crystal Theater, 101
Custer, George Armstrong, 9, 16
Custer, Libbie, 9

Daniels, Ben F., 32
Davisson, Lori, 2
Davlandos, Christo, 72
Decker, ———, 29
Department of Civilian Marksmanship, 145
Department of the Colorado, 24
Development Company of America, 25
Dewey, George, 20
Diaz, Porfirio, 57
Don Luis, Arizona, 55-56
Dos Cabezas Mountains, 101
Douglas, Arizona, 2, 28, 38, 46, 56, 57, 58, 60, 70, 72, 88, 93, 101, 107, 117, 140, 142, 160
Douglas, Cleveland, 128
Douglas, James, 28
Douglas, Walter, 113, 115
Douglas Rifle Club, 70
Dowell, D.H., 117
Downing, William F., 52, 71, 75
Dragoon Mountains, 85, 134

Earp, Warren, 30
Earp, Wyatt, 92
Ehle, A. E., 73
Eighteenth Infantry, 5-7, 11, 16, 20
Eighth Cavalry, 28
Eisenhower, Dwight D., 13, 138
Eisenhower, Mamie Doud, 13
El Cubo, 58-59
El Paso and Southwestern Railroad, 92, 120
El Paso, Texas, 94, 149
Ells, E.P., 59, 69
Emett, James, 51-52
Empalme, 35, 37
Eperson, Charles, 39, 41
Erickson, Jacob, 117
Evergreen Cemetery, 159, 160
Everybody's Magazine, 60

Fairbank, Arizona, 93
"Fate of the Bootlegger, The," 107

Fayson, Matt, 29
Felkner, Jim, 94
Fikes, Mrs., 70
Finley, James, 82-83
First Cavalry, 16, 19-20, 23
Fitzgerald, Albert, 101, 103
Flagg, Charles, 24
Florence *Blade*, 80
Florence, Arizona, 45
Ford, Frank A., 51
Forging the Copper Collar, 119
Fort Apache, 27
Fort Assiniboine, 7, 9
Fort Clark, Texas, 11
Fort Grant, Arizona, 22, 23, 24, 112
Fort Hays, Kansas, 9, 11
Fort Huachuca, 27, 54, 70, 99, 101, 141, 154
Fort Meade, 23
Fort Ringgold, Texas, 12
Fort Sam Houston, Texas, 12-14, 15
Fort Sill, Oklahoma, 16-18
Foster, John, 65
Fourteenth Cavalry, 23
Fourth Cavalry, 11
Fraser, J.A., 59, 73
French, Robert N., 150-153

Gadberry, Tom, 78, 85
Gainesville, Florida, 76
gambling, 50, 56-57, 59-60
Garcia, Judge, 65, 66
Geronimo, 17
Gibson, Lafe, 109-110
Gila Bend, 39
Gila Cuonty, 37
Globe, Arizona, 33, 72, 78, 85
Golconda, Arizona, 114
Gonzalez, ———, 33-38
Goodrich, Ben, 82
Government Hill, 13
Graham County, 31, 40, 81, 133, 134, 135
Graham, Dayton, 94
Greene, W.C., 46
Greenlee County, 135
Greenway, John C., 115-116, 117
Greenwood, John, 36
Guaymas, 35

Gunfight at the O.K. Corral, 92
Gunner, Rudolph, 48, 60-62, 66, 70, 71, 73, 77
Gunsight, 59

Hamlett, Pam, 2, 159
Hayhurst, Sam, 57, 60, 66, 72, 108
Hays City, 9
Haywood, Bill, 114, 124
Heflin, Charles W., 68-70
Helvetia Copper Company, 41
Hereford, Arizona, 94
Hermanas, New Mexico, 124
Hermosillo, 58, 70
Hickey, Dick, 34, 35, 36, 38, 44
Hickey, Mrs., 44
Hickok, Wild Bill, 9
Hicks, O.F., 77
Hill, Leo, 101, 103
Hobbs, Lee, 31
Hoboken, New Jersey, 137, 138
Holiday, Doc, 92
Holmes, ———, 32
Hooker, Henry, 31
Hopkins, Arthur A., 33, 36, 39, 93, 105, 132
Hornbrook, J.J., 120
Horne, R.D., 60, 61, 66, 74
Howard, Harry, 38
Huachuca Mountains, 86
Hudspeth, Lee, 94
Humm, George, 68, 70
Hunt, George W.P., 84, 85, 89

Independent Carnival Company, 30
International Workers of the World (IWW), 113-130, 133, 139, 152
International-American, 57

Jack, William C., 150
Jacksonville, Florida, 6
Jerome, Arizona, 114
Jiminez, ———, 39
Johns, John, 58-59
Johnson, ———, 29
Johnston, James S., 15
Jones, Mary Harris, *see* Jones, Mother
Jones, Mother, 57-58

Jones, Wiley E., 128
Junta Liberal Mejicana, 57

Kelton, Arizona, 110
Kendall, Harry C., 153
Kennedy, Ed, 33, 37
Kibbey, Joseph, 32, 33, 45, 46, 51, 53, 54, 55, 58, 73, 74, 76, 77, 78, 79, 80, 81, 83-84, 137
Kidder, Jeff, 31, 46, 56, 59, 62-67
Kidder, Mrs., 66
Kilburg Canyon, 134
King of Arizona Mine, 40
King William neighborhood, 13
King, Orrie, 77-78
Kingman, Arizona, 114
Kosterlitzky, Emilio, 34
Krag-Jorgensen weapon, 18

La Dura, 35
labor unions, 113-130, 133
Lake Constance, 23
Lake Erie, 144
Larison, Allen, 101, 103
Larn, William A., 52
Larrieu, John, 88
Las Moras River, 11
Lebo, T.C., 23, 24
Lee, Robert E., 11
Lees Ferry, Arizona, 51
Lenz, Emil, 81, 85
Leon Springs, Texas, 132
Leslie, Buckskin Frank, 92
Lincoln, ———, 29
Lindsey, W.E., 124
Livestock Sanitary Board, 31, 71
Livingston, Arizona, 33
Lockwood, Judge A.C., 137
Locust Grove, Georgia, 30
Los Angeles, 38
Lowell, Arizona, 68, 88, 112
Lusitania, 111

Mabry, George, 60
MacArthur, Arthur, 15
MacArthur, Douglas, 15
MacArthur, Pinky, 15
Macias, Shirley, 2

Mackenzie, Ranald, 11
Macy Hotel, 30
Manila Bay, 20
Maricopa County, 79
Mayer, George L., 51
McAda, Oscar, 47
McBride, Robert, 134
McComa, ———, 41
McDonald, C.A., 88
McDonald, James F., 108, 153, 156
McDonald, Porter, 36, 53, 93, 96
McFarland, Daniel W., 89
McGee, E.S., 77
McGee, James, 39, 41
McGonagill, Clay, 55
McKinley, William, 19
McNeal, Arizona, 126
McRae, O.P. 118, 119
Meadows, "Policy Sam," 29
Mediation Commission, 128-129, 130
Mexican Revolution, 99
Mickey, Lew, 41, 53, 78
Miles, Rye, 47, 48, 59, 62, 72
Millay, Jerry, 45
Milton, Jeff, 94
Mimbres, Jesus, 94
Minas Prietas, 37
Mineola, Long Island, 131
Mineral, Arizona, 114
mining industry, 78, 81, 90, 92, 94, 112-130
Moctezuma, 69, 70
Modern Café, 142, 148
Mohave County, 114
Mohawk, Arizona, 40
Moret, Sam, 57
Morgan, William J., 84
Morris, Peter, 85
Morrison, Jessie Wheeler, 2
Mossman, Burt, 26, 27, 51, 82
Mount Graham, 23
Murphy, Mrs. Owen E., 105
Murphy, Nathan Oakes, 26, 27

Naco Amusement Park, 46
Naco, Arizona, 39, 46, 49, 59, 72, 81, 99
Naco Budget, 46
Naco, Sonora, 39, 46, 49, 64, 66, 67, 99

National Guard, 144
National Rifle Association, 109, 143, 144, 145, 153
National Rifle Shoot, 145-146
Nations, O.C., 55
Navarro County, Texas, 68, 84
Needham, W.J., 88
New Mexico Mounted Police, 31
Nez Perce War, 7
Nichols, Harold, 114
Ninth Cavalry, 99
Nogales, Arizona, 37, 46, 56, 63, 141
Noll, Cole, 101, 103
Norcross, Joe, 101, 103

Olcott, Dr., 29
Old, Billy, 34, 46, 52, 59, 72, 73, 74, 77, 80, 93
Olney, Ben, 53
165th Infantry, 131
O'Neill, Eugene Brady, 79, 84
Order of the Indian Wars, 76
Oriental Saloon, 92
Ortega, Pantaleon, 34
Ortiz, 34, 35
Owl Restaurant, 46

Pacheco, Nabor, 58-59
Palace Funeral Parlor, 66, 68
Palace Saloon, 1, 29, 30
Parker, Quanah, 16-17
Parks, Jim, 31
Patagonia Mountains, 64
Pattee, S.L., 151
Payne, Mrs. Edward, 68
Payson, Arizona, 55
Pearce, Arizona, 101
Pearce Cemetery, 93
Pecos, Texas, 55
Perry, Oliver Hazard, 144
Peterson, William S., 33
Phelps Dodge Company, 28, 46, 112, 113, 115, 120, 128
Philippines, 20-21
Pickett, Bill, 55
Pima County, 58, 82, 101
Pinal County, 44, 58, 80, 81, 82, 101
Pinto Creek, Arizona, 33

Pirtleville, Arizona, 94
Plunkett, Sam, 33, 34, 37
Poole, Travis, 51, 59, 73
Powers, John, 134-135
Powers, Thomas J., Sr., 134
Powers, Tom, 134-135
Prescott, Arizona, 32, 46, 55
Prewitt, Deputy, 101
prohibition, 98, 100, 106-108

Quias, Dolores, 64

Rainbow Division, 131, 139
Red Cross, 140
Reddoch, Arcus, 41
Redmond, John McKittrick, 48, 71, 85
Reed, George, 99
Reese, Clarence, 94
Reserve Officers' Training, 112, 131-132
Rhodes, John, 59
Riggs, B.K., 153
Ringo, Johnny, 92
Robertson, Peter, 57, 60, 61, 62
rodeos, 55-56
Roosevelt, Franklin D., 145, 146
Roosevelt, Teddy, 22, 27, 32
Rose, Allen, 85
Roskruge, George J., 145
Ross, John F., 150
Rough Riders, 20, 27, 28, 52, 115
Rountree, Oscar, 31, 32
Rucker, Arizona, 154
Rurales, 34
Rynning, Thomas H., 25, 27-28, 29, 30,
    32-33, 36, 38, 39, 40, 42, 44, 45, 51,
    52, 53, 61

Safford, Arizona, 134
San Antonio, Texas, 11, 12-13
San Bernardino Ranch, 82
Santa Cruz County, 72
Santa Rita Hotel, 145
Sarabia, Manuel, 57-58
Saunders, B.F., 52
Schieffelin Hall, 92
Sedberg, W.R., 24
Seventh Cavalry, 16
Sexton, J.P., 145

Shattuck-Denn Company, 112
Sheridan, Phil, 9, 16
Sherman, William T., 16
Short, Luke, 77, 92, 93
Shute, Eugene, 34, 38
Sieber, Al, 33
Sierra Bonita Ranch, 31
Silverton, D.W., 41-44
Silverton, Mrs., 41-44
Sisson, Tom, 134-135
Sitting Bull, 7
Slaughter, John, 89, 92
Smalley, George H., 106
Smith, Bill, 27
Smith, E.O., 29
Smith, James, 51, 59
smuggling, 49, 58, 83
Snow, Bud, 71
Solomonville, Arizona, 40
Sonora, 34
Southern Pacific Railroad, 25, 26, 30
Spanish-American War, 18-20, 27
Sparks, "Timberline Bill," 31, 32
Speed, Billy, 36, 52, 59, 71, 74, 75, 85
Springfiled (1903), 74
St. Charles, Kean, 79
Stanford, Tip, 59, 64, 65, 66, 72, 77
Stanley, Walter F., 30
steer tying contests, 55-56
Stewart, William F., 22
Sullivan, P.J., 61
Sulphur Spring Valley, 30, 31, 66
Sutherland, John, 64
Sylvanite, 77

Tafolla, Carlos, 27, 67
Taft, President, 89
Ten Miles Well, 58
Tenth Cavalry, 141
Texas Rangers, 26
Texas Military Institute, 14
Thompson, Ray, 36
308th Cavalry, 137
Tombstone, Arizona, 25, 88, 89, 91, 92,
    95, 99, 140, 151
Tombstone Canyon, 116
Tombstone City Cemetery, 104
Tombstone Courthouse, 90, 98, 160

Tombstone Courthouse National Historic Site, 2
Tombstone *Epitaph,* 92
Tombstone Mining District, 92
Tombstone *Nugget,* 92
Tombstone *Prospector,* 92
Tombstone Rifle Club, 109, 143, 145, 146, 153
Torres, Luis E., 39
Torres, Rafael, 58, 70
Tracy, J.A., 1, 41-44, 46, 110
Tucson, Arizona, 25, 29, 38, 49, 101
Tucson Chamber of Commerce, 82
Tucson Country Club, 153
Tucson Rifle Club, 153
Tule Desert, 40

U.S. Customs Service, 87
U.S. Military Academy, 5, 16, 77
Union Hall, 117, 119
United Verde Copper Company, 114
United States v. Harry Wheeler, et al., 138, 141
USS *Maine,* 18

Vail's Station, 41
Val Verde County, 12
Villa, Pancho, 105, 117, 152
Virginia Hotel, 41, 42

Walker, John C., 137
Wanda's Restaurant, 29
War Department, 18, 19, 23, 31, 120, 140
Warren District, 112, 116, 117, 119, 120, 124, 128, 153
Warren District Trades Assembly, 133
Webb, Sam F., 79, 84-85
Weedin, Thomas, 79, 80, 81, 84, 85
Welch, Guy, 89, 98, 99, 104, 105, 110, 138
West Point, 12, 14
West Texas Military Academy, 15
Wheeler, Allyn (son), 18, 23, 30, 77, 90-91, 93, 94, 96, 101-105
Wheeler, Annie Cornwall (mother), 5, 6, 12, 76, 77
Wheeler, Debbie, 159
Wheeler, Fern, 160

Wheeler, Frank, 57, 60, 61, 72, 73
Wheeler, Harry C.: administrative efficiency of, 54, 60, 76, 85, 91, 108; in Arizona National Guard, 132; as Arizona Ranger (acting commander of), 32, 33, 42, 44, (becomes captain), 46, 49, (joins), 28-29, (offers resignation as), 82, (position dissolved), 86, (strict code of), 49-51, 73, 77; and auto theft, 194; birth of, 5, 6-7; and Bisbee Deportation, 115-130, 138-139, 150-153; and bootleggers, 87, 100-101, 106-108, 109-110, 142; campaigns of, 87-88, 96, 108, 154, 156; as captain, 308th Cavalry, 137-141; and cattle rustlers, 30-31, 70, 100; in cavalry, 2, 16, 23, 28, 137-141; charges himself with careless discharge, 95; childhood of, 7, 10; children of, 18, 154, 156; criticized for deportation, 125, 141, 156; as customs officer, 2, 87; death of, 158; as deputy sheriff, Cochise County, 87-89; described, 11, 14, 16, 18, 23, 29, 46, 58, 89, 108, 120, 124, 129, 143, 158; discharged from army, 141; divorce of, 148-149; enlists/reenlists in army, 16, 23; eulogy for, 158; forms posse, 117, 121; funeral of, 158; on gambling, 50, 56, 57, 59-60; general orders issued by, 49-50; gravestone of, 159, 160; in gunfights, 29-30, 41-44, 46, 68, 72, 94, 110; homes of, 93, 96, 105, 149, 156; and horse thiefs, 67-70, 75, 81, 86; and Indian scouts, 19; indicted for kidnapping, 138-141, 150; injured, 24, 42, 44, 112, 138, 156; as marksman/gunman, 2, 9, 17-18, 28, 29, 62, 70, 97, 109, 110, 143, 145, 146, 154, 156; marries, 18, 149; medical discharge of, 24; men killed by, 1, 29-30, 44, 110; military influence on, 7, 10, 11, 12, 13, 14, 23, 49, 112; in military school, 12, 14, 15; as miner, 25, 115; in mining business, 156; on motorcycle patrol, 147; orchard of, 156, 160; patriotism of, 115, 125, 128, 129, 130, 133, 140, 152; on patrol, 38, 47, 62, 75; petition to remove as sheriff, 126; as pitcher, 91, 96; platform of, 108; praised for deportation work, 120, 124, 126, 129; and prohibition, 98, 100-101, 106-108; promotions of, 29, 32,

40, 44, 45-46, 49, 76; pursues out-laws, 11, 30, 33-38, 40-41, 58-59, 60, 63, 66, 70, 74-75, 81, 91, 94, 108, 109, 134; as rancher, 154; records con-cerning, 2; rejected by military, 112, 130, 132-133; rewards offered to, 38, 44; in rifle competition, 109, 143-147, 153-154, 156; salary of, 89, 137; as sheriff, Cochise County, 1, 89-137, (re-elected), 98, 108, (resigns), 137; as spe-cial officer, Douglas police, 2, 142-147; and Texans, 73-74, 77-78; uniform of, 18, 27; and use of automobile, 91, 93, 98, 108, 117, 120, 141; volunteers for military service in WWI, 2, 112, 131-133, 135, 137

Wheeler, Jessie (wife), 154, 156, 158-159

Wheeler, Jessie Jacqueline (daughter), 2, 156, 157

Wheeler, Mamie (wife), 18, 23, 77, 90, 91, 93, 96, 99, 103, 104-105, 109, 112, 125-126, 138, 140, 141, 142, 147, 148-149

Wheeler, Robert W. "Bobby" (son), 156, 159

Wheeler, Sallie (daughter), 5, 12, 77, 140

Wheeler, Sunshine, 91, 93, 99, 112, 140, 141, 142, 147

Wheeler, William Allyn, *see* Wheeler, Allyn

Wheeler, William B. (father), 5-7, 9, 12, 20, 76

Wheeler, William D. (brother), 10, 15, 20, 76, 77, 131, 139, 140

Wheeler, William J. "Jack" (son), 154, 157, 159, 160

White, Jack, 36

White, John, 45-46, 53, 69, 89

White, Lorenzo, 108

White, William, 88

Wild West shows, 55, 74

Willcox, Arizona, 25, 39, 30, 37, 71, 88

Willcox Drug Store, 30

Willcox, George, 115-116

Willcox House, 30

Williams, Arizona, 80

Williams, James, 39

Williams, Starr, 101

Wills, Jessie, 142-143, 147-148, *also see* Wheeler, Jessie Leona

Wilson, Guy, 112

Wilson, Owen, 57

Wilson, Woodrow, 108, 111, 112, 124, 128

Winchester (1895), 27, 37, 74

Winslow, Arizona, 80

Winsor, Mulford, 81

Wobblies, *see* International Workers of the World

Women's Loyalty League of America, 116, 126, 133

Wood, George, 67

Wood, Willis, 40-41

Woods, H.E., 85

Wootten, H.E., 151-152, 153

World War I, 111-112, 131-141

Yaqui Indians, 34-35, 36

Yorkville, South Carolina, 6

Yuma, Arizona, 40, 60-62

Yuma County, 57, 72

Yuma Territorial Prison, 32, 40, 45, 61, 71